The Colfax Massacre

LeeAnna Keith

The Colfax Massacre

 *The Untold Story of Black Power, White Terror, and the Death of Reconstruction*

OXFORD
UNIVERSITY PRESS

OXFORD
UNIVERSITY PRESS

Oxford University Press, Inc., publishes works that further
Oxford University's objective of excellence
in research, scholarship, and education.

Oxford New York
Auckland Cape Town Dar es Salaam Hong Kong Karachi
Kuala Lumpur Madrid Melbourne Mexico City Nairobi
New Delhi Shanghai Taipei Toronto

With offices in
Argentina Austria Brazil Chile Czech Republic France Greece
Guatemala Hungary Italy Japan Poland Portugal Singapore
South Korea Switzerland Thailand Turkey Ukraine Vietnam

Published by Oxford University Press, Inc.
198 Madison Avenue, New York, NY 10016

www.oup.com

Oxford is a registered trademark of Oxford University Press

First issued as an Oxford University Press paperback, 2009

Library of Congress Cataloging-in-Publication Data
Keith, LeeAnna.
The Colfax massacre : the untold story of Black power, White terror, and
the death of Reconstruction / LeeAnna Keith.
p. cm.
Includes bibliographical references and index.
ISBN 978-0-19-539308-8 (pbk.)
1. Colfax (La.)—Race relations—History—19th century. 2. Grant Parish (La.)—Race
relations—History—19th century. 3. Reconstruction (U.S. history, 1865–1877)
—Louisiana—Colfax. 4. Massacres—Louisiana—Colfax—History—19th century.
5. Violence—Louisiana—Colfax—History—19th century. 6. Racism—Louisiana
—Colfax—History—19th century. 7. African Americans—Crimes against—Louisiana
—Colfax—History—19th century. 8. Contested elections—Louisiana—Grant Parish
—History—19th century. 9. Grant Parish (La.)—Politics and government—
19th century. I. Title.
F379.C59K45 2008
976.3´67—dc22   2007023368

9 8 7 6 5 4 3

Printed in the United States of America
on acid-free paper

To Brian

All history is only one long story to this effect: men have struggled for power over their fellow men in order that they might win the joys of earth at the expense of others, and might shift the burdens of life from their own shoulders upon those of others.

—William Graham Sumner

Contents

Introduction: On Bones and Their Markers   xi

CHAPTER 1   Alabama Fever   3

CHAPTER 2   The Philosopher   21

CHAPTER 3   The Fall   32

CHAPTER 4   Led by a Damned Puppy   46

CHAPTER 5   A Town Called Fight   62

CHAPTER 6   Carnival of the Animals   82

CHAPTER 7   Battle of the Colfax Courthouse   88

CHAPTER 8   Voyage of the *Ozark*   111

CHAPTER 9   Getting Away with Murder   131

CHAPTER 10   The Legacy of *Cruikshank*   153

Acknowledgments   173

Notes   175

Bibliography   201

Index   211

Introduction: On Bones and Their Markers

LET THE GHOSTS OF COLFAX HAVE THE FIRST WORD. THEY DO not rest in peace; their bones have been restless.

The bones rose with the flesh still intact on the third day after Easter 1873, preserved by the unseasonably cool Louisiana spring weather. Scattered like boulders across the riverbottom landscape of the town of Colfax, their bodies stirred to motion under the painstaking ministrations of government investigators. In numbers the dead dwarfed the living: the two arrivals from New Orleans, carpetbagger outsiders, assisted by a clutch of local volunteers, buried the corpses of 59 of an estimated 150 homicide victims in the vicinity of the smoking ruins of the Grant Parish Courthouse. Until Easter Sunday morning, in their company of African American militia, free and living men, the 59 had occupied a pair of shallow earthworks on the courthouse lawn, fortifications for their claim to equality and freedom on their home turf. As corpses they would occupy the loamy soil of their entrenchment forever afterward, their mass grave unmarked and the victory of their cause deferred.

The bones were moved a second time in 1899 when prospectors sunk a 1,103-foot shaft through the grave and tapped a small supply of natural gas. Speculative prospecting was not new to Central Louisiana, known as early as 1873, the year of the Colfax Massacre, to possess reserves of petroleum and its invisible by-product, made up mostly of methane. Tapping into deep, subterranean chambers of gas was dangerous work. On numerous occasions, the friction of broken rocks had ignited torrents of fuel into columns of fire that could scarcely be contained by human effort. The white sponsors of the Colfax venture confronted no such hazards, despite the audacity of their violation of the burial site. Instead, a trickle of natural gas percolated to the surface amidst a gentle stream of spring water, a fairly uncommon phenomenon thought to be the scientific explanation for the biblical encounter between Moses and the Burning Bush. In 1902, the site was wordlessly marked by a decorative fountain and eternal flame. Colfax's black inhabitants had to be enjoined by officialdom to keep their hands and faces out of the water.[1]

Over the course of decades, the town uncovered bones during the excavation of the foundations of new courthouses, a highway, and a gas station with underground tanks, and the flow of water and flame from the gravesite continued uninterrupted. In 1927, the survivors among white veterans of the massacre stood by ceremonially to witness an incidental excavation and dispatched two human skulls to an exhibit of Civil War relics at Louisiana State University.[2]

The flaming fountain—featured in *Ripley's Believe It or Not!*—continued to bubble and burn. Drawn by its magic, local children and at least one eccentric old man engaged in furtive splashing and bathing in the basin.[3]

Then, one night in 1951, the unearthly effervescence of the courthouse fountain abruptly ceased. According to the local tradition, the well exhausted its supply of both water and gas without warning on the very day that the State of Louisiana installed a historical marker on the site:

> On this site occurred the Colfax Riot in which three white men and
> 150 negroes were slain. This event on April 13, 1873 marked the end of
> carpetbag misrule in the South.

Superstition would trump skepticism in every surviving account of the result. Local whites built a new artificial flaming fountain and speculated on the supernatural in a series of playful, unremorseful articles in the hometown paper.[4] Local blacks exercised a rigorous taboo about discussing the flaming fountain and the Colfax Courthouse in general, keeping silent for almost as many years as the victims of the Easter Sunday massacre had been buried in the trench below the courthouse and the sign.

Almost sixty years after it was first erected, the "Colfax Riot" marker remains their only headstone.

The most critical of readings must allow a certain admiation for the eloquence and power of the marker's two-sentence summary. It survives as the definitive statement of the event, in part because of the reflection it offers of the state of the twentieth century and its representation of the past. In the words of author James W. Loewen, who condemned the Colfax marker in *Lies Across America,* "historic sites are always a tale of two eras."[5]

In fact, "Colfax Riot" was first used by whites to describe the events that preceded what happened at Colfax on April 13, 1873. There were other notorious riots during the era of Reconstruction, including a disproportionate number of violent confrontations in Louisiana. The grandfather of these was the 1866 New Orleans Riot, a political melee that culminated in characteristic fashion, with a pogrom of blacks, fatal casualties in the dozens, and scores of injured.

By applying the term "riot" to certain racial incidents, white opinion-makers struggled to adjust to the transformation of the South by Emancipation. Ascribing a tendency to riot to the freedmen, the unvanquished defenders of the Old South served notice of the deadly consequences of ideas and behavior that disrupted the antebellum status quo. In a related accommodation, criminal justice was adapted to the management of other categories of crime applied exclusively against the black population, taking care to allocate the benefits of convict labor to the masters of the local hierarchy.[6]

By the standard of riots established as "typical" by the 1920s, when Wilmington, North Carolina, Rosewood, Florida, and Tulsa, Oklahoma had experienced the ordeal in full force, Colfax 1873 was not properly a riot, after all. In light of the high state of military preparedness in the all-black courthouse defense, the confrontation better approximated a battle. Remembering it as the "Colfax Riot" revealed the white will to maintain order.

"Massacre" is the proper term for what happened, given the number of black fatalities, including 48 executed as prisoners hours after the fight was ended. In the 1870s, "massacre" referred traditionally to the murder of civilians or prisoners by armed men, as in the death-and-captivity scenes from the Indian Wars that had provided fodder for the first American thrillers. Thus the term acquired a loose association with white victimhood, evidenced in its wide usage for the murder of numbers of whites, such as the attack, within days of Colfax, by Captain Jack of the Modoc Indians on U.S. soldiers or the public execution of Republican officials in Coushatta, Louisiana in 1874.

In those days, only white conservative newspapers reported on the "Colfax Riot." "Massacre" was the preferred term in Louisiana's black-owned Reconstruction-era newspapers, and in publications partisan to the dominant Radical faction of the national Republican Party. Open meetings of African American men, including high-ranking officials of the Reconstruction government in New Orleans, denounced the Colfax Massacre. The term appeared in numerous federal government documents of the 1870s, generated by overlapping trials, investigations, and reports on the violence at Colfax and elsewhere in the South. President Ulysses S. Grant employed the term in a message to Congress decrying what had happened.

And yet the designation Colfax "Riot" would prevail, a testament to the success of the reactionary white establishment in controlling the history of the Civil War and Reconstruction in Louisiana. In the case of Colfax, the semantic victory reflected above all the determination of local whites, who began commemorating the event in public in the early twentieth century. In addition to the historical marker, a National Forestry Department medallion was put on the tree on which black men were hanged after the fight. One local woman wrote an M.A. thesis on it and collected oral histories, another compiled scrapbooks, and a third composed a theatrical novella. After 1921, an engraved marble obelisk to honor the three whites who fell "fighting for white supremacy" stood half a block off the town square formed by the courthouse, the fountain, the marker, and the unmarked grave.

The historical legacy represented the views of only one constituency, the one that had the clout to air its views in public, at a time when Klansmen claimed influential state and local offices, even in towns not known for being redoubts of white supremacy. Despite its fame in the Klans, however, the story of Colfax vanished from national and even state histories of Reconstruction. The Colfax Riot marker attracted few acknowledgments, especially from those living in the immediate environs, where silence on the subject of the killings soon became a matter of courtesy.

Claims about "carpetbag misrule" therefore escaped critique by those with opposing ideas about the era of the Thirteenth, Fourteenth, and

Fifteenth Amendments, which made citizens of slaves. Granted agency, the 59 souls interred beneath the sign would have certainly employed a more generous characterization. The carpetbaggers' cause had been theirs, too. In behalf of fair elections and peaceful coexistence between races, blacks at Colfax and their courageous white allies had campaigned for self-rule, not misrule. The placement of the marker itself rebuked the social and political order that conceived the lie.

The reference to "negroes"—atypically without capitalization—projects the antiquated origins of the sign into the present, making it a jarring throwback to a bygone time. Due to the twisted influence of Southern charm (spiked with fear), town and country of both races seem to prefer the outdated term to any public conversation on the nature of a slur.

The number 150, despite its divergence from the carpetbaggers' on-site tally of 63 (four of whom were buried separately by relatives), is the least controversial claim on the marker. For all its brutality, the acknowledgment in the body count provides the least offense to the memories of the men buried in the shadow of the sign.

Poised near State Road 8, a highway spur serving Colfax alone, the Colfax Riot marker survives in obscurity. While Louisiana and the country as a whole pursued a different conversation about Reconstruction and its legacies, its version of the past remained out of the spotlight. Colfax became a remnant of the era when cotton was king. The number of influential visits to the town dwindled to nothing, excepting only the Duke Ellington Orchestra's one-time appearance for a whites-only crowd in the 1930s. And yet when it was first raised in 1951, the marker represented the mainstream by what it ignored or obscured. Popular representations of the Civil War and Reconstruction for the nation, including two of the greatest early films, turned a blind eye to incidents of white violence such as Colfax, spellbound by the romance of the South's lost world. With the artistry of *Gone With the Wind* (1939), even the faces of convicts on lease as chain gangs were purged of color, and *Birth of a Nation* (1915) wrapped the Ku Klux Klan in patriotic glory with endorsements from the Oval Office.

As embodied in the Jim Crow notion of the riot, cruelty and self-destruction were construed to be the provinces of black men alone, a view sustained by leading northern academic experts on the history of Reconstruction. Professor William Archibald Dunning of Columbia

University, the founder of the predominant "school" of Reconstruction scholarship, endorsed the notion of carpetbag misrule in the state, declaring "reconstruction through Negro suffrage and [the] regime of carpetbaggers" in Louisiana to be "the *reducto ad absurdum*" of the errors of the plan.[7] The root problems of what Dunning scholars called the "tragic era" stemmed from the abuses of exploitative new arrivals and their credulous African American allies, emboldened by Republican Radicals who "waved the bloody shirt" of Civil War–era sacrifice. Until after World War II, presenting African Americans as victims did not fit the prevailing model of Reconstruction historiography.

Historians were disinclined to probe gravesites in small Southern towns, leaving such matters as the Colfax Riot marker to the powers at hand.

Even W. E. B. DuBois, the first African American to obtain a Harvard Ph.D., missed the Colfax Massacre when he wrote his great 1935 history, *Black Reconstruction*. Forced by segregation laws—and the likelihood of violence—to eschew archival research in the South, he relied on published accounts that omitted the story entirely. DuBois's oversight delayed the acknowledgment of the significance of the Colfax Massacre and its related trial of white perpetrators, *U.S. v. Cruikshank,* the subject of the 1875 Supreme Court ruling that overturned the federal Ku Klux Klan enforcement laws. "*Thus ending carpetbag misrule in the South*": confined to the Colfax historical marker, the claim languished in obscurity, vivid evidence of DuBois's observation that Reconstruction history was "a field devastated by passion and belief."

A Second Reconstruction, brought about by a new campaign of freedom fighters and latter-day carpetbaggers in the 1950s and 1960s, transformed Reconstruction scholarship but left the matter of Colfax and its marker untouched.

A hundred years would pass before the publication of an exposé in one of the few American publications addressed explicitly to a biracial audience, *The Angolite,* a prison magazine published at Louisiana State Penitentiary at Angola. In recognition of its prizewinning journalism, the *Angolite*'s crusading editor, a black, self-educated death-row veteran, and its most trusted reporters were allowed to travel in pursuit of stories, including a profile of the Colfax Massacre that appeared in the winter issue of the magazine in 1989.[8]

Face to face with hardened criminals, including lead author Ron Wikberg, then serving a life sentence for murder, and his coauthors,

E. J. Carter and Floyd Webb, the black citizens of Colfax felt empowered to issue the first challenge to the marker's version of history.

As the first black journalists ever to visit the town, the *Angolite* reporters inspired the confidence of shared perspective. Their status as convicts may have given them credibility among a black population with one of the highest rates of incarceration in the country.[9] In a state that had historically put its criminal justice system at the service of white supremacy and the social order, the *Angolite* reporters invited a discussion about the nature of crime.

"Bones wash up out of the ground," black residents complained, explaining that for generations they had quietly reburied any bones that were exposed. They told reporters of the flaming fountain, of their ancestors' Easter vigils in the swamps. They expressed their outrage at the historical marker. "The well stopped working the same day they put that sign up in front of the courthouse," said Willie White, a man of 60. "I believe God put a curse on [Colfax] when they set that sign up."

Illustrated and meticulously documented, the *Angolite* article, entitled "Tragedy at Colfax," broke the silence of respectable opinion. Appearing simultaneously but briefly in Eric Foner's definitive account of Reconstruction, details of the event marked the first progress toward a just reckoning since the abandonment of the Radical experiment in the middle of the 1870s.[10]

One reader of the *Angolite*'s account was Lalita Tademy, a genealogist and author living in California who became the first to publicize her family's link to Colfax victims and the crime. Tademy was descended from longtime residents of Central Louisiana, including slaves belonging to the area's white and Creole aristocracy. As happens among Louisiana families, the white identity of many of her forebears appeared plainly in the public records she began to research early in the 1990s. *Cane River*, a national best-selling roots story of 2001, included an unflattering depiction of 20th-century Colfax, which appeared in her reflections on the 1930s as a bastion of bigotry and pettiness.[11] Her own memories of the town derived from regular summertime visits in the 1950s and early 1960s, before integration transformed the social and political landscape. Lalita Tademy read the marker and resolved to learn the truth that her relatives were loath to disclose.

"Our people were there," said an aunt, who refused to say anything more. "Some got out, and some didn't."[12]

The result of Tademy's research and imagination was *Red River,* a novel that focuses upon the history of the participants in the massacre, including black and white ancestors on both sides of her family tree. Strikingly authentic, documented liberally by the substantial hidden record of events, her story lets the spirits speak. "I think on those colored men in the courthouse every day," says a great grandmother in the book: "dog-bone set to fight for an idea, no matter the risk."[13]

Like Tademy's novel, this book continues the project of recovering the lost history of the Colfax Massacre, pursuing origins, characters, and legacies in the fragmented documentary record of events. It relies heavily on the work of scholars with particular interest in legal and political dimensions of *Cruikshank* and the Colfax Massacre—most written since the 1990s.

Equal parts outrage and admiration for the courage of its subjects drive the inquiry across the years. Its reconstruction of the rhetorical site of the massacre builds on the foundations of earth-shattering change in the contemporary era, as a Second Reconstruction joined African Americans and their allies in pursuit of equality and the truth about the deadliest incident of racial violence in the history of the United States. Empowered at last by the world's turn, the ghosts of Colfax have mustered in these pages to provide the fullest account of their fate.

The Colfax Massacre

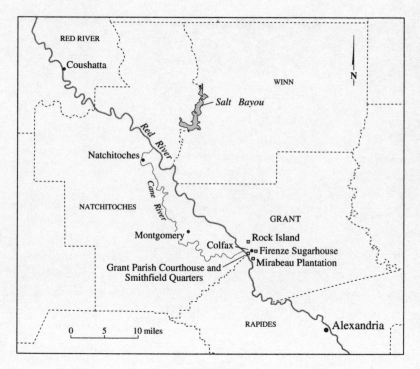

Grant Parish and environs

ONE

Alabama Fever

THE FORCES THAT CREATED THE COMMUNITY AT COLFAX
sprang into motion with a churn and crack in 1832, as a
U.S. Army Corps of Engineers snagboat removed the first of millions
of submerged trees from the Great Raft of the Red River. The logjam
had been the wonder of its ancient environment: more than 100 miles
in length, stronger than the river itself, and older at nearly 1,000 years
than the fresh, alluvial soil of the valley. Louisiana had been made
in this way over the course of millennia, by the buoyant migration
of dirt and organic material from the farthest reaches of the North
American continent. Confounding navigation, moving water and
earth unpredictably, dwarfing human effort in its geologic immensity,
the Red River and its Great Raft had presented an insurmountable
obstacle to settlement and commerce. Deep into the era of Louisiana's
globalization, the Red River valley remained the wilderness within the
southeastern frontier.

The river had met its match in Captain Henry Shreve. In an era of
technological innovations and bold commerce, Shreve made his mark
as a master of the Mississippi watershed. His modifications to the original
Robert Fulton steamboat design and his challenge to the Fulton mono-
poly after 1812 had facilitated the transportation revolution that made New
Orleans the first great boom town of the nineteenth century.[1] Shreve's
alliance with the Corps of Engineers symbolized the momentous engagement of federal power in the development of the western frontier: the
first application of the power invested by the interstate commerce clause
of the Constitution, harnessed to the ambition of private entrepreneurs

such as Shreve. The lure of a government contract turned Shreve's attention to the project of designing his original snagboat, which netted a
large share of a $75,000 federal appropriation in 1824. As superinten-
dent of a $300,000 river improvement program in the 1830s, Shreve drew
a handsome salary, supervised the purchase of three snagboats for the
Corps of Engineers, and profited by his insider's awareness of the future
transportation trajectories.[2] The removal of the Red River Raft was the
crowning achievement of his career, symbolized by the designation of
the new head of commercial navigation on the Red River as the city
of Shreveport.

Shreve's attack on the raft, using steam power and human muscle,
proceeded with astonishing success. His snagboats battered the gates
of the logjam at full speed and lay claim to dislodged trees, using giant
pincers and lengths of chain. Ratcheting the wood above deck, Corps
of Engineer crew members used cross-saws to break the mass into man-
ageable pieces before sending them downriver. In their first day on the
job in 1832, Shreve's crew cleared four miles. By 1838, the Red River
was open for commerce to the headwaters of Caddo Lake in East Texas.
Hailed as a heroic feat of engineering, the victory of man over nature
on Red River proved deceptively simple. The essential hubris of the act
remained invisible for generations afterward.

Terrible consequences in two discrete series of events flowed out of
the removal of the Great Red River Raft. First, the tragedy of slavery
descended on the land. Where Caddo Indians had shared the hills and
swamps with scattered white families, tremendous estates rose, offering
products to the world market. Shreve himself facilitated the sale of Red
River tracts to slave-power investors. Upon this transformed landscape,
the new arrivals built a towering hierarchy of race and class, compromised
from the outset by the unseen fissures of black ambition. Where floods
and land crevasses still threatened, Red River planters used human fuel
to fire a tremendous engine of wealth creation. Where the river ran red
with dirt and hurtling logs, carrying five times the sediment load of the
infamously muddy Mississippi, the African American community accumulated grievances of historic proportions. A reckoning to dwarf the
raft removal would charge the gates of this impregnable morass during
the Civil War and Reconstruction era.

A second, unseen horror commenced immediately but imperceptibly,
as Shreve's snagboats liberated forces of nature beyond the control

of humankind. In fact, the actions of the Corps of Engineers—in particular, the decision to dredge across a log-jammed bend of one of the Red River's 29 switchbacks—merely accelerated a process already under way for at least a century, by which the Mississippi River was leaking into the Atchafalaya River. The sharply steeper and shorter course of the Atchafalaya has ensured the constant escalation of the water transfer, as water in the Mississippi seeks the most direct course to the sea. The breakup of the Great Raft moved up the geological time-table for a momentous shift in the course of the Mississippi River, with fateful consequences for New Orleans, the river deltas, and the social order they sustained.[3]

The material changes under way intruded literally overnight at the site that would become Colfax. In 1832, during heavy rains some months after the initiation of the raft project, the Red River jumped its banks and claimed the circular channel that locals immediately christened the Rigolette de Bon Dieu.[4] The visible cut in the river's path created a high bluff that would later serve as the steamboat landing for one of the most profitable ventures in the history of agriculture. Shreve himself would pay the first call, to inquire about the current owner of the adjacent land on behalf of an associate from out of state.

The chain of intermediaries in the sale of the Colfax land gives a clue to the elaborate means of profit-taking in the late-era frontier environment of 1830s Louisiana. When Shreve sounded his boat's sig-nature hail on the site above the Rigolette de Bon Dieu, he was heard throughout the river bottom and piney woods and at points beyond the reach of sound. The captain's choice of local brothers, John and Peter Hickman, as his agents in a sale was the talk of farming households scat-tered on a broad arc. Remarkably, the river champion would deliver a total of $200,000 to the brothers, who in turn contracted Jean Baptiste Prudhomme of nearby Natchitoches, himself an agent of the French owner of the House of Bourbon title to the property.[5] The sale even-tually encompassed 15,000 acres of land fronting seven uninterrupted miles of the Red River.

Captain Shreve was perhaps the only man who did not claim a fee, and his services to his out-of-state friend exceeded the typical exchange of courtesies among gentlemen. Shreve's associate had probably done most of the time-consuming research into titles and provenance for himself, as his responsibilities as the junior U.S. senator from South Carolina had included service on the Committee on Private Land Claims, the federal agency charged with the resolution of colonial and current land tenure. The distribution of the Louisiana Purchase, with its overlapping U.S., French, and Spanish administrations, had been the chief preoccupation of the committee since its creation in 1826. From his just-vacated position in Washington, Senator William Smith had accumulated very useful insight into eligible sites for development along the river reaches Shreve knew best. More important still, Smith's influence might help keep river management appropriations flowing to the Corps and its Louisiana projects, including the Great Raft removal, still years away from completion.

Indeed, the former senator from South Carolina was a powerful man at the time of the Red River sale: the recent chairman of the Judiciary Committee, former justice of the South Carolina high court, and a personal friend of the sitting president, Andrew Jackson, with whom Smith had attended a one-room school in the South Carolina backcountry. In 1829, Smith had turned down Jackson's offer of a seat on the bench of the United States Supreme Court, giving as his reason his reluctance to be constrained from speaking out on political issues.

Residing in New Orleans in the winter months of 1832 and 1833, the senator, then aged 70, must have seemed to Shreve the embodiment of power and influence. But in fact, his political fortunes would turn for the worse in his twilight years for want of winning elections. Appointed twice to fill South Carolina seats in the Senate under special circumstances (1816–1823 and 1826–1831), William Smith was losing ground to John C. Calhoun, his Senate partner and bitter rival from the home state. Smith had fallen out with his more famous colleague over the issue of the "nullification" of federal legislation by states, occasioned by the passage of what Calhoun called the "Tariff of Abominations" in the 1820s. In the words of an admirer, Smith, "though a very good States-rights man, was not exactly ready for disunion." Smith watched as his rival came to be regarded as conscience and voice of the South.[6]

Taking up residence in Alabama and Louisiana in the early 1830s, the old judge stoked the embers of his political ambitions as a representative in the Alabama state legislature and in an overture to faithless electors that almost delivered him the vice presidential nomination in 1836. His chief occupation in his last decade would be the acquisition and development of plantations.

Some of William Smith's best-known political convictions stood sharply in opposition to his real estate ventures. In a conflict that did not go unnoted by South Carolina critics, the judge's investments on the frontier of sugar cultivation placed him in the minority of southerners whose business interest favored tariffs, a device which Smith had publicly denounced as an abomination. More inflammatory still, the judge, who enjoyed his reputation as one of the most dogged critics of federally financed public works, reaped the benefits of federal development expenditures amply in his Louisiana purchase. Smith had voted against the admission to statehood of Mississippi, Alabama, and Missouri during his first term in the Senate in protest against the designation of one-twentieth of the territory as public lands—"monstrous donations," in his view, to the overreaching government in Washington. Buying into the territory opened by the Corps of Engineers Mississippi watershed management program, he took advantage of the greatest peacetime federal expenditure for public works yet authorized by Congress.[7]

In the course of his dogged resistance to public financing for improvements in North Alabama, Smith took pains to "solemnly declare" during an 1835 dispute in the Alabama legislature, "that during my twelve years in the Senate, I never voted to appropriate one cent in money, or one inch of public lands for works of Internal Improvement, or for any other purpose beyond the purposes specified in the Constitution."[8] By virtue of distance and the primitive communication networks of the time, the old conservative (who in fact served just ten years in the Senate) managed to conceal his private speculation on the federal project in Louisiana. The contradiction between his political principles and his acts on his own behalf remained undiscovered.

In the matter of another pillar of William Smith's political outlook, however, the purchase and development of the Louisiana land was a seamless fit. A longtime slave-owner, Smith made his name as one of the Senate's most passionate defenders of forced labor. He became almost notorious for his willingness to endorse slavery in unconventionally unequivocal terms. In contradiction to Thomas Jefferson's prediction (in *Notes on the State of Virginia*) that the sin of slavery would haunt the households of the South, Smith denied that mutual hostility structured the relationship between masters and slaves. Instead, he argued, self-interest on the part of masters favored humane considerations on the model of family life. "The whole commerce between masters and slaves,"

he argued in an 1816 speech, "is patriarchal." Against those who called
for abolition, however, the vituperative Smith invoked the authority
of Jefferson, that "venerable patriot," and of Moses in Leviticus, and of
"the only true and living God," comparing his enemies to Robespierre
and the "praetorian guards of the Romans," denouncing slavery in defiance of tradition and natural law. "It is very easy for those who have
their fortunes secured in bank stock...or money at interest," he complained, "[to] deliberately proclaim a jubilee to our slaves, in which
they have neither interest to lose nor danger to fear."[9]

Smith was so outspoken that he was able to preserve his reputation
as a champion of slavery in spite of his objections to the admission of
new slave states, including Alabama, his adopted home, during his first
term in the Senate.

Smith had inherited a single slave from his parents, who both died
young in up-country South Carolina, then the frontier of Revolution-
era America. The slave Priam would live to be more than 100 years old,
and his assistance to Smith in the early years of the 19th century must
have been invaluable. By 1820, the aspiring politician managed a size-
able workforce on his York, South Carolina plantation, with roughly 50
of his 87 slaves at the peak of their working and childbearing years.[10] In
Dallas and Autauga counties in the southern Alabama "black belt," the
judge accumulated 6,000 acres worked by a very large number of slaves
in the 1820s and 1830s. With yields of 400 to 500 cotton bales annu-
ally, the Alabama plantations would have had to employ upward of 100
slaves, some of whom may have made the journey west after the sale
of the properties in York.[11] A townhouse and plantation in Huntsville,
Alabama, where Smith established his primary residence, employed a
slave population of about 30, including the original, Priam. According
to their skills and age, their value in 1840, the year the judge died, ranged
from $300 to $1,000 apiece.[12]

Land made up the lion's share of the old judge's personal assets. Smith
was first and foremost a frontiersmen, an early victim of the "Alabama
Fever" that swept a new generation of slaveholders into the southeast
after 1812. Smith bought into the territory that became Alabama when
Tecumseh still walked its paths—before the initial cessions of land by the
Cherokee and Creek Indians—acting on a tip from General Jackson.[13]
His push toward the Red River anticipated the fateful westward tra-
jectory of cotton cultivation, which supplied the bustling demands of

Northeastern and English textile factories even as it tore at the fabric of national unity in the decades before the Civil War. Given to plain living and hard travel, the old judge knew how to grow cotton, with expertise that extended to plantation medicine and the diet of slaves. His insider's knowledge of the adjudication of land claims and appropriations for infrastructure development had yielded tremendous dividends in fertile land and market access.

William Smith's personal westward migration, however, also underscored the volatility of land as a means of producing wealth. The high demands of cotton cultivation had exhausted the productivity of his holdings in South Carolina and Huntsville by the 1830s, and his properties in South Alabama inexorably yielded nutrients with every crop. Expansion into Louisiana's Red River country and other undeveloped spaces offered the only hope for sustaining the profitability of his life's work. Having failed in politics, Smith would have to break new ground for plantation agriculture or else surrender to old age.

Embarking on this major venture late in life, Smith relied on the energy and insight of the younger man who married Smith's orphaned granddaughter, whom he had raised as if she was his own child, shortly after the Red River acquisition. At age 24, slightly above the national average age for first marriage, Mary Smith Taylor had languished in the service of her grandfather's ambition, riding rough roads to his far-flung obligations in Washington, South Carolina, Alabama, and Louisiana. A Carolina suitor had described Mary as "not beautiful" and "taciturn." Upon learning of her decision to vacate the state with her grandfather's move to Huntsville, the young man would call her "ugly [and] cold-blooded."[14] Attractive enough when ornamented by her grandfather's sprawling domains, she found an intimate companion in Meredith Calhoun, whom she probably met in the vicinity of Natchez, Mississippi. The couple was married at the handsome Trinity Episcopal Church in that city on May 24, 1834.

Meredith Calhoun was perhaps the only man ever to contract the Alabama Fever in the exchange floors of European ports. At age 28, Calhoun had already compiled a storied career in international trade. He was only a boy when he made his first journey in the service of the great American merchant and financier Stephen Girard. Girard, an avowed atheist who would accumulate one of the five largest fortunes in the history of the United States, with a 21st-century value of $83 billion, was an acquaintance of Calhoun's father and uncle, the Colhouns, Irish immigrants engaged in Philadelphia's maritime trade.[15] The placement offered young Meredith an unparalleled opportunity for advancement as an apprentice and journeyman in Girard's sprawling enterprises.[16] Trained as an accountant under the personal supervision of the master, Calhoun took to the sea at age 12 and soon after earned the rank of supercargo in Girard's merchant fleet. The supercargo took responsibility for the cargo of goods, beginning typically in Philadelphia with shipments of manufactured goods, luxury items, and wines destined for ports in the U.S. South, where they would be exchanged for agricultural products and carried to Europe. Girard's fleet of ships—nicknamed the Philosophers for the Enlightenment values honored in such names as *Voltaire, Rousseau, Montesquieu,* and *Liberty*—remained constantly in motion, loading and discharging cargo in every ocean, and sailing for years at a time between calls at the home port.[17]

Girard's confidence in protégés such as young Calhoun (the second or third most favored of his apprentices in a class of two dozen) exceeded the standard business models of the era by a wide margin.[18] In his capacity as supercargo, Calhoun supervised the exchange of hundreds of thousands of dollars in goods and cash, personally determining the global price structure for commodities and currency. The supercargo made meticulous reports to Girard on the content of every transaction, but in an age when letters made ocean voyages by private means alone, the true extent of Girard's oversight was minimal. His willingness to risk his initial investments in Calhoun's hands gave Girard the flexibility to follow opportunities that other traders missed and to collect a portion of the profits Calhoun could obtain for himself. Calhoun accumulated capital, business acumen, and cosmopolitan panache. For 13 years, he scarcely knew the feel of dry land.

Calhoun's moral education under the tutelage of one of the 19th century's most notorious unbelievers proved more ambiguous. A typical cargo included mundane evils such as tobacco, sugar, and rum en route from the Americas, copper, iron, and flax from Russia, Indian textiles, or luxury and manufactured items taken on at Le Havre or Amsterdam. After the British navy made its historic commitment to uprooting the trade in the early 19th century, Girard's vessels rarely carried slaves, although Calhoun was probably involved as a junior partner in an unsuccessful slaving scheme involving two human cargoes in the late 1820s.[19] As a matter of course, however, Calhoun regularly traded in opium intended for the China market, where traditional trade goods were in low demand. Girard's ships took on most of their opium in the East, where the illicit wares of India and Afghanistan found their markets, but his supercargoes carried explicit instructions to buy it wherever it could be found. Calhoun fulfilled his master's wishes amply, securing virtually all of the available supply at the European ports he usually visited. "It would be mortifying to me," Girard wrote to another agent on a ship frequently supervised by Meredith Calhoun, "if after the *Rousseau* has been at or near a port or a place where opium can be obtained on reasonable terms, she should go to China without reaping the same advantage as others will do."[20]

Calhoun's journeys also introduced him to a breathtaking range of cruelties in human interactions. The seafaring life was notoriously hard, as sailors on merchant ships endured the same harsh discipline as those impressed into naval service. In the prevailing attitude toward the corporal punishment meted out to slaves, a visitor to Calhoun's Red River plantations in the 1850s would hear something "exactly like what I have heard again and again, *ad nauseam,* from Northern ship-masters and officers."[21]

On land in Europe and Asia, the young Philadelphian encountered stark contradictions to the doctrine of brotherly love. In Russia, he watched his local ombudsman knock a livery servant to the ground and viciously apply the horsewhip when Calhoun's carriage was delayed. He visited textile mills and ironworks in England and on the continent in the same era that inspired the denunciations of Marx and Engels. Calhoun recoiled from the "pestilential and destructive system" that debased factory laborers. Even slavery, he would later explain, was not as cruel as those industrial masters, "possessed of most sumptuous abundance," whose laboring millions knew hunger, filth, and isolation.

> [M]illions of them were driven into a dreary exile, voluntarily destroying their social happiness by sundering their family ties and withdrawing themselves from all that they loved, to gratify the meanest and most material wants. What kind of morality was such a state of society likely to produce?

Calhoun had seen the 19th-century world and found it hard, unfair. It was his good fortune, he observed, to find himself among the favored classes of the most hierarchical and most productive era in the history of human enterprise.

Educated at firsthand about the booming opportunities of the age, Calhoun would choose to stake his all on slavery. Leaving behind the merchant city of his youth, declining the opportunity to employ his knowledge in the growing network of financial institutions in New York, and disdaining the emerging industrial economy in New England and Midwestern towns, when he finally chose to put down roots after all his years of wandering, he went south. Like his uncle, Gustavus Calhoun, who had established a plantation in the wilds around Natchez in the 1820s, Meredith Calhoun deemed the slave economy to hold the greatest opportunity for profits in any kind of business. In partnership with Judge Smith, Calhoun invested his personal capital in the construction of a network of plantations that ranked among the great entrepreneurial ventures of the day.

Calhoun bought slaves, making Huntsville, Alabama the base of the operation. Huntsville was a pretty market town in the foothills of the Appalachian Mountains, the first settlement of white migrants and their slaves within the boundaries that became Alabama in 1819. In Huntsville, cotton was king—its cultivation and delivery to markets occupied the energies of nearly everyone in town. A thriving cotton market brought wagons from miles around to the rows of storefronts surrounding the courthouse square, where the names of bankers and cotton brokers were stenciled on plate glass. On the Tennessee River and on one of the earliest railroads built in the South, Huntsvillians shipped the white gold of the Tennessee Valley to Memphis and New Orleans and beyond. By the 1830s, stately avenues of mansions composed the nucleus of an urban elite. Schools, theaters, and handsome churches cultivated the gentry of what became the most refined inland city of the Deep South. Judge Smith, a Huntsville old-timer and representative in the Alabama legislature, took his place among the leading citizens and ensured a favorable reception for the Philadelphian among Huntsville's best families. Out of respect for his grandfather-in-law, whose hatred for John C. Calhoun of South Carolina was well-known, the young man employed the Old Country spelling of his name around town, introducing himself as Colhoun for the remainder of the old judge's life.

Already in the 1830s, however, the red clay soil of North Alabama showed signs of diminished fertility. As planters such as William Smith began to retire or to trade out their Alabama farms for opportunities out west, Huntsville's storefronts and the pages of its newspaper advertised a growing supply of surplus slaves. Having arrived at the right place at just the right time—holding ready cash—Meredith Calhoun stood poised to assemble the human assets of his enterprise with Smith under the most favorable market conditions.

A lifelong commodities broker, practiced at assessing value with his own hands, Calhoun brought tremendous expertise and skill to the purchase of slaves. Slaves sold as individuals or in lots appeared in his fixer's eye in the image of other commodities, with calculable values in currency, hogsheads, or bales. He could also benefit from the insight of his brother William Calhoun, Stephen Girard's longtime agent on the wharves of Charleston, Alexandria, and New Orleans, for whom the sights and sounds of slave auctions were as commonplace as salt air.

Calhoun could calculate with actuarial certainty the skew of slave productivity and profits across the demographic indices. Older slaves and children constituted disproportionately small numbers on his Louisiana plantations—16 and 150, respectively, out of the total population of 738 slaves that appeared on the 1850 census. Less than 5 percent were over 50, and only 20 percent were children. In contrast, 27 percent of slaves on his Uncle Gus Calhoun's Natchez plantation were 50 or older, with 22 percent under 12 years of age.[22] The young man who recoiled at the horror of wage slavery in the industrial city matured on plantations managed by factory values: life itself was found to have a price.

Only the meanest class of southern men was designated as slave traders. The opprobrium directed at this kind of exchange inspired the only attack on slave power ventured by the federal government before the Civil War, when Congress prohibited the import of slaves from overseas in 1808. The role that Meredith Calhoun performed for the benefit of his grandfather-in-law's investments in Louisiana might be better understood as slave brokerage, except that his specific purchases and sales cannot be reconstructed by documentary records. Secrecy surrounding transactions in the internal trade in slaves was a hallmark of the general taboo. William Smith's insatiable political ambitions, moreover, required extensive subterfuge to deflect constituents' attention from his business out of state.[23]

During the winter of 1836, Calhoun and Smith assembled a transport of roughly 1,000 slaves destined for the Red River plantations. Market conditions had been favorable: oversupply in the vicinity of Huntsville made it possible to dispense with some of the ordinary inconveniences of human chattel. Rather than purchasing whole families of slaves, for example, Calhoun and his buyers chose about 700 healthy teenagers and women and men near the age of 20. The new arrivals joined the mixed-age lot of about 300 slaves that had worked the old judge's South Alabama plantation and the farm east of Huntsville, which now provided temporary shelter for the group. Bargain prices for slaves offset some of the extraordinary expenses of other necessities for the trip, during a period when the high cost of flour, potatoes, and other necessities made newspaper headlines.[24] The partnership paid dearly for the 100 wagons and 1,000 mules that would accompany their slaves to Louisiana. Leaving under cover of darkness (so as not to attract the attention of Smith's political enemies), the caravan was thought to be the largest overland transport in the history of the cotton frontier. In its cargo, Calhoun assembled his outrageous aspirations to the sumptuous abundance of the world.

The path from Huntsville to the southwest had been worn by millions of footsteps, spanning the millennia in its Indian origins and serving as an artery of the American westward migration of the 19th century. In recent decades, the overland route out of Huntsville had come to specialize in forced migrations. The expansion of the cotton frontier required the transfer of at least 600,000 slaves between 1810 and 1860, with points west of Huntsville in Mississippi, Louisiana, and Texas claiming the largest share.[25] The 1830s were peak years, not only for slave crossings but also for Indian transports. Under military supervision, the federal government removed some 20,000 Choctaw, Creek, and Chickasaw between 1830 and 1836 to Indian Territory north of the Texas border, with additional thousands, including 16,000 from the Cherokee Nation, to come in 1837 and 1838.

Along the trail of Cherokee tears as far as Muscle Shoals, the Smith and Calhoun caravan made its sorrowful way. At the intersection with the Natchez Trace, the company of slaves was redirected to the Deepest South.

As a business venture under expert management, the Red River transport probably avoided the most terrible blunders of Indian removal. The migration of the Choctaw had produced a fiasco that even government could not abide and was seeking to redress during Calhoun's own

planning stages. Removal agents had received inadequate funds, as little
as $100 per day to protect and feed hundreds of animals and migrants.
Provisions had run short, even where forward units of the U.S. Army
had placed resupply caches at 80-mile intervals. Due to corruption, bad
luck, and cheap service, water transportation was uncomfortable and
terrifying. The harrowing scene witnessed by Alexis de Tocqueville,
who saw Choctaws near Memphis cross the Mississippi on a flatboat
ferry that their dogs were afraid to board, would have been an inevitable
requirement of the slaves' journey. Floods, low water, and bad directions waylaid parties in unfamiliar settings remote from settlement. The
high mortality of the Indian migrations—ranging from 15 to 25 percent—illustrated starkly the high stakes of the Calhoun transport.[26]

Depending on the season of the year 1836 in which the caravan
departed, Smith and Calhoun's slaves faced the challenges of either
winter or summer in the elements. The ferry scene that disturbed de
Tocqueville owed its special horror to the icy condition of the river, in
which jagged floes moved with enough velocity to knock the flatboat
off its course. Harsh winters in 1831 and 1832 had contributed to the
mortality and privations of the initial Choctaw transports. Summertime
transport might prove even more dangerous in an age when dysentery
and bacterial infections stalked communities everywhere. The warm-
weather cholera epidemics of 1831 and 1832 killed tens of thousands
in North America, including uncounted numbers of migrant slaves.
Exacerbating ordinary risks, a final spasm of southeastern Indian resistance, the so-called Second Creek War, saw Indians targeting U.S. mails
and other potentially valuable transports in Alabama and Mississippi
from May 16 until the end of the year.[27]

Slaves in Calhoun's caravan to Red River, like the Indians in their
similar journeys, would have been required to abandon their dead. For
most, this indignity would have come at the end of a series of forced
interruptions of friendships and family life. The interregional slave
trade of the 19th century imposed a harsh economy on slave families. In the eastern seaboard slave states of Maryland, Virginia, and the
Carolinas, commercial agriculture experienced declining productivity
due to market saturation in traditional products such as tobacco and
the exhaustion of the soil by centuries of cultivation. By the time of
the American Revolution, elites in these states had become preoccupied with the problem of surplus slaves. The expansion of the cotton

frontier stimulated the economies of both slave sections, opening up profitable new fields or commercial production and buoying the price and demand for East Coast slaves. For the hundreds of thousands who made the journey to new western plantations, migration severed even the most intimate family connections. Sales broke up as many as one in three slave marriages, and separated half of all children from their parents.[28]

Calhoun purchased most if not all of his slaves from plantations in Alabama, which began to experience its own problems with surplus slaves in the 1830s. Because cotton placed such high demands on the nutrient content of the soil, land tended to lose productivity after about 20 years of cultivation. The immediate vicinity of Huntsville, therefore, which had served as the first Alabama frontier during the early years of William Smith's ventures in the town, included a number of exhausted plantations where owners were eager to sell their human property. Between 1830 and 1840, the slave population of the town and its vicinity actually decreased by about a thousand.[29] Some proportion of these losses made up the transport of 1,000 to the Red River property of Smith and Calhoun, for which probably 750 new slaves were purchased. Most—as reckoned by the shockingly small range of ages on the 1850 slave schedule—were 15 to 25 years old. Roughly half of these migrants were old enough to remember their first sale and transport, which had brought them to Alabama from the East Coast states.[30]

Sarah Thomas, whose parents made the migration as slaves from Virginia to Rapides Parish, Louisiana, provided a fragment of song to an interviewer in the 1930s that captured some of the horror of forced separation.

> You're selling me to Georgy,
> But you cannot sell my soul,
> Thank God Almighty,
> God will fix it for us some day!
> I hope my old gran'mother
> Will meet poor John some day,
> I knows I won't know him, when I meets him,
> Cause he was so young when dey sold him away.[31]

Illiteracy and poor communications technology made the separation of family members total and permanent. Only after Emancipation would a lucky few be reunited with loved ones who survived.

The "coffle" provided the primary means of transporting slaves overland. Coffling employed a variety of means to prevent runaways, the most severe of which was the coffle yoke. Coffle yokes bound a slave to a partner, using a smaller version of the wooden yoke used to harness oxen; another strategy joined slaves in a line by chaining their necks or shoulders along a length of pole. When the need for security was less pronounced or where terrain was more difficult, a transport might join slaves by generous lengths of chain at the wrists and ankles. Whatever the means of binding the slaves, standard coffles proceeded no more than two abreast, with slaves at four-foot intervals. Thus the Calhoun caravan, excluding the wagons and mules, extended roughly half a mile in length.

With good luck and good planning, the journey to Red River would have been completed in about a month. Calhoun would have incurred the expense of contracting with one of the many emigrating companies conducting the lively business of westward migration from Huntsville. Experienced slave-traders and aspiring overseers may have also played a role. Adding fees to the cost of provisions and equipment, the journey probably cost Smith and Calhoun about $15 per slave. With the average price of slaves on the New Orleans market spiraling as much as 100 percent over the Huntsville price in 1836, the overland transport saved Smith and Calhoun about $500 per capita.[32]

The timing of the venture was equally fortuitous. The Calhoun slaves crossed over to the left bank of the Red River some months before the onset of the depression caused by the Panic of 1837. The huge sums of capital expended by Smith and Calhoun in the 1830s fit the trend toward easy credit and inflation, fueled in part by foreign investment. The sudden contraction of the money supply in the Panic resulted in nationwide bank failures and widespread unemployment. Prices of commodities such as cotton and sugar dropped precipitously. Smith and Calhoun, however, had already made plans to miss 1837 and subsequent markets, as their slaves devoted their labors to clearing fields and filling swamps. Protected within the concrete assets of their investments in the previous decade, the partners waited out the economic turbulence by the turgid waters of the Red.

Upon arrival at the site that became Colfax, the managers of the Calhoun transport were free to unshackle their charges. The wildness of their new environment ensured the improbability of escape now that roads and footpaths veered away. The curiosity and obligations of whites in the surrounding area likewise cut off the possibility of flight. Few were old enough to know the labor of carving out a space for cultivation by experience, but all would learn the brute requirements in the months to come. The slaves felled and trimmed thousands of shrubs and pine and cypress trees, some of which were used to build the log cabins that would house the early generations of slaves. Magnificent timbers of giant cypress shaped the galleries and rooflines of a quartet of majestic dwelling houses for the masters and their wives. Calhoun had delivered lumber mill machinery to the site, the first farm for miles around to cut its own lumber, and slave-and-mule crews spent many hours hauling trees to the mill. His chattel filled swamps and broke 5,000 acres of raw land using fire and plows, benefiting from the relative scarcity of rocks and tree roots in the alluvial soil. The original parcel of land included overseers' housing and other basic improvements, but the great work of fencing, housing, and warehouse-building on the 15,000-acre spread consumed tremendous effort. On the riverbank above the Rigolette de Bon Dieu, modern capital gave form to an edifice of barbarous hierarchy.

Like Thomas Sutpen of Sutpen's Hundred, the tragic patriarch of William Faulkner's novel *Absalom, Absalom,* Meredith Calhoun built a plantation—"tore violently a plantation," as Faulkner described it—to crown the institution. In 1840, upon the death of the judge, Calhoun became the sole proprietor of four contiguous Red River operations— the Mirabeau, Smithfield, Meredith, and Firenze plantations—that would cultivate cotton and sugar at the state of the art. Calling on his personal connections (as well as his mighty capital supply), he imported a state-of-the-art sugar refinery, the second of its kind in the country, designed by the Louisiana-born mixed-race Parisian Norbert Rillieux. Ten Rillieux boilers—each 96 feet in length— occupied the interior of the brick building. Special chutes allowed laborers to unload wagons of wood directly into the fireboxes for each boiler from the outside. The Smith and Calhoun sugarhouse was the second largest in the United States, constructed at a cost of nearly $200,000. Rising on the banks of what became known as Sugarhouse Bayou and surrounded by acres of outbuildings, the Firenze sugar house was the largest and most extravagant structure for hundreds of miles around.[33]

Sugar was risky business on the Calhoun properties, the northern-most outpost of sugarcane cultivation in Louisiana and perhaps the world. The investment in the Rillieux evaporator aimed to offset the hazards of the latitude by processing cane juice faster than standard machinery.[34] Although Firenze reaped impressive yields in 1853 and 1854, sugar rarely accounted for a significant share of plantation revenues.[35] The investment in sugar aimed to offset the plantations' vulnerability to fluctuations in the cotton market. More important, perhaps, the sugar operation initiated Meredith Calhoun into the elite fraternity of Louisiana sugar planters. In their ranks, Calhoun found a community after decades of wandering.

Cotton was the lifeblood of the Calhoun plantations. On Mirabeau, Smithfield, and Meredith, the rich soil yielded bounteous harvests. With more hands than any other cotton planter in the state (and more than all but a handful of planters in the United States), the plantations tilled the most acres in Louisiana. By the late 1850s, the combination produced the largest cotton yields by far in the state. Calhoun produced 3,800 bales in 1859, a quantity that outstripped the second-largest Louisiana grower by 50 percent and the third-largest by 90 percent. With cotton selling for $44 a bale that year, the total value of the crop was $167,000—worth more than $3.5 million in 21st-century terms.[36] Coming on the heels of several bumper harvests for both cotton and sugar, the 1859 revenues swelled one of the greatest fortunes of the day.

Plantation revenues supported two sharply divergent lifestyles, with only five white employees, a manager and four overseers, to occupy a kind of middle ground. The Calhoun family dwelling houses on the four estates were fine but not opulent, built in the prevailing Louisiana style with steep pitched rooflines, inset porches, and narrow columns. In fact, the family visited rather than resided on the Louisiana proper-ties until right before the war. The Calhouns made their permanent residence in Huntsville in the fledgling city's largest building, the 12,000-square-foot townhouse constructed by William Smith in the years leading up to his death. Even in 1840, before the rich yields of the Red River properties started rolling in, the house and its appointments were the talk of the town, with a library valued at $1,000 and $4,000 in silver serving pieces.[37] A priceless collection of European art—thought to be the finest in the southern states—reflected the growing prosperity of the Calhoun estate and the family's extensive travels in Europe in the 1840s and 1850s.

The Calhouns actively took part in Huntsville's version of high society, forming close relationships with leading families and endowing the establishment of an Episcopal church on a lot adjacent to their hometown property. Between visits to Europe, the ongoing renovation and refinement of the Huntsville house and gardens, and the management of the Louisiana plantations, Meredith Calhoun found ample energy to manage the affairs of the local Episcopal church he had endowed and its long-suffering minister, Henry C. Lay. The construction of an opulent sanctuary and rectory on a lot adjacent to the mansion attracted the old supercargo's excess of energy for business.

"Friend [Colhoun] has a great deal to say to me about church," Lay wrote to his wife in 1853. "It does not suit him to see us go [about our business] without his co-operation, and he remonstrates accordingly." Calhoun's motivations seemed more sociable than spiritual to Reverend Lay, who complained, "He has not put his foot inside the church," for all his willingness to intervene. Indeed, Calhoun's refined sensibilities stood at odds with some features of Old Time Religion in the Deep South. "Mr. Col. says it is a most intolerable thing that I should undertake to put down dancing," wrote Lay, "and that he has a great mind to build a handsome opposition church on his lot opposite."[38]

As their income rose in the 1840s and 1850s, the Calhouns spent more of their time in Europe, acquiring chandeliers, carpets, and more precious works of art. In the court of Emperor Napoleon III of France and the Empress Eugenie, Meredith Calhoun and his wife and daughter joined the ranks of a coterie of U.S. admirers. Their enthusiasm was reputed to have extended to the purchase of a pair of aristocratic titles—Count and Countess Calhoun—in exchange for $100,000 for the treasury of France.

Wealth served to insulate the family from the moral hazards of its acquisition, allowing them to avoid the sights and sounds of forced labor on the plantation for years at a time. Staging slavery as costume drama for the European class, the Calhoun patrimony maintained the greatest possible distance between their persons and the bodies held in bondage in their name.

TWO

The Philosopher

REAT PHILOSOPHERS WHO DO NOT WRITE FIND A HARD road to fame. Preoccupied with the requirements of business—tongue-lashing, fence-mending—men of means with agendas to develop had little time for scholarly reflection. Meredith Calhoun had been known to dabble with a pen, producing a pamphlet on the subject of the philanthropy and patriotism of his first patron, Stephen Girard. What he mainly wrote was numbers, more than most men could dream about: credits, debits, receipts; bills of sale to millineries, art brokers, and portrait artists; hogsheads and bales; bushels, barrels, and tons; female, 25, her son, 6.

A mover and shaker like Calhoun required a scribe, a young man, perhaps—learned, upright, and eager for the royal entertainments reserved for the rich and their guests. It was Meredith Calhoun's great fortune—in keeping with his running streak of luck—to host an intellectual of this description near the peak years of his glory as a slave master.

Frederick Law Olmsted was 30 when he made his way to the Calhoun Plantations on the Red River. In 1853, the Calhoun family made its first sojourn in Louisiana since 1848. In all probability, the encounter was not accidental, though the destruction of both men's personal records by fire makes the reconstruction of the invitation impossible. Olmsted was not yet widely respected for his Civil War–era service as the head of the U.S. Sanitary Commission, supervising soldiers' medical care, and his greatest fame still lay decades in the future, awaiting the fulfillment of his design for New York's Central Park. In 1853, Olmsted's talent and helpful associations had won his appointment as a special correspondent for the *New York Daily Times* to report on a subject of burning interest to many northerners inspired by the heightening controversy over slavery and its southern defenders. To satisfy the curiosity and budding outrage of its readers, the *Daily Times* commissioned Olmsted to journey to the belly of the beast, to observe the South's peculiar institution firsthand with a critical eye.

Far from making Meredith Calhoun a household name, Olmsted would guard his identity securely, taking greater pains to prevent his identification than he did with any other character that appeared in his column and his subsequent book. Based on what he saw on Calhoun's plantations and what he came to know about its master, the Yankee journalist took extra care to cover his tracks, even placing the story of his visit to Calhoun out of sequence in his journey from Virginia to Texas.[1] On Calhoun's Red River plantations, Olmsted would encounter a display more cruel and a defense of slavery more defiant than all the rest.

Olmsted traveled up the Red River by steamboat in the spring of 1853. He would have his first glimpse of the four Calhoun plantations well before his arrival, passing the small clusters of plantation buildings, approximating villages near steamboat landings, and the rolling lawns of four stately Calhoun dwelling houses, spread along the family's seven-mile stretch of the riverbank. He disembarked in the old city of Natchitoches, 30 miles to the north, and traveled overland to Firenze, the finest of the family estates.[2] With the indulgence of the master, Olmsted enjoyed virtually unfettered access to the plantation, accompanying the plantation manager and overseers on their rounds. In the evenings, the Yankee traveler was invited to the family table at Firenze, where he received ample portions of Calhoun's hospitality and outspoken opinion.

"The proprietor believed the negro race was expressly designed by Providence for servitude," Olmsted wrote. In support of his case, Calhoun referred to his broad experience of the world. One need only look at "the condition of negroes where they were allowed their freedom," he opined, to find them "in a most melancholy condition." On the other hand, "their condition when in slavery he thought to be superior to that of any white laboring class in the world."

Everywhere the laborer was degraded, stupid, unable to take care of himself. In Slavery he had a master, who, unlike a free laborer's master, had a direct pecuniary interest in taking care of him, in protecting him and supporting him in his rights.

Calhoun had been to England, and seen working men "entirely at the mercy of any bad man who chose to...secure his private ends by [their] ruin." In the North, only the relative prosperity of manufacturing towns obscured the basic evil of the relations of production. Calhoun told Olmsted about his observations in Russia of the brutal suppression of the laboring class.

> As to the moral condition of the slaves, he asked me who there was to throw a stone. Look at the condition of things in New York, where thousands of virtually disposed women were forced by the state of society and their inability to take care of themselves, to a most loathsome prostitution—a state of things that had no parallel, and never could have, in a slave country.

"What kind of morality was such a state of society likely to produce?" he asked Olmsted rhetorically, without apology for his unveiled reference to the sexual abuse of slave women by their masters. At the same time, he admitted that he did not encourage religious observations among his slaves, being equally suspicious of black preachers and of white clergymen who ministered to slaves. "[A] religious negro generally made mischief and trouble," he believed. He had found "the public religious exercises of the negroes," he observed, "to be exactly similar, in their intellectual and moral character, to the Indian feast and war-dances, and [he] did not encourage them."

Olmsted recorded that most slaves on Firenze, Smithfield, Mirabeau, and Meredith lived in detached cabins—although some of the rough log cabins from the early years had not yet been replaced in the early 1850s. In keeping with the local style, newer slave cabins tended to be miniature versions of the master's dwelling houses, with peaked roofs and deep porches, although typically without windows. Lots around each of the houses were home to chickens and a family hog, with individual and community gardens nearby. Calhoun's overseers offered generous provisions, including cornmeal, pork, molasses, and salt. Coffee and hard liquor appeared only rarely, but slaves received wine in a gallon-sized crockery jug as part of their regular rations. The quality and amount of the jug's contents, according to local memory, varied according to the slave's individual standing with his master—a trick that Calhoun likely picked up in his seafaring years.[3] Sales of eggs and other produce from the slaves' own stock could be applied toward the purchase of barrels of flour at below-market prices, a practice intended to discourage illicit trade in liquor.[4]

"[S]hops kept by unprincipled white people," as described in a court document from the 1850s, appeared occasionally upon the edges of the Calhoun domain. Here, slaves could purchase whiskey "in exchange for articles pilfered from their masters," including agricultural produce. One such establishment, operated by the widow Antoinette Boulard and a man identified in the census as J. Rancho, attracted the personal attention of the master with devastating results. As described by the widow in the lawsuit *Antoinette Boulard v. Meredith Calhoun:*

> [B]y the advice and procurement of the defendant, certain white men, named Murray, Shelton, Johnson, Hamilton, and Houton [likely Calhoun's overseers], together with about twenty-nine slaves, all belonging to the defendant...came to the residence of the plaintiff, in the night of the 19th May, 1856, and forcibly and violently ejected her from her house, and removed her stock of goods, wares, and merchandize, from a store which she kept there; which, together with the person of the plaintiff, the said white men and slaves placed in a flatboat, and turned the same adrift in the Red River.

The Louisiana court refused Boulard's petition for $20,000 in damages, agreeing with Calhoun that such a merchant was "a nuisance to the community in which she resides."[5] Everything that passed for leisure and sustenance on the Calhoun plantations would come from the master or not at all.

Work started before sunrise, pausing briefly for breakfast and for a more extended period after lunch, and continued until after dark. Olmsted observed the plantations in early March, when crews of women drove plows behind single or double teams of mules. The men were primarily occupied with ditch digging, a critical task for irrigation and flood control. (A so-called task ditch, through a stretch of the toughest clay soil on the property, existed primarily to punish slave offenders with hardship duty.[6]) Under the supervision of a black driver armed with a whip, almost a hundred children were engaged in planting corn, moving in parallel lines with a machine-like rhythm that

Olmsted found unsettling.[7] These three sets of responsibilities fit into the seasonal pattern of agricultural work, with the busiest season getting under way with cotton picking in August and September and culminating in the rush to harvest and process sugarcane before the first freeze in November. Hoeing, weeding, harvesting, and the collection of wood for the sugarhouse fire kept the Calhoun slaves occupied full-time for all but a week or two each year.

The crack of the whip sounded constantly, Olmsted observed, but rarely touched the working crews, "except very lightly, or as a caution to smaller children when they did not move fast enough."[8] He interviewed the overseers, the general manager, and Calhoun very closely on the subject of corporal punishment, forcing each to acknowledge its central place in maintaining plantation discipline. His most telling encounters, however, unfolded in front of his eyes. A disturbing exchange between a seven-year-old girl and an older man revealed the everyday texture of whipping in the lives of slaves. "If you don't do as I bid you, quick," said the girl, "I will tell the overseer to have you flogged."[9]

The onset of the busy season in spring inspired the boldest and most recalcitrant of the Calhoun family slaves to shirk their responsibilities where possible. A repeat offender in this category became famous locally as "Bloody Sea" Duncan. Duncan spent his nights during planting season at home in the slave quarters, but escaped each day before dawn to the woods and thereby avoided his duties. As they became familiar with the trick, overseers on the plantation learned to set a pack of hounds on Duncan's trail. "Bloody Sea" took to the bayous, earning his colorful name by cutting the throats of the swimming hounds and turning the water red with their blood.[10]

Though the name of the slave is omitted, a local story about the execution of an especially recalcitrant man survived in the account of Calhoun's next-door neighbor, published in the 1890s. Sometime in the 1850s, on the instructions of Meredith Calhoun himself, a slave was burned alive before a crowd of 300 others on the Smithfield plantation. "The story made a great sensation at the time, but it could never be proved," explained the neighbor.[11] "Bloody Sea" Duncan, the only slave known to have risked such a terrible penalty, may well have been brought to reckoning after all.

The discovery of a young slave woman hiding in a creek bed in the woods during Frederick Law Olmsted's tour of the property confirmed the persistence of "Bloody Sea"–type malingering into the 1850s. To Olmsted's horror, her offense resulted immediately in the most brutal beating he would ever witness. The overseer in Olmsted's party (which also included Meredith Calhoun's teenaged son, William) delivered 30 or 40 blows with a rawhide whip to the woman's bared shoulders and upper back. After questioning, the overseer required her to pull up her dress and undergarments and lie on the ground, then administered the horsewhip to her naked legs and buttocks.

"Oh, don't, Sir!" cried the slave, as Olmsted recorded it, "oh, please stop, master! Please, sir! Oh, that's enough, master! Please, sir! Oh, that's enough, master! Oh, Lord! Oh, master, master! Oh, God, master, do stop! Oh, God, master! Oh, God, master!"

Overwhelmed, the Yankee traveler rode a short distance away, clumsily mounting the crest of the creek bed and breaking through a cluster of bushes. "The screaming yells and the whip strokes had ceased when I reached the top of the bank," he wrote. "Choking, sobbing, spasmodic groans only were heard."[12]

Olmsted noted the incidence of violence on the plantation with particular scrutiny in light of sensational allegations surrounding the Red River plantations in general and Meredith Calhoun in particular. Red River provided the backdrop for the best-selling book of the 1850s, Harriet Beecher Stowe's *Uncle Tom's Cabin*. *Uncle Tom's Cabin* appeared in 1852, only months before Olmsted's journey, awakening a generation to the cruelty of slavery. Olmsted no doubt included the otherwise remote reaches of the Red in order to satisfy the interest of readers of the *New York Daily Times* in the reality behind Stowe's maudlin tale of a family destroyed by slavery. Indeed, as evidenced by his observations of Calhoun's plantations, he found ample evidence of physical and psychological distress. He refused, however, to speculate on the real-life identity of the brutal Simon Legree, the novel's pitiless slave master. Committed to preserving the anonymity of his southern hosts, Olmsted omitted any reference to *Uncle Tom's Cabin* in his direct observations of Louisiana plantations and their owners.

Who was Simon Legree, the cruel master in the book, who murdered Tom and otherwise embodied all the evils of the system? Olmsted did not pretend that the question was not on his mind, admitting that the peddlers of "cheap literature" on his Red River steamboat had sold three copies to other passengers during his journey to Natchitoches.

Engaging some Louisiana natives on the topic in the elegant stateroom, he learned that there were two planters in the Red River valley considered "bad enough to do it."[13]

In fact, two names would be associated with Legree, although neither was identified in print until well after the Civil War. Locals tended to favor a middling planter named Robert McAlpin, who owned property in the Cane River community of Cloutierville, about 15 miles from the site of Colfax. Subsequent owners of the McAlpin plantation would later sell a slave cabin from the property which became part of a traveling exhibit as "Uncle Tom's Cabin," and would change the name of the Cloutierville place to Little Eva Plantation in honor of the young white character who loved Uncle Tom.[14] A more high-profile exposé appeared in the *Washington Post* in July 1896, shortly after the death of Harriet Beecher Stowe. "Model for Mrs. Stowe," declared the headline, "Meredith Calhoun Was the Original Cruel Simon Legree."

The *Post* article described an 1878 encounter between Stowe and the *Post* reporter and Washington author William Hugh Robarts, in which Robarts inquired about the identity of the infamous Legree. Robarts claimed that Stowe said she had obtained her insight into Red River circumstances in conversation with a Cincinnati steamboat captain who regularly plied those waters. The character Legree, she explained, was based on "the man who before the war operated the only profitable sugar estate on the north bank of the Red River." Guessing the identity of the literary fiend in conversation with the author, Robarts himself supplied the name Calhoun, which Stowe confirmed, saying that she had never drawn a character more true to life. In the 1896 article, Robarts proceeded with a handful of florid tales about Meredith Calhoun, whom he described as "strange," and also as "one of the most accomplished gentlemen I have ever known."

Although much in the story was untrue—in particular a sequence in which Calhoun used a Bowie knife to gut a local ne'er-do-well, a version of the legendary "sandbar fight" of Natchez, Mississippi—unmistakable details reveal the author's familiarity with the family history before and after the Civil War.[15]

Regardless of its accuracy, the Robarts article reveals the extent of Calhoun's infamy in the Red River community and beyond. Robarts had spent several months at Fort Jesup, an army barracks roughly 20 miles from the Calhoun estates, during the mobilization for the Mexican

War from 1845 to 1848. The old soldier had maintained his contacts from Fort Jesup, where notables such as U.S. Grant and Robert E. Lee had also served, writing a history of the Mexican War and its officer corps. With little to do during their stay except swap stories and explore the countryside in their free time, the soldiers must have been aware of their proximity to Calhoun's great fortune and his multitude of slaves. During their tour of duty in the area, Calhoun happened to be engaged in a campaign to enlarge his local profile. In 1847, he purchased a newspaper that he renamed *The Red River Republican,* dedicated to the issue of states rights and emblazoned on the masthead with the promise of the 10th Amendment, guaranteeing the powers of states. Calhoun made a contribution of $350 that year to buy a cannon for a volunteer company called the Rapides Guards, who probably served alongside soldiers from Fort Jesup. Also that year, Calhoun scandalously purchased a large lot of fresh captives from Africa in a transaction later sensationalized by an Oregon newspaper as "The Last Cargo of Slaves."[16]

One of Robarts's principal informers for the 1896 article was Montfort Wells, a steamboat pilot and scion of the Rapides Parish planter clan with the second-largest holdings on Red River, whose land abutted the Calhoun property below Rigolette de Bon Dieu. As Calhoun's colleague in the sugar elite, Montfort's father, James Madison Wells (later to be appointed the first Reconstruction governor of Louisiana), was in a position to know of any stains on his neighbor's reputation, especially in light of a long-standing dispute between the two men about their adjoining property boundaries.[17] For her part, Stowe may well have spoken to a Cincinnati river captain, but she had a more intimate source in her brother Charles Beecher, who passed part of the 1840s as a clerk in a New Orleans cotton brokerage firm. At his urging, for example, Stowe depicted Legree (like Meredith Calhoun) as northern-born transplant to the region.[18]

Simon Legree probably reflected a composite of the worst characteristics of a number of infamous slaveholders, as Stowe suggested in her 1856 *Key to Uncle Tom's Cabin.*[19] Significant details of the fictional tyrant's behavior and persona are entirely inconsistent with the worldly and refined character of the man who met with Frederick Law Olmsted. But in one crucial particular, the management of the Calhoun estates confirmed and perhaps even exceeded the cruelty that inspired Stowe and her readers. Like Legree and other members of the sugar-planting caste,

Calhoun acceded to the demanding pace of sugar production even at the cost of the lives of his slaves. To *"use them up,"* as Stowe recorded in her own italics in the *Key to Uncle Tom's Cabin*, to *"sacrifice a set of hands once in seven years,"* was the original sin of the Louisiana sugar economy.[20]

The truth behind the accusation appears beyond dispute in Calhoun's slave schedules for the 1850 census. Of 738, as previously noted, only 16 slaves were 50 or older. The percentage defies the typical life expectancy for slaves in that era. In light of the difficulty of selling or trading superannuated slaves, it is unlikely that Calhoun managed to pass those of his slaves in their 50s to new owners. Although Calhoun selected slaves in a particular age range to create his 1836 cohort, the family holdings from South Carolina and south Alabama included many who would have been older than 49 in 1850. Statistics on fertility provided additional evidence of harsh conditions. According to Olmsted's rough calculations, the rate of increase on the Calhoun farms stood at 4 percent, significantly lower than similar projections he prepared in the seaboard slave states.[21]

In pursuit of profits in sugar so far north of the proven line of successful cultivation, Calhoun worked his slaves to death to avoid sacrificing his cane to the chill of the season in which it reached maturity. His laborers may also have perished in the more ordinary pursuit of profits in cotton or plantation maintenance.

Whatever the cause of the high mortality among his slaves, Calhoun found it necessary to resort to extraordinary measures to replenish his supply. The purchase of captives from Africa was illegal in the United States after 1808, a prohibition enforced with increasing vigilance by the British royal navy, but high demand kept a thriving black market trade in the vicinity of sugar crops. Near Galveston, Texas, the stronghold of the pirate Jean Lafitte served as a conduit of fresh labor captured on the high seas. Entrepreneurs, including the frontiersman Jim Bowie, a pioneer of the Red River country who would lose his life at the Battle of the Alamo in 1836, purchased Lafitte's slaves for as little as a dollar per pound, discreetly distributing their cargo to prearranged buyers by beaching ships along Louisiana's waterways.[22]

As late as 1847 and perhaps afterward, Calhoun purchased a number of teenage boys newly arrived from Africa. The illegal transaction, sensationalized by a post–Civil War newspaper as "The Last Cargo of

Slaves," took place amid a temporary spike in the price of slaves during a time of high demand for both cotton and sugar. According to the account of a survivor, the boys had been kidnapped while loading coconuts onto a ship that suddenly took to the high seas. The boys were stuffed into shipping boxes, which were nailed shut and delivered after several weeks to Cote Blanche Island in Louisiana's Atchafalaya Bay.[23]

Calhoun purchased the largest lot of this cargo, according to the article, but no accounts of Africans among the freedmen on his former plantations have survived. Perhaps like many of their predecessors, they had succumbed to the rigors of their new environment and died before their time.

A final vignette illustrates the complex blend of paternalistic care and profit-driven cruelty that characterized Meredith Calhoun as a philosopher of bondage. In the early 1840s, the Calhouns took up residence in Paris, occupying a mansion that had previously served as Benjamin Franklin's pied-à-terre on the outskirts of the city. In their company they carried two slaves, as well as the teenage daughter of an elite Huntsville family whom the Calhouns had offered to introduce to society. In Paris, the Calhouns posed as living symbols of American slavery, displaying their human chattel like a version of Franklin's famous coonskin cap. During an era when "America" appeared in a living tableau presented in the court of Louis Napoleon as a master in a hammock attended by black-face slaves, Meredith Calhoun flaunted his status as a slave-master in pursuit of big-city notoriety.

Mary Calhoun's personal maid, known only as Margaret, created a sensation among Parisians unaccustomed at that time to seeing real black people or slaves in the streets. The Calhouns kept her close at hand and immaculately dressed. Napoleon himself, encountering the family in the street, paid his respects to Margaret's exotic appearance, leaning forward in his carriage and bowing politely as he passed.[24]

The family's peculiar claim to fame may have smoothed the Calhouns' bid to take part in the storied court of Louis Napoleon and his accomplished wife, Eugenie. Social climbers from the United States, snubbed in London, were welcome in the Tuileries, where the "Noblesse of the Dollar" enjoyed wide recognition. Similar displays may have created a sensation in the various Italian towns where the family purchased artwork in the 1840s and the 1850s, mostly destined for the Huntsville townhouse. The Grand Duke of Tuscany, for his part, was less than impressed, intervening to rebuke the master painter Geniseppi Sabatelli for the sale to Calhoun of two precious original paintings, "Tasso Reciting His Poems at the Court" and "The Mother of the Gracchi." Too late to stop the sale, Leopold prohibited the future export of Sabatelli's works without his personal permission. Undaunted, the Calhouns continued to assemble a world-class collection of paintings and sculpture, attracting notice wherever they traveled because of their unusual company.[25]

For all the excitement, however, these were unhappy years for the Calhouns, who had departed for France on the heels of the death of one son and a tragic accident that had left their eldest crippled for life. Margaret, the gilded mascot of the Calhoun entourage, also felt pangs of anxiety in her long absence from her own children, each of whom was approaching the prime working years. Mary Calhoun was especially solicitous of Margaret's desire to send greetings and hear news from home. Writing to her Alabama friends, she urged them to give Margaret's love to the children.

"Poor things," she wrote, "I often think of their unprotected state." As the wife and daughter of slaveholders, but one without legal agency in business matters, her views on the institution of slavery were of little consequence. As a mother, however, she knew the pain of losing a child, having buried her own son before the family's abrupt departure for Europe. Making the association between the likely relocation or sale of Margaret's children and her own recent loss, she veritably shuddered in the page. "I can write no more," she continued, "my heart swells almost to bursting when I contemplate upon my home, and the last sad weeks I passed there."[26] To lose a child was the universal currency of mothers' pain.

THREE

The Fall

M EREDITH CALHOUN WAS NOT SO POWERFUL THAT HE could not be hurt. In November 1836, in Huntsville, William Smith Calhoun, aged one and a half years, the future heir to the Smith and Calhoun fortune, broke his back in a catastrophic fall. The exact circumstances of the accident are unknown, the date itself an approximation. His age and the fact that he fell from the arms of a maid were the only details to survive, stripped bare of the horror of the child's improbable injury and of any speculation on the motivations of the slave woman who dropped him. His miraculous survival, succeeded by the equally miraculous slow recovery that made it possible for him to learn to walk and work and raise a family, perhaps obscured a fraction of the trauma of the defining moment. Delicacy, too, discouraged overly elaborate discussions about the hump on William Calhoun's back.[1]

No surviving account suggested that the baby's maid intended to hurt him. To do so would have violated one of the South's most fundamental and instinctive taboos: to speak of the hatred of slaves for their masters. To raise the possibility was to defame the benevolent influence of the Calhoun family within the most intimate sphere of its household. And the maid may well have been entirely innocent. Judging by the record of Margaret's experience in France a few years later, the Calhouns treated personal servants with kindness and a measure of respect.

The injury to the eldest son, however, occurred amid a series of unfortunate events, the most extreme of which arose from the departure of the caravan of 1,000 slaves and mules. The tragedy occurred only six months after the rattling passage rolled out of town, poisoning the psychological environment. For months beforehand, the assembly of the transport of one thousand had been the consuming horror of slaves in Huntsville and for miles around. Forever afterward, the broken families would suffer the effects. The nursemaid alone would know the contents of her heart in the flashing instant of the baby's brush with death. In the fall of 1836, however, a thousand grieving parents knew the shock.

For Meredith and Mary Calhoun, the injury served to introduce a tragic era in their family life. Within four years after the fall, Judge Smith and his wife, who had raised Mary as an orphan, succumbed to old age, leaving an estate valued at more than $1 million. John Taylor Calhoun, William's younger brother, died suddenly at age four in July 1842. Meredith Calhoun, Jr., born in 1840, died at age six, leaving only a daughter, Marie Marguerite Ada Calhoun, known as Ada, and William, called Willie, to grow to adulthood.[2]

In the summer of 1842, shortly after the death of John Taylor, the Calhouns moved suddenly to France, where Meredith and Mary would spend most of the final three decades of their lives. The discovery of a doctor who could claim to hold a cure to Willie's spinal deformity provided the major impetus for the move. Dr. Jules Guerin was a giant of 19th-century medicine, the founder of one of Europe's most respected medical journals, and an experimental scientist of broad and significant accomplishments. In the late 1830s, Guerin had abandoned his studies of infectious disease to concentrate on deformities of the spinal column with a specialty in children's medicine. He established a clinic on the grounds of the Chateau de la Muette in Passy, a suburb of Paris. The chateau had been the former country estate of Marie Antoinette and more recently had served as a scientific laboratory, the site of the first hot air balloon flight.[3] Here Willie and a servant, Frederick, would occupy a suite of rooms during several rounds of surgery. Guerin promised Calhoun that his son would walk and that the hump would disappear.[4]

Guerin was a pioneer of the concept of social medicine, convinced that settings, class, and lifestyle choices determined people's health. His clinic in Passy imposed a regimen to reflect the doctor's prevailing theories on socialization, diet, and physical fitness.[5] According to prescription, the seven-year-old would be confined indoors; baths were prohibited, and Frederick was instructed not to carry him downstairs. Guerin was a believer in the nutritional powers of cheese and onions, which no doubt appeared with regularity on Willie's tray. Guerin's interest in the quantitative study of "excreta of the body" imposed additional requirements for his care.[6] To a boy Willie's age, Dr. Guerin, the French nurses, and the mysteries of the palace must have cast intimidating shadows. As revealed to le tout Paris decades later, when the 85-year-old Guerin physically assaulted his esteemed colleague Louis Pasteur in an academic conference, the doctor could indulge a furious temper.

Combined with the surgery and the loneliness occasioned by the frequent absence of his parents, the hospital era must have been a harrowing experience. The letters of Mary Fenwick Lewis, who accompanied the Calhoun family to France, reveal a measure of the young hunchback's distress during the first two years of his hospital stay. "Willie says—off with your silk dress and bonnet and play with us," she wrote in March 1843. "Show me how to make my boat sail, sit down on the mattress with me, play cards with me, and tell me tales about Napoleon and Josephine. What demands!" In other moods, he was wistful, giving Mary a letter from his mother, and after "making me read it two or three times, wish[ing] to know if I did not think it pretty." By April 1844, "poor Willie" expressed some bitterness: "He complains of bad fate as usual and has of yet not left his room though the weather is very fine."[7] The emotional legacy of the experience would bear on his unconventional outlook as an adult, which revealed the strain in his relationship with his parents. Old resentments, the acquisition of a French accent and mannerisms, and the persistence of his status as a hunchback contributed to his eccentric and sometimes perverse persona.

By the age of 15, Willie Calhoun had returned to the United States and learned to ride on horseback, a detail that survives in Frederick Law Olmsted's account of his 1853 visit to the Red River. Willie was present on the plantations during his family's second stay upon the properties in a five-year period and rode in Olmsted's company on the day that he witnessed the flogging of a Calhoun slave. Olmsted recorded that the "delicate and ingenuous lad" who rode beside him "betrayed not even the slightest flush of shame." Young Willie's sangfroid, combined with the fact "that I constrained myself from the least expression of feeling of any kind," Olmsted remembered, "made the impression in my brain the more intense and lasting." The beating was a "red-hot experience" for Olmsted, who said the incident remained "a fearful thing in [his] memory" for years afterward.[8] Like Olmsted, William Smith Calhoun

was a stranger to the harsh realities of corporal punishment on the plantation. Unlike his guest, however, he would be constrained by his position from revealing his emotional reaction to the blows.

The young master did not shrink from the ugliness of plantation
life. In 1859, at the close of another visit to the United States, Meredith,
Mary, and Ada Calhoun would return to Europe, leaving Willie in
Louisiana.[9] Young Calhoun became the first resident master of the Red
River plantations. The arrangement promised to be mutually beneficial
for father and son. Meredith Calhoun would delegate authority in keeping with his own coming-of-age tradition in the service of Stephen
Girard, and hope to benefit by William's supervision of day-to-day
operations. William gained control of the plantations in their top productive years and also won a measure of distance from his parents that
he probably valued. During his first two years on the farms, he did not
write to his mother even once.[10]

The family wealth smoothed young William's entrée into the
Louisiana elite, among whom French manners were a matter of course.
He was a hunchback, plagued by asthma and diminutive of stature,
but he doggedly pursued acceptance, joining the Masonic lodge at
Cloutierville, where he received his "degrees" in 1860.[11] Cloutierville,
near Colfax in Natchitoches Parish, formed part of the original arc of
settlement on the Red River, along the stretch abandoned by the main
current after the Great Raft removal project flooded the Rigolette de
Bon Dieu. Now poised along the banks of a river-shaped lake called
Cane River, the great Natchitoches plantations had surrendered some
of their economic clout but retained their distinctive cultural cachet.
Here, mixed-race and francophone families cultivated sugar and cotton,
built lavish plantation homes, and developed a lively town life with ties
to New Orleans, the Caribbean, and the Continent.

Despite his family name and Episcopal upbringing, Young Calhoun
shared more in common with Cane River creoles than with the prot-
estant community that coalesced around the Rapides Parish seat of
Alexandria, 25 miles below Calhoun's Landing. Producing sugar in
much greater volume than the Calhouns and occupying majestic riv-
erfront estates, Rapides planters from old Louisiana families formed
a clique that no amount of wealth could help an outsider to pene-
trate. As the former head of navigation on the Red River, Alexandria
had developed the amenities of a country town, including telegraph

service and the best local options for lodging and dining. Known about town for his crumpled posture and deep pockets, Calhoun remained apart from the social scene that his fellow Rapides Parish planters called home.

Outside the river bottoms, a different Louisiana could be found. Rising up from the alluvial plain, fertile, shaded acres stretched for miles in the Louisiana piedmont. The settlement of piney-woods country, as the locals called it, traced its roots to the 1700s, and early on included English-speaking families of rugged frontiersmen. In the first half of the 19th century, this Deep South yeomanry grew and prospered on the proceeds of a bale or two each year of market cotton. Scattered widely and politically subordinated under the Bourbon slave interests, the pinewoods population of Central Louisiana parishes such as Rapides, Winn, and Catahoula established few significant towns. In hamlets such as Cheneyville and Montgomery, in the vicinity of the Calhoun plantations, white men identified themselves as farmers, storekeepers, or sometimes doctors. Lawyers, schoolteachers, and judges, the backbone of the nonagricultural elite, practiced almost exclusively in the river-bottom courthouse towns.

Secession and Civil War would bring these disparate communities together in a common cause. The Confederate States of America made ample distinctions among the categories of men eligible for military service under the first Conscription Act, passed in April 1861. Plantation owners, overseers, Confederate officials, and a wide variety of craftsmen and technicians could claim exemption on the basis of their nonmilitary service to the cause. Draft-age men with the means to hire a substitute were likewise excluded from call-up.[12] Well in advance of the draft, however, Red River valley residents had formed volunteer companies and elected officers. The Rapides Invincibles, Cheneyville Rifles, and the Stafford Guards traveled from the region to serve under Robert E. Lee in the Army of Northern Virginia.[13] Others, including the Red River Rebels, the Rapides Rangers, the Louisiana Tigers, and the Pineville Sharp Shooters, joined the Army of Tennessee.

Rich and poor, slaveholder and independent laborer alike joined the ranks of men in gray. Among area elites who took up the charge were brothers from a Rapides estate with more than 300 slaves. The young men of the Stafford clan formed the nucleus of the Stafford Guards, with the elder, Leroy Stafford, destined to rise in the ranks to brigadier general before losing his life in the Battle of the Wilderness.[14] James W. Hadnot, a 38-year-old farmer worth $40,000, did not serve, but his brother A. J. Hadnot left his $30,000 Rapides plantation to join the Consolidated Crescent Regimental Infantry. Wealthy soldiers carried their personal servants to war, sometimes forming companies served by a detachment of picked hands. The best-known slave trooper in Natchitoches, "Old Buck" Frazier, had first accompanied his master in the Mexican War of 1846–1848, and reprised services as drummer for a unit of local elites.[15]

Men of more modest means gave their all in the war to sustain the slave system. A middling family in Natchitoches dispatched a father, Denis Lemoine, and two of his sons to an artillery unit.[16] Clement Penn, an Alexandria shoemaker with no property and no family in the area, signed on with the 18th Louisiana Infantry and later the 2nd Louisiana Cavalry, where he served alongside David Paul, a clerk in a Rapides Parish store owned by his brother.[17] Paul, known forever afterward as Captain Dave Paul, also commanded an influential unit of Home Guard with an impressive record of subduing jayhawkers, runaway slaves, and Union troops on the Red River bayous and uplands.[18] Their military service bestowed a sense of importance and entitlement on yeoman participants that would not be forgotten after the war. Many in their ranks, including Paul, would play a major role in the political reorganization of Central Louisiana after the war.

The career of Christopher Columbus Nash, the organizer of the white militias at Colfax in 1873, illustrated the war's capacity to elevate humble men who fought well and survived. Nash joined the Sabine Rifles, a detachment from hardscrabble pinewoods Sabine Parish, where his father's $10,000 operation made him something of a local elite. He became a junior officer in the 2nd Louisiana Infantry, arriving in time for the first major engagement of the war, in Manassas, Virginia, and fighting to the bitter end with the celebrated brigade led by General Thomas J. "Stonewall" Jackson. In Virginia, Nash fought against and alongside other future players in the Reconstruction of Colfax, tasting victory in 1862 against Nathaniel P. Banks, the Union general who would govern Louisiana by fiat during and after the war. Taken prisoner at the Battle of Chancellorsville, where Stonewall Jackson fell mortally wounded in spring 1863, Nash returned to the Confederate front in time to serve under General James Longstreet, who later pledged his loyalty to the Yankees as the militia commander for Louisiana's Republican governor. At the Wilderness in 1864, the Confederate lieutenant surrendered to General Philip Sheridan, who would arrest Nash during the Louisiana Ku Klux Klan roundups of the early 1870s. Ulysses S. Grant issued the order to parole Nash from the prison camp at Johnson's Island at war's end. As president, Grant would approve Nash's indictment on federal charges of murder and conspiracy in connection with the massacre at Colfax in 1873.[19]

The wartime career of Meredith Calhoun's contemporary and next-door neighbor demonstrated an alternative path. James Madison Wells was one of the few men on Red River who dared openly to defy the Confederate cause. From a large family of elite sugar planters of old Rapides Parish stock, Wells was an unlikely slaveholding Unionist, championing Stephen Douglas, the Northern Democratic candidate, in 1860 and aggressively opposing secession. Upon learning of the death of Stonewall Jackson at Chancellorsville, Wells publicly and elaborately expressed the wish that the Confederate champion would rot in hell.[20] Threatened with assassination for this offense, he withdrew to his family's Bear Wallow hunting preserve and amassed a guard of dozens of deserters and anti-Confederate jayhawkers. Wells's oldest son, James Madison Wells, enlisted in the Army of the United States as a private, losing his life in the fighting around Vicksburg or Port Hudson in 1863.[21] Another son—Thomas Montfort—enlisted instead in the Confederate First Louisiana Cavalry, maintaining his gallant local reputation as a riverboat pilot, expert dancer, and horserace champion.[22]

The elder Wells made his way to Union lines north of Baton Rouge and lived the duration of the war in New Orleans, which had been occupied by the United States since 1862. He would return to his home parish in the company of General Nathaniel P. Banks and U.S. troops during the Red River Campaign of spring 1864, sporting the title of Lieutenant Governor Madison Wells, the second-ranking member of Louisiana's first Reconstruction government.[23] The opprobrium associated with his branch of the Wells family name would only increase during his term as governor of the state in 1865 and 1866.

During the 1864 invasion of the Red River country, William Smith Calhoun, whose disabilities precluded military service, would become acquainted with the elder Wells when the new lieutenant governor came with cash in hand to purchase cotton and sugar from loyal planters for transport by the United States Navy. The encounter made public the young master's unqualified commitment to the preservation of the Union. Finding acceptance among a small community of Unionists in Alexandria and the surrounding plantations, Poor Willie could do little to prevent the inexorable assault upon his family's domain by the forces of change. While his views on slavery remained obscure, his allegiance to the agents of Emancipation became a matter of enduring local infamy.

Meredith Calhoun himself remained well above the fray in Europe, distancing himself emphatically from Unionists and Rebels alike. His politics had emphasized the rights of states and property owners versus the encroaching power of the federal government. The newspaper he had published from Alexandria in the late 1840s had placed the 10th Amendment to the Constitution—with its reference to rights reserved to the people—prominently in the masthead. A second short-lived paper in the election of 1860 had brought Wells and Calhoun together in the enterprise of promoting the candidacy of Stephen Douglas, who stood for Union and slavery.[24]

The election of Lincoln and the secession of Alabama and Louisiana from the Union were anathema to Calhoun, whose few recorded displays of wartime bonhomie seemed calculated to conceal the worrying outlook for the family estate. "The unhappy man that is distracting the country greatly distresses me," wrote Mary Calhoun to her husband in January 1861, "and [yet] I sometimes imagine that things cannot be so bad as the horrid *Herald* represents them to be." Another letter, dated April 1861, provided a report on the Calhouns' manic expenditures from a Huntsville girl living in Paris:

> Colhoun had given several grand entertainments and had fed all the bon ton in Paris. At their last ball, Ada appeared in a little theatrical performance, a scene from Ester by Racine. Their *fête chametre* at Nunilly was delightful. The young people dressed [in country costumes] and enjoyed themselves amazingly.[25]

Après moi, le déluge, Calhoun may well have imagined. Displaying sublime confidence in the ultimate resolution of the conflict in his favor, he purchased 800 acres in public lands adjacent to his Louisiana properties. The deeds to the properties, dated April 1861, bore the personal signature of Abraham Lincoln.[26]

Among Confederates, Calhoun presented an equally bluff façade, organizing an extraordinary passage from Europe to the war-torn South in the fall of 1861. "He evaded espionage and ran the gauntlet of Northern rebel-hunters," the *Huntsville Democrat* reported of the 56-year-old's visit, "by studiously ignoring the English language after he arrived in Canada," and pretending to rely on his French attendant as interpreter. By such elaborate precautions, the old philosopher could hope to evade the scrutiny of Confederate as well as U.S. interrogators. His contributions to the urgent cause from exile were scarcely commensurate with his capacity, and he had fortified himself with seemingly insincere assurances of rising Confederate sympathies on the Continent. Within weeks of his return, he reported, he expected Britain and France to act together to break the U.S. naval blockade and liberate southern cotton and sugar for European markets.[27]

The Red River Campaign of 1864 created an additional category of combatants from the area around Colfax. With the arrival of U.S. troops supported by a 50-boat naval flotilla, African Americans defected in droves from the plantations they served as slaves. An exodus of 4,000 massed around the federal column in Rapides.[28] Families crowded the riverbanks in order to greet their liberators and express their joy.

> Great day!
> Great day, the righteous marching
> Great day!
> This is the day of the jubilee
> God's going to build up Zion's walls
> The Lord has set his people free
> God's going to build up Zion's walls

Their spirituals embraced the obligation to continue the fight, as championed in another version of the song, "Great Day":

> Gwine to take my breast-plate, sword in han'
> God's gwine to build up Zion's walls
> And march boldly in the field
> God's gwine to build up Zion's walls
> We want no cowards in our ban'
> God's gwine to build up Zion's walls
> We call for valiant hearted men[29]

A proportion of the men held as slaves found their way to Union lines and joined the army. The number of black soldiers drawn from the local population cannot be determined in aggregate, as census data omitted names on the 1860 slave schedules. The difficulty of accounting for blacks in military service is further compounded by substandard army record-keeping, in particular the practice of enlisting new men under the names of absent or deceased black soldiers. An official roll of 186,017 African Americans joined one of the 154 Negro regiments created by the United States Army during the war, and an additional 200,000 served as laborers, servants, and spies for U.S. forces. Louisiana, home to the longest federal occupation and the headquarters of the Department of the Gulf, led the way in tapping the energies of this new class of fighting men.[30] Among those who experienced the thrill of wearing the Union blue were at least three former slaves of the Calhoun plantations: Cuffy Gaines, Edmund Dancer, and Alabama Mitchell.

Alabama Mitchell did not know his last name when he joined the army on May 1, 1864. The recruiting officer at Natchez, Mississippi, with whom Mitchell signed on within a week of the Union victory at Monette's Ferry near Colfax, enlisted him under the name Alabama Calhoun and assigned him to the 70th United States Colored Infantry. Later, his unit would be joined with the 71st United States Colored Infantry. Like many slaves, he knew neither his birthday nor the year of his birth, but he was born in Colfax to Fanny January, a slave of the Calhoun family, and was approximately 18 years old in 1864. Alabama Mitchell, who learned his father's name only after the war, performed garrison duties at Natchez for the duration, and did not see combat. Quite likely, he took advantage of his time in the army to learn to read and write his name. In later years, he would sign in his own hand—not using the surname he discovered after the war—as Alabama Calhoun.[31]

Loyal Gaines, known as Cuffy in the black community, grew up on the Calhoun plantations as a slave and married Alabama Mitchell's sister, Missouri. Gaines joined the 4th United States Colored Cavalry, participating in the siege of Port Hudson in southeastern Louisiana, where black troops had their first sustained exposure to battle. As Gaines later explained to army pension officials in a sworn affidavit, his duties provided an unexpected opportunity for a reunion with his brother-in-law.

[D]uring the war some time after the capture of Port Hudson and
while his the fourth regiment U.S. Colored Cavalry was doing gar-
rison and scout duty at Port Hudson his company rode thru Natchez
Mississippi. While there he saw Alabama Calhoun alias Alabama
Mitchell[. He] knew him well and stopped and talked with him.
Alabama had on the uniform of a U.S. soldier.[32]

A third former Calhoun slave, Edmund Dancer, served alongside
Mitchell in the 70th and 71st colored infantry, and may have also been
present during the chance encounter of Mitchell and Gaines.[33]

The breakdown of order that facilitated the call to arms of slaves such
as Mitchell, Gaines, and Dancer reflected the overwhelming chaos of the
Red River campaign, which developed in a series of feints, retreats, and
acts of destruction. Charged by speculators such as Lt. Governor Wells,
who arrived in his hometown with $10,000 in cash to buy up available
stores, the military action served the interests of commerce as much as
strategic necessity. Filling the holds of Union gunboats with cotton and
sugar, General Banks (and naval commander David D. Porter) set off
a scramble for saleable goods that resulted in massive damage to local
properties. Officers of both armies ordered the destruction of commercial stores that could not be secured amid the fighting, burning docks,
warehouses, and homes in the process.

The scathing retreat of Union forces over the falling waters of the
Red River, aided by removeable wing dams of ingenious design, added
significantly to the ruins, as Confederate artillery and mounted divisions in hot pursuit shot up steamboat landings and buildings on shore.
With jayhawkers and civilian criminal elements joining in the free-
for-all—for example, with the vengeful destruction of the Wells family
home—the consequences of the abortive Union campaign were mili-
tarily insignificant but locally devastating. "We traveled like the Israeli
armies of old," remembered one Union soldier, "lit by burning fires at
night and a pillar of smoke by day." Another account, published in 2001,
compared the burning landscape in the vicinity of Calhoun's Landing
to a scene from the Lord of the Rings.[34]

Amid the chaos, the blood of innocents soaked the shores of the
Red River below Calhoun's steamboat landing. A Confederate battery
placed on the opposite bank took aim at the *Cricket,* flagship of Admiral
Porter, and at two pump-boats—*Champion No.* 3 and *Champion No.*
5—who had recently engaged with the *Cricket* in an effort to salvage the

ruins of the *U.S.S. Easton,* sunk by a rebel torpedo. Near dusk on the evening of April 26, the *Cricket* and its small company encountered the Confederate artillery and the 200 rifles of the 28th Louisiana Regiment. The bombardment of cannon, canister, and minié balls took out the cannonade of the *Cricket* and brought the Admiral's flagship to a perilous, drifting halt. "Finding that the engine did not move," Porter later reported:

> I went to the engine room and found the chief engineer killed, whose place was soon supplied by an assistant. I then went to the pilot house and found that a [solid] shot had gone through it and wounded one of my pilots. I took charge of the vessel, and as the battery was a heavy one, I determined to pass it, which was done under the heaviest fire I ever witnessed.[35]

Despite the *Cricket's* tinclad armor, roughly half of its crew was killed.

The crew and human cargo of the unprotected pump-boats proceeded at considerably greater risk. In a move that would later be excoriated by Confederate witnesses (in the only firsthand accounts of the tragedy that would appear in print), Porter's Navy had taken on hundreds or thousands of black refugees from plantations upriver and jammed them onto the open decks of the unarmored steamboats used as tugboats and personnel transports. Some 150 or 200 persons crowded the two decks and cabins of the *Champion No. 3,* which looked almost exactly like a traditional river steamboat with dredging and hauling equipment attached. As recorded by a rebel artilleryman working the cannonade, their desperate bid for freedom reached a sudden and catastrophic end.

> The transport *Champion No. 3,* was struck in the boiler by a solid shot, and was enveloped in hot steam and water. This transport was loaded with near two hundred negroes, consisting of men, women, and children, taken from the plantations above, and most recklessly and cruelly attempted, under the convoy of gunboats, and under actual fire, to be run through the lines of our army.
>
> The twelve pound gun solid shot which struck the boiler of the transport, was probably the most fatal single shot fired during the war, producing the death of one hundred and eighty-seven human beings, over one-half instantaneously, and the remainder within twenty-four hours. All on board except three perished by the most frightful of deaths, and the steamer fell into our hands.[36]

Its crew scalded to death along with the would-be freedmen, *Champion No. 3* lurched and grounded in the loam beneath the gun emplacements. Porter returned fire, taking out two of the Confederate guns and a portion of the brick stable of Calhoun's Mirabeau Plantation before fleeing to the safety of Union-controlled Alexandria.

Slaves from Mirabeau, mobilized by the victorious rebels to assist in raising the damaged vessel, removed the scalded bodies of the dead and dying and attended to the three survivors, burying the remains in the soft soil of the riverbank.[37] Theirs was truly the "Old Ship of Zion" described in the Jubilee songs of freedmen who survived.

> What ship is that a sailing, Hallelujah
> What ship is that a sailing, Hallelujah
> Do you think that ship is able to
> Carry us all home to glory?
> Hallelujah. ....[38]

Porter, chagrined, took pains to conceal the incident from his superiors, even omitting the names of the four naval officers who perished in the crew of the *Champion No. 3* from his final report. It would later be reckoned as the most deadly instance of black civilian casualties in the Civil War.[39]

William Smith Calhoun, who remained at home during the war, probably witnessed the destruction of the *Champion No. 3* and its fearful aftermath. Skirmishes during the federal retreat had brought Union and Confederate troops onto the family properties near Colfax, where the defeated U.S. Army reconnoitered with their naval transports on April 25, 1864.[40] The Louisiana-born Confederate commander, Major General Richard Taylor, described the destruction of this stage of the campaign as complete. "For many miles," he wrote on April 24, "every dwelling-house, every negro cabin, every cotton-gin, every corn-crib, and even chicken-houses have been burned to the ground."[41]

What local property owners experienced as disaster introduced the era of Emancipation for their slaves. Especially where responsible whites had fled, explained a planter who stayed home, slaves took advantage of the arrival of federal troops to celebrate and defect. "[T]hey turned out and I assure you for the space of a week they had a perfect jubilee," complained John H. Randell of Rapides Parish, writing to his absent neighbor, Confederate Governor Thomas O. Moore. Slaves rounded up cattle and hogs for massive barbeques, raiding masters' supplies of liquor and other valuables. "Your furniture was taken out of your dwelling house and distributed among the Negroes," Randell wrote, adding that portraits of the governor's wife had been stolen and mutilated.

Getting the crews back to work after the withdrawal of the Union force would prove difficult, Randell predicted. "Several have been shot and probably more will have to be."[42] In fact many, such as the black soldiers represented by Mitchell, Gaines, and Dancer from Calhoun's quarters, were forever beyond the control of their former masters. One tumultuous year after Banks's retreat, Red River African Americans—freed forever by the Confederate surrender—would have the chance to celebrate again.

FOUR

Led by a Damned Puppy

CROSS RAPIDES AND THE SURROUNDING PARISHES, families shared in the bitter legacy of defeat. Statistics on agriculture, once the pride of the region, reveal the depth and breadth of the suffering. Losses in livestock imposed immediate obstacles to economic recovery: with fewer than half of the prewar number of horses, asses, and mules, inhabitants of Rapides Parish were insufficiently prepared for lifting, timbering, and plowing damaged assets. Food stocks were similarly low, with half of all milk cows dead or missing, along with three quarters of the prewar stock of pigs and cattle. Yields of corn dropped from 820,000 bushels in 1860 to 261,000 bushels in 1870, during years when the value of garden produce brought to market fell from $7,830 to $800.[1] The loss of split-rail fences to the campfires of armies on both sides posed a substantial obstacle to the recovery of agricultural yields. For Louisiana's sugar plantations alone, the overall wartime losses amounted to $190 million of an estimated $200 million in antebellum assets.[2]

Nature compounded the destruction that humans had wrought. A flood of the Red River in late May 1866 destroyed the season's cane seedlings and cotton crop on alluvial lands, while an extended drought parched the family farms in the pinewoods country. That summer, an epidemic of cholera sent workers and overseers scrambling for higher ground to the detriment of crops.[3] A second series of floods breached the plantation levees two times in June 1867. Later that summer, a plague of caterpillars stripped tens of thousands of acres of cotton to the bare stalks.[4] Occupying the only Louisiana territory destroyed by fighting and afflicted by natural disasters to a greater extent than other commercial farms, Red River plantations experienced devastating harvests during years when sugar and cotton planters elsewhere in the state did well.[5] Severe dislocation arose from the wartime globalization of both markets, as manufacturers developed alternative sources of sugar and cotton overseas.

Big planters such as William Calhoun faced the additional difficulty of securing the labor of former slaves. Questions about alternatives to slave labor on southern plantations had preoccupied natives and U.S. government officials since early in the war. Many whites were convinced that people of African descent would not work except when compelled, a conviction drawn from observations of resistance and malingering by unfree laborers. In fact, severe challenges confronted the recovery of the workforce on big commercial farms. In the first place, the number of blacks on the river bottom plantations contracted significantly after the war. Liberated from bondage, many fled the scene of their former degradation while others set out to reunite with family members back east. In Rapides Parish, to which the area around Colfax remained joined until 1869, the prewar population of 15,000 blacks was reduced by 5,000 in the late 1860s.[6]

Freedmen's rising expectations further complicated the overall shortage of labor. The most striking set of changes transformed the demographic profile of agricultural workers, as black families withdrew women and children from the fields. Black families took pride in their ability to confine women's work to the domestic sphere, in contrast to the experience of generations in slavery.

> No more auction block for me
> No more, no more...
> No more mistress' call for me
> Many thousand gone.[7]

Children—formerly deployed in planting, picking, and even the sugarcane harvest—enrolled wherever possible in school. Compounding this shortfall, men engaged on plantations chose to work fewer hours themselves, approximating the workdays of free laborers on family farms and in factories. Calculated in working hours per capita, the highest average number of hours worked each year fell from 3,047 in the 1850s to 2,187 in the 1870s.[8]

The sweet potato was the deadly enemy of sugar and cotton crops. Wherever black families obtained access to land, subsistence farming based on the cultivation of high-yield and nutritious tubers prevailed. In Rapides Parish, during the period in which stocks of every other category of agricultural produce collapsed, the total production of sweet potatoes rose from less than 10,000 bushels in 1860 to more than 54,000 bushels in 1870.[9] Food crops allowed families of freedmen to withhold their labor from commercial markets, at least during years when terms of employment seemed unfavorable. With start-up farms of 40 acres and equipment priced at more than $300, even in an era of reduced land values, few freedmen commanded the resources to buy land in the years following the war.[10] Renting, leasing, and the emerging practice of sharecropping land provided black families with the means to shrug off the old pattern of gang labor on commercial plantations.

Planters of Rapides Parish were quick to recognize the threat posed by independent black farmers. Black Codes, championed by Governor James Madison Wells and other conservative Unionists, attempted to restore some of the conditions of slavery by prohibiting ownership and leasing by freedmen. When the Civil Rights Act of 1866 and the proposed 14th Amendment to the Constitution struck down Black Code restrictions, Louisiana planters resorted to informal conspiracies to achieve the same effect. In December 1868, a meeting in Alexandria secured the unanimous agreement of all present to the proposition that landowners in the parish discontinue the practice of allowing freedmen to cultivate vacant lands. The planters agreed not to sell or rent parcels of their property to any blacks except those who had demonstrated their loyalty and adherence to the old order. Any planter who violated this standard, they agreed, would be considered an enemy of the public.[11]

The December agreement formalized the standard already in practice on most of the great plantations in Rapides. On two plantations owned by the family of a local doctor, William Cruikshank, for example, a total of 55 hands were employed but no lands were rented or sold in 1868. The Stafford Plantation near Cheneyville had 300 acres in cultivation, but did not rent or sell any land. Lewis and Joseph Texada, on twin plantations named Castile and China Grove, worked 400 acres with 80 hands, but offered nothing for sale or rent.

Completing his preprinted 1868 survey of crops and employment terms in Rapides, Natchitoches, and Winn parishes, a Freedmen's

Bureau agent credited only three plantations with acres "Rented or Sold to Freedmen." Firenze, Meredith, and Mirabeau—owned and managed by William Smith Calhoun—provided the only lands available to black farmers in his part of Louisiana.[12]

Willie Calhoun's status as an enemy of the public in his home parish extended well beyond matters of land tenure. By December 1868, the behavior of the heir to the Calhoun estate had scandalized the white population of the region. Equipped with a power of attorney giving him control of all his parents' assets in Louisiana, young Calhoun had set out to rebuild his father's devastated plantation operation by icono-clastic methods.

The renting of land—100 acres or more on each plantation—was one of many business strategies his neighbors found objectionable. In the cash-strapped harvest season of 1868, more than half of Rapides Parish planters employed laborers in exchange for a share of the crop. With significant variations, planters provided one-third to one-half of the annual harvest to workers who paid for their own food and cloth-ing; wages, alternatively, ranged from $10 to $12 a month. As the largest employer in the region by a wide margin, with more than 1,600 acres in cultivation, Calhoun's employment policies set the regional standard for labor contracts. Aside from those fortunate enough to rent land directly from the former master, freedmen on the Calhoun plantations earned a quarter-share, a surprisingly low amount.[13]

Calhoun had credit. In a region strapped for cash, the heir to his father's broken fortune was one of the only local planters with enough assets to stock plantation stores. In 1867, using his legal power to lever-age his father's remaining assets, he obtained a total of $15,000 in loans from First Citizens Bank of New Orleans. Later that year, Calhoun opened the first store in the territory that became Grant Parish, con-verting a brick stable in the cluster of buildings near the steamboat land-ing.[14] Poised on the riverbank, the Calhoun store became the center of the emerging community life of free black laborers.

The store and the promise of opportunity to rent or own Calhoun's land attracted laborers to his four plantations. The hunchback was also willing to offer fringe benefits that few other planters in the region would dare.

Near the sugarhouse on Firenze Plantation—once the jewel of his father's and grandfather's investments but recently out of use—Calhoun operated a school for colored children. With 20 boys and 15 girls as its pupils, the school was one of three serving black families in the sprawling parish of Rapides.[15]

The education of black children addressed one of the touchstones of white supremacy. After generations of denying the privileges of literacy to their slaves for fear it would be used against them, southerners instinctually shrank from proposals to establish schools. Indeed, the idea of free or low-cost schools regardless of race cut against the grain in the South, where public schools of any kind had scarcely existed before the war. The federal role in promoting education for freedmen grew out of wartime literacy training for black soldiers. The first federally sponsored program for public education was established in Louisiana in 1864 on the orders of the United States Commander of the Gulf, Nathaniel P. Banks, who imposed a property tax on citizens in the occupied portion of the state to defray the cost of equipping schools and employing teachers.[16] Continued and expanded by the Freedmen's Bureau, with support from northern charitable and abolitionist associations, programs to instruct children and adults became a hallmark of early Reconstruction policy.

The freedmen embraced education with a fervor that thrilled sympathetic witnesses. People of all ages clamored to learn how to read and use numbers. From their own meager resources, African Americans in southern states contributed $1 million to educational programs in the late 1860s. By 1868, the Freedman's Bureau monitored the operation of 1,600 schools in the former slave states and Washington, D.C.; 178 of these schools were in Louisiana, mostly in the area around New Orleans. The Louisiana schools served upward of 14,000 students, many of them adults. In one measure of the effectiveness of Freedmen's Bureau programs, an agent concluding a tour of educational facilities around the state reported with pride his conviction "that a greater number of colored than white people in this State can read and write."[17]

Teachers in the freedmen's schools represented a wide spectrum of differences. During the earliest years of operation, the majority were white male soldiers in the Union army, but at war's end new populations stepped up to meet the growing demand for education. Northern abolitionist societies had long cherished the idea of education for African Americans. In 1865 and 1866, large numbers of northern teachers traveled to war-torn southern communities, although Louisiana received a smaller number of these missionaries than other states. By 1868, most Louisiana teachers were natives. Of 543 freedmen's school teachers around the state, more than half were African Americans themselves.[18]

The first effort to establish schools for freedmen in the area soon to be named Colfax grew out of the Freedmen's Bureau and missionary effort in 1866. The Freedmen's Bureau agent in Montgomery, a former U.S. infantryman from New York named Delos W. White, secured space for six or eight schools and obtained a guarantee of substantial salaries for teachers. The first cohort of instructors included mostly northerners, sent up from New Orleans. Cholera and the opposition of local whites resulted in an early end to the school year, and the retreat of the first generation of teachers.[19] The school at Firenze, established the following year, probably relied on Calhoun family resources for the teacher's salary and teaching materials. The possibility that William or Ada Calhoun provided the instruction cannot be discounted; a Freedmen's Bureau agent reported that former masters and their families taught school in "a great number of cases" in the area.[20] More likely, Calhoun offered the teacher housing and a measure of protection from the hostility of the white population of the area.

The contents of the Calhoun curriculum were never recorded, but basic instruction in reading, spelling, and simple arithmetic provided an academic core for typical freedmen's schools. Perhaps equally important, schools served to educate African Americans on national institutions and values. A Louisiana schoolteacher testified that one of her colleagues made a point of decorating the classroom with American flags and bunting on national holidays, a deliberate act in a state where the 4th of July had fallen out of fashion. Students learned "national" and patriotic songs: "Hail, Columbia," "Yankee Doodle," and "The Star-Spangled Banner." Teachers introduced the Declaration of Independence, the Constitution, and the Emancipation Proclamation as key texts in the American experience.[21]

The political orientation of freedmen's schools—combined with their open solicitude for elevating the oppressed race—made them targets for organized violence. "The feeling [among Louisiana whites] is unanimous that [freedmen] should not own an acre or land nor have any schools," wrote the Freedmen's Bureau superintendent for the state. "They are more hostile to the establishment of schools than they are to owning lands."[22] Surrounded by Calhoun's extensive domain, without white neighbors in the immediate vicinity, the Firenze school evaded the most severe response of local conservatives. Other programs in Rapides and the neighboring parishes, however, were less secure. A school near Cheneyville—next door to the Stafford plantation—closed late in 1868, after repeated threats to the teacher's life. On the Sabine River, near the birthplace of Christopher Columbus Nash, a black schoolteacher was lashed with a whip and released, only to be kidnapped, his horse stolen, and his saddle burned. In addition to two assassination attempts on his clerk, a Freedmen's Bureau agent in the North Louisiana district reported, "Threatening letters have been sent us; bricks have been thrown through our windows; [and] dead cats dropped into our cistern." Fifty school facilities stood idle for lack of teachers, he explained, because "[t]his district is so remote, lawless, and violent, that teachers from the North and from other parts of the South justly hesitate to come here."[23]

Calhoun's commitment to educating black children derived from personal sympathy as well as business calculations. His sensitivity to the ambitions of slave parents for education developed close to home. Though his childhood provided few examples of humane relations between masters and slaves, Calhoun's parents had permitted or perhaps even facilitated rudimentary schooling for the children of their personal servants.[24]

More important, his sensibilities were enhanced in the late 1860s by his intimate experience as the head of a mixed-race household. Sometime after his return from Europe, Calhoun took up residence with Olivia Williams, a woman described as mulatto on the 1870 Census. According to the family tradition, the couple was married under the great white spires of the St. Louis Cathedral in New Orleans. Though the census taker recorded a different last name for Williams and her son Eugene, then two years old, the terse available notations provided a flash of insight into the novel status of her relationship with Calhoun. In a year when estimates of the value of personal property and racial categories appeared on the census, William Calhoun and Olivia Williams—occupants of the same household—each claimed a separate and equal share of the household's wealth, making her one of the richest black women in the state.

In presenting a mixed-race woman as his wife or near equivalent, Willie Calhoun stared down significant risks. His political activities would prove more dangerous still. Prior to the momentous events of Reconstruction, the fragmentary record of the hunchback's life provides no insight into the views that propelled him onto the barricades of the struggle for black equality.

Neither his parents nor his sister seemed to share William's drive to contribute to the cause. Indeed, in January 1867, around the time that his freedmen's school and labor policies began to attract the unfavorable attention of his neighbors, William's family remained in Paris, where Ada sat for a likeness by the leading portrait artist of the European courts. Meredith Calhoun accompanied his daughter to the studio, resolute in his determination to pretend as if nothing had changed. The old philosopher, in the twilight of life at age 60, could scarcely imagine the transformation of his former domain.[25]

Whether true conviction or some hope of personal advancement motivated William's unorthodox outlook cannot be determined, and sheer perversity or rebellious spirit cannot be ruled out. In the era of military Reconstruction, Calhoun aligned himself with the radical element in local politics with fateful consequences for Louisiana and the nation. His brief, unhappy career in politics would transform his troubled inheritance in unanticipated ways.

The spark that ignited Calhoun's political ambition consumed the more celebrated political career of his neighbor, James Madison Wells. Wells had presided over the creeping restoration of the old order in Louisiana, including the establishment of the infamous Black Codes. In the summer of 1867, General Philip H. Sheridan, commander of the newly created Fifth Military District administration, dismissed Governor Wells along with other officials of the reconstructed Louisiana government. "[H]is conduct," complained the general, citing well-known instances of Wells' granting state commissions to men still wearing their gray Confederate uniforms, "has been as sinuous as the mark left in the dust by the movement of a snake."[26] Sheridan's clean sweep of Louisiana offices set the stage for the implementation of Congress's revolutionary agenda for Reconstruction.

The frustrations of the Congress with President Andrew Johnson mirrored General Sheridan's mistrust of Governor Wells. Like Wells, the president regarded down-on-their-luck southern aristocrats with a sympathy that seemed to outweigh his obligation to represent the victorious national cause. Popular sentiment in the North and West increasingly despaired of southern recalcitrance in the months after President Lincoln's assassination. Fuelled by outrage at southern practices that aimed to replicate the conditions of slavery and return prominent Rebels to positions of influence, the 1866 congressional elections empowered the self-styled Radical faction of the Republican Party with a massive majority. Refusing to seat the pro-Confederate delegations sent to Washington by southern states, congressional radicals imposed tough new requirements for readmission to the Union. The Reconstruction Act of 1867 invalidated the state constitutions adopted since the war, calling for the election of delegates to new constitutional conventions. Army commanders were authorized to register voters under explicit instructions to include eligible African American men.

Radical Reconstruction, which began in 1867 and continued for nearly a decade, was a unique era in the history of the United States and the world.[27] Never before, in any setting, had a repressed minority ascended so quickly to the enjoyment of the rights of the majority. The embrace of black suffrage in 1867 derived in part from hard-boiled political calculations, including the issue of population and apportionment in Congress and the Republican Party's desire to expand the ranks of its loyalists. In a fundamental way, however, the move reflected a rare spirit of humane idealism growing out of the experience of civil war. Inspired by the Union's late awakening to the evils of slavery, obliged by their unanticipated status as champions of Emancipation, Radical advocates placed their hopes for national unity and grace on the shoulders of black voters.

A season of heady political excitement had begun. In Louisiana, as in other southern states, Congressional Reconstruction sprang into motion with a series of three momentous elections. First, army registrars swept into plantation communities and towns to register voters. Holding white southerners to strenuous requirements for wartime loyalty and registering any black man of legal age, the army created a black-majority electorate: Louisiana's 127,639 voters included less than 45,000 whites.[28] In the summer of 1867, elections to a constitutional convention dispatched 50 black men and 48 whites to New Orleans. Nine months later, voters were asked to ratify a covenant that permanently disenfranchised Louisiana Confederates, established public schools, and required officials to acknowledge the inalienable equal rights of all citizens.

The April 1868 vote revealed the persistence of bitter divisions. With every office in the state in the balance—and with U.S. Grant, the architect of Union victory, initiating his bid for the White House— the people of Louisiana took sides in the most democratic election in the history of the state.

The scalawag Willie Calhoun won election to the upper house of the Louisiana legislature, joining a Rapides Parish delegation that included two African Americans, Samuel E. Cuney and George Y. Kelso, both of whom had been free men and property owners before the war. The victor in the race for the sheriff's office in Alexandria was another black man, William J. DeLacy.[29]

Among the new class of state senators, William Smith Calhoun presented a most unusual profile. The fact that he spoke English with a French accent mattered little in Louisiana, where distinguished Francophones in the *gens de coleur* predominated among the African American officeholders. His physical disabilities were profound—contemporaries described him often as a cripple—and yet not nearly as severe as those afflicting his fellow Radical Marshall H. Twitchell, who would later serve in the same house of the legislature after an assassin shot off both of his arms. In a state where a native son and Confederate general, Longstreet, served as head of the Republican militia and called openly for the protection of black voters, Calhoun could hardly be seen as the biggest rascal among Louisiana scalawags.[30] It was his wealth that made him different. In all the South, he was probably the greatest slave master ever to embrace the cause of black equality.

Great planters had been known to cast their lot with the Republicans. Former Governor Wells, for example, had not let the matter of his 100 slaves deter him from his loyalty to the government that set them free with the Emancipation Proclamation. As the party of Lincoln moved sharply to the left in 1866 and 1867, however, the early generation of slave-owning scalawags retired to the sidelines. White Republicans drew their ranks almost exclusively from poor and middling natives and carpetbaggers from out of state.[31] No other planter in the top-ten list of largest U.S. slaveholders was known to cooperate with the Republicans, much less to join the Radical faction and run for office. Compounding the oddity of it all, Calhoun's candidacy for the Louisiana Senate was his maiden engagement in political matters. Only strong conviction—or a perversely ill-timed bid for attention—could account for his leap into the political melee.

No fragment of William Calhoun's stump speech has survived to shed light on his political platform, but his strengths as a candidate derived from the same source as what remained of his economic clout. Black enfranchisement transformed his Red River plantations into a center of emerging political power. In a pattern replicated around the state and all across the South, Republican Party organizers sought out the population of eligible voters that continued to live and work on the plantations. The "coalition of 1867–1868" joined representatives of the national organization to sympathetic communities in the South. The proliferation of Union Leagues and other Republican political clubs galvanized the black electorate in even the remotest rural areas.[32] Union Leagues adapted Masonic rituals and secrecy oaths to a real-world setting in which clandestine operations and membership saved lives. Operating mostly in defiance of the wishes of big employers and former power brokers, party cadres seized the opportunity to organize workers on Calhoun's farm, possibly offering to sponsor his candidacy to reward his indulgence. In a parish where black voters outnumbered whites 999 to 157, the five family plantations emerged as a kind of political machine in which farm workers championed their employer in exchange for his patronage and protection.[33]

New friends had encouraged and supported Calhoun's candidacy. In keeping with the stereotype of Reconstruction-era carpetbaggers, particularly in Louisiana, Calhoun's two white Republican allies had arrived from out of state. Both had fought in the war: the Alabama carpetbagger William B. Phillips as a Confederate and his sometime housemate Delos W. White in the Union Army. Phillips had arrived in Winn Parish in 1865 from his native Alabama, possibly as a deserter. Meeting with "kind and respectful treatment from the citizens," the 24-year-old established a farmstead at Rock Island near the Winn Parish portions of the Calhoun estate. Closed-lipped about his political leanings, Phillips learned a local secret concerning the nearby murder of several Union officers after Appomattox, and the disposal of one of the bodies in a roadside well.[34] He prospered amid adversity, accumulating a significant amount of personal property, valued at more than $2,500.

The radicalized electorate created in 1867 brought the political identity of William Phillips into the open. As a devoted Union Leaguer, Phillips frequented the black communities of Rapides Parish, organizing and speaking. Frequently in the company of Calhoun and Delos

White, the Alabamian also developed a close relationship with the non-white family who lived in an area of Grant Parish called Rock Island and the Devil's Backbone, astride a narrow ridge in the vicinity of Rocky Bayou. The Fraziers, a family of freedmen, had bright economic prospects and political ambitions. Phillips set up household nearby in a cypress cabin with a mixed-race teenager named Bella Weathers. In 1869, the girl gave birth to a son, Robert Phillips, characterized in the 1870 Census as a mulatto.[35]

Phillips would pay a price for his nonconformity. In March 1867, he received a visit at his home "by a party of some fifteen persons, with the avowed purpose, to use their own language, of 'putting him out of the way.'" He survived, but remained in the Red River country under threat. As he later described it in a sworn affidavit:

> On or about December 17, 1867, as said Phillips was traveling in the public road, nine men, most of whom were armed, attacked him and struck him over the head, and ordered him to leave the country, as they would have no damn Yankee in that country; that they were not whipped, etc.

Four months later, the threat was broadened to include William Smith Calhoun. Phillips and Calhoun, said the men, should be aware "that there was no law for them, and [their enemies] intended to make and carry out their own laws."[36]

Delos White appeared on the 1870 Census as a member of the Phillips household, listing his occupation as bookkeeper and $500 in personal property—not much to show by the standards of the carpet-bagger caricature. White, a native of Queens, New York, had first passed through the area that became Grant Parish at the head of a column of Union invaders during the Red River campaign and retreat of 1864. Mustered out of his cavalry unit with a distinguished service citation, Captain White made his way back to northern Louisiana as an agent of the Freedmen's Bureau.[37] His responsibilities included the care of needy freedmen, the arbitration of labor disputes, support for freedmen's schools, and the investigation and adjudication of racially motivated violence. As a loyal official with knowledge of the area, he also facilitated law enforcement, riding with U.S. soldiers in the pursuit of a gang of infamous Winn Parish outlaws.[38] White's association with Phillips and Calhoun during the 1868 election complemented the overtly political character of his work. From his base of operations at Rock Island, the captain rode the footpaths and steamboats between Alexandria, Montgomery, and Natchitoches as a kind of police escort for Republican notables.

Security precautions proved urgently necessary during the presidential campaign of 1868. Having witnessed the power of black enfranchisement in the April balloting, southern conservatives were determined to stem their losses in the presidential election of November 1868, held separately that year in the newly Reconstructed states and widely viewed as a referendum on the future direction of southern policy. Their own ranks swelled by the influx of poorer white voters into the reformed electorate, conservatives loosely associated with the Democratic Party coordinated a twisted version of a traditional campaign. Black voters would not be spared the appeal: Democrats rewarded "loyal" black men with jobs and symbolic favors, such as a gala affair for colored Democrats at Alexandria's Ice House Hotel. Employers distributed campaign buttons and monitored their display.[39] The threat of punishment or death shadowed every exchange with the freedmen and emerged with particular ferocity when Republican whites and outsiders played a role.

Across the South, the Ku Klux Klan and related organizations emerged as armed wings of white political movements. Louisiana klans included the Knights of the White Camellia, the Southern Cross, and Seymour and Blair Societies, named for the heads of the Democratic presidential ticket.[40] Although such clubs existed as real organizations, with secret membership, rituals, and costumes, participation in white supremacist direct action was not limited to initiates. A single klansman—or an unaffiliated racist willing to pose as such—might inspire his neighbors to act in the spirit of the movement. Klan activity ranged from "patriotic" displays and barbeques to night riders' raids on political meetings or the homes of their enemies. Murder played a central role in Louisiana and throughout the region.

The display of muscle by white conservatives served only to reinforce the determination of African Americans to make a political stand. As observed by a Freedman's Bureau agent in the summer of 1868, "Leading minds among [the freedmen] were fully occupied...under strange and novel excitement." Evidence of "[o]pposition to reconstruction [sic], especially to the negro vote, intensified this excitement," as Union League and other new Louisiana clubs urged solidarity.[41]

The candidacy of General Ulysses S. Grant and Schuyler Colfax encouraged Republicans who saw the victory of the hero of Appomattox as an antidote to southern militancy, as expressed in a ditty from the *Grant and Colfax Songster:*

> He'll make the nation brighten up,
> Just like his own cigar;
> And all "discordant elements"
> He'll quiet, near and far;
> So "on this line we'll fight it out!"
> It's sure to be our plan, sir,
> Then "three times three for U.S.G.,"
> Oh! General Grant's our man, sir.[42]

Musical rallies of political associations such as Grant and Colfax Clubs provided memorable fragments of the party line for the encouragement and education of illiterate voters. As the season progressed, Republican campaigners increasingly relied on secret venues and word of mouth to publicize such meetings, usually held in inconspicuous locations such as black churches, warehouses, and barns.

An incident in October illustrated the dangers of the discovery of black political meetings. In a hamlet called Holloway's Prairie near the future site of Colfax, armed whites disrupted an evening event in a building used for church services. An eyewitness described what happened: "The colored people in the building, finding themselves surrounded, attempted to escape from the building and one of them was shot and killed while jumping through the window." Afterward, "the party of white citizens entered the room and selected from the congregation two men and one colored woman, whom they tied and took to a neighboring house, and there hung until they were dead."[43]

The last weeks of the campaign season witnessed a sharp escalation of violence, as evidenced by the Holloway's Prairie murders. Bands of night riders—"mounted and fully disguised"—made regular appearances around Alexandria.[44] Twice in October, militants smashed up the offices and printing press of a Republican newspaper, the *Alexandria Tribune,* and threatened the life of its editor. W. B. Phillips also received death threats—perhaps, like a Republican in neighboring Catahoula Parish, including letters depicting gallows and signed "K. K. K." A gang of whites informed him to his face that "there were not United States

troops enough in Louisiana to protect him if he attempted to live there."
Phillips and Calhoun would learn "that there was no law for them," and
the latter "should never see the legislature" should he prevail in the
polls.[45]

Convinced, Phillips and hundreds of other Republican activists fled
to New Orleans before the election and was not present to cast his own
vote. Calhoun, for his part, did not encounter threats of violence in
person, whether in deference to his wealth or because of his disability.
However, as he later explained, "I was told by at least fifty colored men"
that white vigilantes intended to flog him with a whip if he carried
through on his support for the Republicans.[46]

Election Day unfolded as a series of armed skirmishes within a
30-mile radius of Calhoun's Landing. In the predawn hours, a gang
of whites in Natchitoches blindfolded a black Republican activist and
beat him almost to death, then threatened to burn the home of a white
town councilman, Alfred Hazen, and shot him to death in a hail of
gunfire.[47] At 6 A.M., W. S. Calhoun arrived at the polling place for the
Plaisance Ward of Grant Parish, located in his own storefront near the
riverbank. There he discovered a gang of Democrats "in a beastly state
of intoxication," as he described it, threatening to disrupt the voting.
One of them, the notorious local thug and future sheriff J. G. P. Hooe,
"made a Democratic speech to the colored people" while holding a club
in one hand and a revolver in the other.

"[T]hey were free to vote for whom they chose," Hooe told the freedmen in Calhoun's presence, "but not to be led by a d—d puppy."[48]

Similar acts of intimidation inflamed the state. In exile in New
Orleans, W. B. Phillips saw three white men confront an African
American on Election Day, saying that "if he did not want his brains
blowed out, he had better vote for Seymour and Blair."[49] After-hours
raids on ballot boxes and assaults on couriers occupied much of the first
week of November.

Despite the risks, Republicans in both racial categories turned out
in force on Election Day, urged by the party to "do their duty man-
fully…and vote as their consciences shall dictate."[50] Calhoun did his
utmost to ensure that black voters on his plantations had their chance,
by personally supervising the submission of 150 ballots and riding 25
miles to Alexandria with a group disqualified by the Plaisance Ward
registrar. At the parish seat, Calhoun and his men encountered a civic

spectacle of historic proportions. "The town was filled, jammed, and crammed by the impouring masses of our Nation's wards," reported the *Alexandria Democrat*. "[All were] marching to the music of the blue [Grant and Colfax] ticket and the promised land."[51]

Violence carried the day in Rapides Parish and Louisiana as a whole. The final statewide tally of 33,000 votes for Grant fell nearly 30,000 short of the number that had elected Louisiana's 21-year-old carpetbagger governor, Henry C. Warmoth, six months earlier. Horatio Seymour won the electoral delegation for Louisiana, Georgia, and six states outside the former Confederacy, receiving 100 percent of the votes cast in seven parishes and more than 99 percent in eight others, all of which included significant numbers of African American voters. The fraudulent results did not derail the rise to power of U. S. Grant—destined to be one of the most popular politicians in the history of the 19th century—who defeated Seymour with an electoral majority of 214 to 80.[52] Fraud and intimidation, however, posed a substantial and continuing threat to the survival of Louisiana's nascent Republican establishment.

More threatening still, the pattern of violence initiated during the 1868 election continued afterward, gaining significantly in momentum and deadliness. In a series of attacks thought to have claimed the lives nearly 800 people in the state, an estimated 40 to 50 Republican voters lost their lives in the area that would become Grant Parish the following year.[53] Although most of the victims were black, white activists such as Phillips, White, and Calhoun assumed terrible risks in the months following the election. Rising to the challenge, Calhoun worked aggressively to counter the threat of white supremacy in his home domain. Passionate and inexperienced, his response provoked the escalation of the conflict on the bloody ground of his Red River estates.

If he conceived of his foray into Reconstruction politics as a path to redemption for his father's sins, his good faith would be put to a severe test in the years to come. The hunchbacked, misfit, peripatetic scalawag Willie Calhoun had yet to experience the true character of outcast.

FIVE

A Town Called Fight

VEN AFTER A GANG OF WHITES SHOT AT THE TEACHER, breaking the window and tearing up the classroom walls, pupils of all ages continued to attend classes at the freedmen's school at Frazier's Mill. "The attendance during the month has been good," wrote Delos White, in his report to the Freedmen's Bureau in August of 1868. "Should the threats of burning the school house not be carried into execution, there will be one hundred pupils before the present session closes." Captain White kept an eye on the Frazier's Mill school from right next door, where he lived in the house belonging to William Phillips and his mixed-race romantic companion. White's presence reassured the black community of Rock Island. As the chief government gunslinger in the region and a personal friend of Hal Frazier's, White made it known in conservative circles that threats carried into execution would meet maximum reprisals.[1]

Hal Frazier, the proprietor of the mill and farmstead where the school was constructed, also sought to minimize risks, employing his son as the teacher and erecting the schoolhouse on the lot adjacent to his own home. Frazier was known as a man who could get things done, having purchased his own freedom and 2000 acres from his former master before the war. He stayed close to the premises, keeping critical documents and cash in his pockets to ensure against fire. When he was killed, the gangsters took nearly $400 from Frazier's wallet, along with "valuable notes" on loans to freedmen he had helped get started. The black community between Montgomery and Calhoun's Landing had lost its godfather and favorite son.

Frazier had seen the bullet coming. It entered through his right eye at point-blank range and followed months of vividly explicit threats from local whites. His employee Jesse Robinson, who had accompanied one of the strangers to the mill to measure lumber, took his fatal shot in the back of the head, but he had been warned as well. John Frazier himself, the former master of the place, had told Robinson that the two of them would "smell bullet packing" if they did not shut down operations at Frazier's Mill. "D—n you," said the white man, sometime after Thanksgiving 1868, "we will break up that nest of radicalism."[2]

The murder of Hal Frazier and his hired hand on December 12, 1868 set in motion a cycle of political and violent reprisals. Itself arising from the escalating tensions surrounding the recent elections, the incident galvanized the determination of Red River radicals to meet fire with fire. Captain White swore revenge and hailed a steamboat to New Orleans. "I left the parish, as I know that I will be murdered in the same manner as Frazier was," he wrote to a Republican newspaper, in a letter publicizing the atrocity at Frazier's Mill. With the backing of the U.S. government and his friend William Smith Calhoun in the Louisiana Senate, which would soon conduct a full investigation of political violence in the state, White could anticipate bringing the killers to justice. Less than three months later, in fact, the scene of the crime would be incorporated into a new political and law enforcement jurisdiction in which White himself would be appointed as sheriff.

The establishment of the new parish and its parish seat on March 9, 1869 represented something more than an act of vengeance for the murder of a radical boss. Indeed, white citizens of Montgomery in Winn Parish had first circulated the petition that inspired the legislature to act. The vast boundary of Rapides Parish yielded most of the land for the new entity, with the Montgomery pocket of Winn Parish and a parcel of Natchitoches tacked on.

In the designation of names and locations for the parish and parish seat, however, the town boosters perceived the blunt defiance of the bill's steward in the statehouse, William Smith Calhoun. Using scissors—according to the local legend—Calhoun removed the recommended name, Red River Parish, and pasted in the hated name of U. S. Grant. Instead of Montgomery, the new parish seat was Colfax, named for Grant's radical vice president and located on the site of Calhoun's country store and freedman's school above the Rigolette de Bon Dieu.[3]

Within weeks of the establishment of Grant Parish, William Smith Calhoun and others in the Senate executed one of the duties imposed upon the new legislature by the Reconstruction Act of 1867, voting to ratify the 14th Amendment. According to its authors in Congress, the language of the new law empowered freedmen by investing the federal government with the power to enforce all the rights of citizens identified in the Constitution and the Bill of Rights. In combination with the 13th Amendment and pending voting rights authority, the 14th Amendment promised a new birth of freedom for African Americans and others traditionally subordinated to the interest of the white, male ruling class.[4]

The 14th Amendment's potential to empower the experimental political alliance in Grant Parish, however, remained unrealized in the spring of 1869. In light of the killing of Frazier, Senator Calhoun and his allies had lost much of the exuberance conveyed by the place names Grant and Colfax. Describing the murders and providing security details about White's departure in a letter to William Phillips in New Orleans, Calhoun noted his own precautions against assassination. "The fact is, Phillips," he wrote, "if you was here I wouldn't give two bits for your hide."[5]

White and Phillips would be back, holding the newly created titles of Grant Parish sheriff and judge. White would return early in the New Year in the company of members of the 4th United States Cavalry, with whom he would conduct the initial investigation into the Frazier's Mill killings.

White and his posse took over the job initiated by a Winn Parish constable, who arrested a white man in January 1869 on charges of beating a freedman in an unrelated incident. A party of nine armed whites had rescued the prisoner, a "man calling himself Davenport but bearing the aliases of Carpenter, Baker, etc.," who then flamboyantly confessed to having murdered Hal Frazier before riding away. The conspiracy revealed the extent of popular support for continuing violence against blacks and radicals, reaching well beyond the new boundaries of Grant into Winn and Claiborne parishes.

Frazier's murderers, it appeared, had ties to a criminal organization known as the West and Kimbrell clan, whose campaign of violence and theft in Central Louisiana targeted political leaders alongside more commonplace prey. The gang was notorious at the local level, where they were considered bloodier and more successful at looting than their better-known contemporaries, Frank and Jesse James. Their participation in the Frazier's Mill murders (or merely their obstruction of justice in the case) raised the stakes for Sheriff White and his posse of U.S. cavalrymen. As one hostile constituent told White to his face, the soldiers would not always be around when White would need them.[6]

The federal agents' authority to take responsibility for the Frazier case derived from a rider attached to the Army Appropriations Act of 1867, one of the landmark omnibus achievements of the first Radical Congress. Since the terrible days of the war, the federal government had relied on the use of military tribunals such as Freedmen's Bureau courts to address challenges to law and order in the South. In 1866, the Supreme Court struck down the use of such draconian measures in areas in which civil courts remained in session with the ruling in *Ex parte Milligan*. "The powers of the Constitution should not be strained to suit emergencies," the deciding opinion observed, "for on its maintenance and its integrity depended our liberties and free government, not only in the present but for all time to come."[7] Interpreting the decision as a call for enabling legislation, congressional radicals provided a slim legal foundation, authorizing Freedmen's Bureau agents to punish acts of whipping and maiming former slaves. Tucked into the army bill— which included the controversial clause disengaging the commander of the army (Grant) from the commander-in-chief (the increasingly conservative Andrew Johnson)—the language elicited little commentary at the time.[8] The provision initiated the establishment of separate, federalized procedures for extraordinary law enforcement in peacetime. As such, it provided a discreet beginning for the widening war on southern terrorism.

The expanded powers of the state government also served as a wedge against the mounting power of white supremacy in Louisiana. Under the newly elected, 26-year-old carpetbagger governor, Illinois-born Henry Clay Warmoth, Radical Republicans in New Orleans, the Reconstruction-era capital, enlarged the number of appointed offices in the state. The creation of new political entities—Grant Parish being one of eight new parishes established in the legislative sessions attended by Willie Calhoun—served this goal most effectively. Empowered to appoint dozens of sheriffs, parishes, judges, recorders, and clerks (as well as to recommend candidates to newly created postmaster offices),

Warmoth and his allies shored up the security and power of the party organization by elevating cadres to responsible positions.[9] In concrete terms, the spoils advanced the cause of party men such as White and Phillips, who used their preelection tenure in office to prosecute the Frazier murders and other pressing dangers.

Warmoth also organized the establishment of a metropolitan police jurisdiction that included five parishes in and around the city of New Orleans, a predominantly white city in those days, home to thousands of reactionary Knights of the White Camellia. The legislature endowed the Metropolitan Police District with overriding authority, independent of the mayor of New Orleans and law enforcement officials in its constituent parishes. With 500 regular troops and the authority to expand to meet emergencies, the Metropolitan Police served as a militia in all but name, subject to the governor's command. In practice, the designation of the force as an urban police unit subverted the spirit of the 1867 federal act to abolish state militias in the occupied states, out of date since the rise to power of Republican government in the 1868 elections. With experienced black soldiers in its mostly nonwhite ranks, the Metropolitan Police Force cut a highly visible profile in the streetwise political struggles of Reconstruction New Orleans. Dressed in black and red uniforms and employed at far distances from the city, Metropolitans provided the battle-ready face of the new Louisiana.[10]

New authority over the conduct of elections emanated from federal and state advances. In February 1869, Congress passed the 15th Amendment, elevating black suffrage toward the highest law. Key language in the 15th granted Congress the power to secure a black man's right to vote, a capacity that Republicans had exercised liberally with similar endowments in the 13th and 14th Amendments. With this capacity dormant, the extremely narrow guarantees of the 15th appeared to exclude only certain forms of discrimination rather than to extend a universal profile of voting rights.[11] Capitalizing on electoral gains, however, sponsors of black suffrage could hope for federal oversight and other forms of voting rights enforcement in the South as the product of ratification of the suffrage amendment and the election of Radical Republican majorities in subsequent Congresses.

The Republican-dominated legislature in Louisiana expanded state oversight of elections, beginning with a sweeping investigation of the violence in November 1868. The Committee on the Conduct of the Late

Elections solicited sworn testimony and documents from hundreds of witnesses, including Calhoun, Phillips, and White. Estimating that one thousand had been killed and hundreds more harassed in political incidents in the previous year, the committee condemned the machinations of conservatives of the state as an "exhibition of the basest human passions [to exceed] any thing to be found in the darkest annals of the Christian era."[12] With hearings extending into the summer of 1869, the report provided the foundation for new legislation to grant Governor Warmoth greater authority in election procedures and the certification of officeholders. The Louisiana Returning Board, not established until early 1870, would answer the complaints of the Committee on Elections with a system of centralized state government control.

William Smith Calhoun played a key role in a controversy that elevated Louisiana's 1868 election dispute to the House of Representatives in Washington. A Warmoth appointee, a carpetbagger and midwesterner named Joseph P. Newsham, had served in Congress since the summer of 1868, but lost his bid to be elected to his seat in November to Calhoun's Rapides Parish neighbor, an Irishman and lawyer named Michael Ryan. Mounting a campaign to get Congress to recognize him as the legitimate victor for the 4th Congressional District, Newsham called on Willie Calhoun, whose testimony on Newsham's behalf provided the centerpiece of the challenge.

Calhoun and Ryan had been intimate friends—brought together by their activism as Unionists during the war and bonded by their mutual experience as recent arrivals from Europe. Indeed, the coziness of their relationship had become the subject of gentle ridicule among their elite neighbors and even the Ryan family slaves. "[Calhoun] was generally charged with following Mr. Ryan in whatever course Mr. Ryan pursued," observed James Madison Wells sometime after the war. "That was natural," he said kindly, "for Mr. Ryan had been his lawyer." A less generous comment on their wartime intimacy, a former slave named Harriett Bissee, testified after the relationship had grown cold that "Mr. Calhoun...was at Mr. Ryan's house every day in the week."[13] Physically and perhaps emotionally estranged from his family, Calhoun grasped the companionship of a like-minded and slightly older man of affairs, whose Irish bonhomie and dashing appearance may have smoothed his entrée in the masculine world of the Red River planters. The relationship also opened contacts and business opportunities to Calhoun, the most important of which paid dividends during the Red River campaign, when Calhoun and other Unionists received permission to move freely and market their crops to the federal invaders.

Like James Madison Wells, President Johnson, and other wartime Unionists, Ryan's views had diverged from the dominant faction of the Republican Party during Reconstruction. The election of 1868 found him squarely in the camp of white supremacy and home rule as the Democratic nominee for the 4th Congressional District. As such, he had led the opposition to his former friend's candidacy for the legislature and moved to check the emergence of the Calhoun plantations as a bastion of black political power. The Newsham challenge to the questionable election returns gave Calhoun an opportunity to block the ascendancy of his most bitter personal rival.

"Judge" Ryan had made the strategic error of appearing on Calhoun's property on Election Day in the company of J.G.P. Hooe and men bearing guns and other weapons. As Calhoun described the scene in sworn testimony, the candidate was drunk, disorderly, and menacing to the black voters of Plaisance Ward. Worse yet, he testified, Ryan was ineligible to hold office under the rigid requirements of the "Iron-Clad" loyalty oath required by Congress of prospective officeholders. During years of intimate wartime conversations, allegedly, the older man had repeatedly condemned the government of the United States. On at least one occasion, Ryan had appeared in a gray uniform, a fact that Ryan did not dispute but did try to make light of as an attempt to impress some ladies.

Ryan's defense (provided to Congress in a printed compendium of favorable affidavits) relied on his claim that, as an Irishman, he had "blarneyed those rebels a good deal," offsetting his Unionist politics with a strong display of southern pride. Ryan ridiculed Calhoun for his handicap, calling him "that little crooked-backed fellow," and laughed with witnesses about his own superior appearance and physical dimensions. Congress took Calhoun's side, expelling Ryan and installing Newsham in his place in early 1870.[14]

Progress against the encroaching power of white militants proved elusive for all these efforts. The membership and influence of Ku Klux Klan–style organizations reached an apex in Louisiana and the South in 1869 and 1870. Subscribing loosely to the goal of overthrowing federal domination and reestablishing the subordination of the black population, white supremacists skirmished everywhere against the Reconstruction order. Their basic strategy targeted the will of Republican and African American participants to persevere, with the threat of assassination and yet-more-indiscriminate killing as its basic tool. Merciless, the Klansmen disregarded innocence, family, or high office, murdering three members of state legislature in Georgia, raping black girls in the presence of their fathers in Alabama, and administering the horsewhip, in a notorious South Carolina case, to the pitifully crippled body of an African American teacher.[15] Klan-style actions united distinguished elites and Confederate veterans with more humble neighbors elevated by their status as whites.

The demobilization of federal troops abetted the rise of the Klans in 1869 and afterward. Readmission of states required a partial recognition of the end of martial law, and reduced military expenditures in the South played well with northern and western constituents. In Louisiana, for all its troubles, the U.S. troop level dropped from nearly 2,000 statewide in 1868 to only 598 in 1870 and 421 in 1872.[16] Left increasingly to their own defenses just as the morale and capacities of their enemies surged, black and Republican voters endured an extended mean season.

Klan violence at the local level drew part of its power from the intimacy of town and rural interpersonal relations. Knowledge of relationships and family circumstances facilitated strikes against Republicans when they were most vulnerable. For example, a gang of Natchitoches conservatives staged a mob visitation on the home of a Republican judge on the night of his young daughter's unexpected death, when the judge himself was out of town attending to his dying father, to demand that he resign his office and leave town. The town undertaker informed the judge's traumatized wife that he would not assist with her child's burial.[17] Where ostracism failed to intimidate, white partisans employed threats or feints at violence, such as the gunshots fired into the school at Frazier's Mill or a number of near-miss encounters on the decks and wheel wells of Red River steamboats. Hoods and costumes were used sparingly in Red River valley demonstrations, but the Klan's signature use of fire, including burning stakes with symbols attached, made its threatening appearance on at least one occasion. Murder, a Klan standby since 1868, marked no moral boundary at Grant Parish, which was destined to deliver the largest number of victims in the history of racial violence in the United States.

The worst of the worst among the murderers made their base of operations in what remained of Winn Parish, staging raids on targets all along the Red River region well into Texas. Keeping its association secret, membership in the West and Kimbrell "clan" overlapped significantly with the leaders and participants in white supremacist movements. Attacks sometimes assumed an explicitly political character, such as in the murders at Frazier's Mill, but other times pursued the more straightforward criminal goals of booty and protection. Targeting pioneer campsites on the old Natchez Trace near Montgomery and camouflaging their low-down ruthlessness as a form of ideological commitment, the West and Kimbrell boys embodied the lawlessness that made Central Louisiana the most dangerous neighborhood in the South.

In riding out against the Wests and the Kimbrells, Sheriff Delos White embarked upon a crusade worthy as a symbol of the irony of the Republican Party's ill-fated effort to transform the South. Committed to law and order and the establishment of effective infrastructure for business and community life, the party offered white boosters in towns like Montgomery and Cheneyville a lifeline to rebuild their shattered economies and broken moral compass. If his pursuit of the criminals who took his neighbor's life was representative of White's capacity to achieve his goals, his constituents in the new Grant Parish may have hoped to benefit from his leadership and courage. With White as guide, the captain of the cavalry detachment had killed one of the Kimbrell brothers and slowly narrowed the range and audacity of gang activity. Everyone had benefited, not least those neighbors who stood most at risk of accidentally discovering a deadly secret. After White himself was murdered, the same white citizens who killed him would finish up his work against the outlaw clan, riding down and executing by firing squad the nine remaining chiefs.[18]

No one who feared death would have lived the life that Delos White had chosen. To his final day, he persisted in his soldierly pursuits in spite of meager rewards for maximum exposure to danger. Relieved of the office of sheriff at the first election and cut adrift by the dissolution of the Freedmen's Bureau in 1869 and 1870, White continued to live and work on William Phillips's Rock Island farmstead, picking up a little income as recorder of the parish. The adjacent territory in his former Freedmen's Bureau district became so overgrown with lawlessness that a bureau agent passing through the area had to flee the main road to avoid being captured by bandits. "I lay out in the swamp all night," he reported, "with nothing to eat for thirty-six hours."[19] Among those benefiting from the chaos were conservatives and racists determined to rid the area of carpetbaggers, federal officials, and white friends of the African American community. The targets of White's own vendetta for the killing of Hal Frazier and Jesse Robinson made no secret of their plans for a preemptive strike.

Around midnight on the night of September 25, 1871, White and Phillips awoke to discover their house on fire. They grabbed their guns and broke for the door. Before he stepped across the threshold, however, as Phillips remembered it, White "was instantly shot dead." A second volley from the doorway caused Phillips to drop to the floor. He feigned death with burning cinders from the roof falling around him, until the unseen raiders blew a whistle and rode away.[20] Emerging from the blaze, Phillips found a burning stake to which the night riders had affixed a copy of one of his speeches from the 1868 election. White's body was burned beyond recognition; friends could salvage only a small portion to place in the grave.[21]

Phillips, who lost his home and $10,000 in personal property in the attack, could hardly hope to turn to parish officials to investigate and punish the leaders of the killing mob, as he believed that the sheriff and his deputy had ridden at the head of the column. Once again a refugee in New Orleans, now penniless, the Alabama radical obtained warrants from a U.S. judge for the arrest for Sheriff Alfred Shelby, Deputy Sheriff Christopher Columbus Nash, Clement Penn, and three others. As reported in Delos White's hometown newspaper, the *New York Times,* the federal charges against the Grant Parish Klansmen included murder and attempted murder, as permitted under the Ku Klux Klan and Enforcement Acts passed earlier that year.[22]

The participation of the parish law enforcement officers in the murder and attempted murder was the latest chapter in the history of violence in the lives of both men. Shelby was a hired gun, brought to Colfax at a dangerous juncture on the strength of his reputation as a fighting man. Born in Nashville, Shelby had embarked on his military career in 1849 as a private soldier in a battalion of filibusters—pro-slavery imperialists, famous for their role in propping up a short-lived U.S.-led regime in Nicaragua. Like C. C. Nash, his junior colleague in the Colfax courthouse, the sheriff served in the Civil War in the Virginia theater. He moved to Louisiana after being transferred west of the Mississippi in the final days of the war. Assassination had been a cherished goal of Shelby's notorious Confederate unit, Wheat's Louisiana Tigers, whose members displayed slogans on their hatbands such as "Lincoln's Life or a Tiger's Death."[23] Deputy Nash's career in the 6th Louisiana Infantry appeared tame by comparison despite his two stints as prisoner of war and his participation in the bloodiest fighting of the 19th century. A man on the make, newly relocated to Grant Parish from Louisiana's Texas frontier, Nash would parlay his role in the 1871 killings into a position of leadership in the white supremacy movement and the community as a whole.

Black gunslingers, recruited to the area early in 1870, responded avidly to William Phillips's call for the arrest of Captain White's killers. The delivery of indictments thrust into public view the most inflammatory Republican secret in Grant Parish: the existence of a unit of the newly created Louisiana State Militia whose members had discreetly established households in the black community.

The occupations and addresses of these part-time soldiers indicated their associations with the top ranks of Republican leadership. Levi J. Allen resided on the Wells plantation, having relocated with his wife and seven children from Tennessee. Peter Borland, a seven-year veteran of the United States Army, opened a general store near Colfax with financial backing from Willie Calhoun and an appointment from the Postmaster General. Borland, unmarried and disfigured by a gunshot wound to the mouth that also claimed part of his hearing and vision, was born free to parents of mixed racial ancestry in Jersey City, New Jersey. He had enlisted in 1863 in one of the first black regiments and remained in the army as a "Buffalo Soldier" after the war. Borland shared his space behind the store with Eli Flowers, his friend from the 25th Infantry, just back from an 18-month stint patrolling the Texas frontier. A Pennsylvania-born mulatto, Flowers obtained a position teaching school, probably on the Calhoun plantations. To finance his share of the imported muscle without attracting scrutiny, Calhoun had lined his pockets with ready cash, obtaining three $5,000 loans in May 1870.[24]

The leader of the Grant Parish militia held a commission as captain in the Louisiana State Militia's 6th Infantry Regiment. William Ward appeared on the federal census conducted in the summer months of 1870 as a resident of Grant Parish with personal property valued at $150. Ward had been one of the first black men mustered into the Army of the United States, joining the 22nd Regiment of the Louisiana Corps d'Afrique in September 1863.[25] He fought in Virginia as a member of the First Colored Cavalry one year later, rising to sergeant, the highest rank available to African Americans in the service. Continuing in the army after the war, Ward had served with Borland and Flowers in the 25th U.S. Colored Infantry on the Texas frontier, where skirmishes with hostile Apaches proved only somewhat more dangerous than coexisting with the white communities they were trying to protect. Tuberculosis cut short Ward's career as a Buffalo Soldier, and he mustered out from Ship's Island to the city of New Orleans in 1868 with a disability pension. Making friends among the statehouse Republicans, he found his way into the ranks of the Louisiana State Militia under the command of the turncoat general James Longstreet.

Ward obtained weapons from the state in October 1870 and instructed his rudimentary company in secret. For nearly a year, no one outside the inner circle of radicals in Grant Parish knew what was afoot.[26]

Literate, articulate, and deliberately vague about his antebellum status as slave or free, Ward was consumed by ambition as well as his wasting illness. The delivery of warrants in the White case presented an opportunity to show his strength to white allies and the black population of the parish. Awaiting the arrival of a U.S. marshal appointed by the U.S. attorney in New Orleans, Ward assembled his company as *posse comitatus* in order to arrest and hold captive the individuals named in the White indictments.

Posse Comitatus law enforcement, despite its long-standing recognition in the common law, coexisted uneasily with the civil liberties guaranteed by the U.S. Constitution. Prior to the Reconstruction-era enforcement acts, the most significant use of *posse comitatus* had derived its authority from the infamous Fugitive Slave Act of 1850, which allowed the formation of ad hoc companies to assist in the apprehension and delivery of suspected runaways. The Civil War, Reconstruction, and western migration elevated the practice of employing members of militia in this extraordinary capacity to the point that Congress finally banned the practice in the *Posse Comitatus* Act of 1878.[27] Loosely organized under Ward's own authority as head of the militia, the 1871 posse of black Union veterans set out in pursuit of Sheriff Shelby, C. C. Nash, and other members of their gang.

Violence inevitably resulted from the confrontation of the rival gunmen. Ward's militia acted decisively, seizing several men and killing two in the process. The existence of a parallel process of law enforcement using parish institutions—the court of John Osborn, a conservative judge elected on Sheriff Shelby's ticket in 1870—made the black police action more audacious. In an incident that became infamous, Ward's men overran the Grant Parish courthouse (formerly Willie Calhoun's stable and storefront near the steamboat landing) while the court was reading a state district court indictment of a party of suspects in White's murder. Seizing the prisoners at gunpoint over the strenuous objections of the judge, Ward claimed superior jurisdiction in the name of the U.S. attorney in New Orleans. He hustled his captives toward a passing steamboat over Judge Osborn's livid objections about the prerogatives of the court. "Damn the court," said Ward. A new era in local history had begun.[28]

Within a month of White's assassination, Ward delivered a full docket of suspected mobsters to the federal bench in the capital city. Dressed in plain clothes, but armed with new weapons and the power of the U.S. government, Ward, Flowers, Allen, Borland, and their men created a perfect spectacle of black Republican aggression before an audience of hostile whites.

The authority that Ward saw fit to flaunt with such belligerence derived from new extraordinary federal prerogatives in law enforcement. Devised as enabling legislation for the voting rights conferred by the 15th Amendment, ratified in March 1870, laws passed in 1870 and 1871 initiated a sweeping reconfiguration of the national understanding of crime. Crimes committed by individuals—formerly the exclusive province of state and local officials—now risked federal prosecution under the first new categories of offense promulgated since the Alien and Sedition Acts of the 1790s.[29] The Reconstruction-era acts took as their model the immense grant of power to federal officials in the 1850 Fugitive Slave Act, which created special federal tribunals to investigate charges against African Americans outside the slave states. Using *posse comitatus* and severely limiting the rights of defendants, the 1850 law proved notoriously effective in representing the interests of slaveholders, who claimed or reclaimed more alleged runaways during 1851 than

the sum total of all those captured in the preceding six decades. Under
the older law, whites and others who assisted suspected runaways were
subject to imprisonment for interfering with property rights, with the
Supreme Court weighing in unanimously in approving such detentions
as a proper exercise of federal power. The Enforcement Acts employed
the same authority on behalf of men seeking to exercise their voting
rights and other privileges. Harnessed to the service of a rival constituency, the power of the federal government to uphold individual rights
took aim at the mounting white supremacy conspiracy in the South.[30]

The language of the Enforcement Act of 1870 evoked the tactics
of the Ku Klux Klan and the texture of the tribulations of Phillips,
White, and other victims. When "two or more persons shall conspire
together, or go in disguise upon the public highway, or upon the premises of another, with the intent to...prevent or hinder his free exercise and enjoyment of any right or privilege granted or secured to him
by the Constitution," the law prescribed, "such persons shall be held
guilty of a felony," and subject to a fine of up to $5,000 and up to 10
years in prison. The far-reaching definition of the threat derived additional force from the law enforcement procedures approved by the act.
District attorneys, U.S. marshals, and commissioners appointed by the
U.S. courts, including William Ward, were empowered to designate
arresting parties "specially authorized and required, at the expense of
the United States, to instigate proceedings against all and every person
who shall violate the provisions of this act" and deliver them to the
appropriate federal court.[31]

Additional acts of Congress in 1871 further enlarged the federal
capacities in the South. Enforcement provisions adopted in February
imposed federal oversight of congressional elections, strengthening
the hand of Republican activists by establishing federal voter registration procedures. In April, the most stringent measures yet gained the
approval of Congress and President Grant. Using language borrowed
from the white supremacists' own rhetoric, the Enforcement Act (or Ku
Klux Klan Act) of 1871 parsed the notion of making war on the United
States, identifying specific criminal acts as insurrectionary. Among the
categories of behavior met with federal sanctions in the act, the murder
or harassment or injury of federal officers and appointees in the conduct of their work assumed new dangers. The Klan Act empowered the
president to designate a state of insurrection in territory hostile to the

government of the United States, to suspend the writ of habeas corpus, and to impose other elements of martial law.[32]

To employ the enlarged powers of the government, the Grant administration expanded the staff and portfolio of the attorney general of the United States, establishing the Department of Justice. The Justice Department coordinated the activity of U.S. district attorneys assigned to the federal circuit courts across the country. New laws and litigation in the South necessitated a centralized legal strategy, including the appointment of a solicitor general, charged with arguing the government's case before the justices of the Supreme Court. In 1870 and 1871, Grant moved to ramp up prosecutions by replacing his sitting attorney general with a determined Georgia Radical, Amos T. Akerman. Under Akerman's supervision, the administration aligned itself firmly with those who would protect the civil and political rights of African Americans and their allies in the southern states, prosecuting thousands of suspected Klansmen and their allies under the auspices of the Ku Klux Klan and Enforcement Acts.[33]

Even among some Republicans, the assumption of new powers by the central government appeared draconian. Some objected that the legislation was unconstitutional because it extended federal oversight to punish acts of private citizens. The majority, however, saw enforcement as an urgent necessity, with life-and-death consequences for Republican activists and their agenda in the South. "These combinations amount to war," insisted one supporter, "and cannot be effectually crushed on any other theory."[34]

Southern communities where the provisions were applied writhed under the federal yoke. The first to feel the full impact of the laws occupied a piedmont zone of South Carolina, where the president estimated that two-thirds of the white inhabitants of the region had taken up arms against federal authority. Soldiers from the 7th Cavalry, including many who would be assigned to Grant Parish after the massacre in 1873, occupied the region, scouring for arrests, holding hundreds without charge, and securing a number of significant convictions against the organizers of white violence. Other major federal initiatives netted Klansmen in Tennessee, North Carolina, and Texas. The total number of individuals prosecuted under the new authority grew from 879 in 1871 to 1,890 in 1872 and 1,960 to 1873.[35] Thousands more fled their strongholds or abandoned their illegal pursuits.

The federal dragnet in Grant Parish and its environs attracted little attention outside Louisiana. Arrests—and the threat of more incidents like the ones that claimed the lives of Jeff Yawn and another white man from Natchitoches, said to be resisting arrest—continued in the weeks after the round-up that sent Shelby and Nash to New Orleans. The arrival of an unnamed federal marshal in Colfax supplemented Ward's authority to expand the investigation. From New Orleans, William Phillips did his part, testifying before the grand jury against the organizers of the fatal raid on his Rock Island home. Using the Enforcement Acts' power to thwart conspiracy, negligence, and obstruction of justice, Phillips executed a handful of strategic coups against white witnesses for the defense who were themselves placed under arrest. Testimony in the grand jury proceedings produced additional warrants, further angering the white population of the area. "The 'boys in blue' and the 'milish' are still making arrests in the Empire of Grant," an Alexandria newspaper complained. "Nearly every boat takes down some good citizen, dragged from his home and family."[36]

The outrageous William Ward exacerbated the emotional tension by disregarding white sensitivity to the appearance of black men under arms. As indicated in the newspaper report, Union veterans in Ward's unit conducted operations wearing old U.S. infantry uniforms, a practice common in the Louisiana militia, which also included men in gray in its motley ranks. Militia commander Longstreet, responding to complaints from the countryside, censured Ward's display of drilling and parade maneuvers—a violation of state policies that aimed to make militia operations as inconspicuous as possible. Ward's personal appearance and demeanor provided additional offense to racist whites. Described as "large frame[d]," a "full-blooded Negro," and "a zulu type," Ward was said to "bear the indications of the worst qualities of his race" in his face. The few surviving examples of the tone and content of his spoken comments at the time—his profane dismissal of Judge Osborn's court, for example—bear witness to the captain's abrasive personal style. Whites saw Ward and his men "running wild over the parish," and "committing deeds highly prejudicial to good order and to the general interests of the community at large." Worst of all, whites feared the infectious spread of Ward's defiance in the black community.[37]

The participation of local African Americans in Ward's militia smoothed the outsiders' introduction to the plantation South, where many families traced their roots in the Red River region to migrations predating the Louisiana Purchase. Although the identity of hometown militiamen was not recorded in 1871, the more complete record of the violence two years later places black veterans from Colfax resolutely in Ward's inner circle. Ward, Allen, Flowers, and Borland benefited from the presence of seasoned military men in the community of freedmen, especially during months when they conducted military drills and preparations in secrecy. Black Union veterans Alabama Mitchell, Cuffy Gaines, and Edmund Dancer had returned from the war to Grant Parish, where Mitchell and Gaines took up residence as free men on the Calhoun plantation. Likely recruits, the local men could hardly refuse the salary for state militiamen, pegged to the U.S. Army's going rate of $16 a month.[38] Their enrollment reinforced the link between the new arrivals and the radical establishment of the parish led by Willie Calhoun.

As the new base for federal and militia operations, the parish seat at Colfax took on the semblance of a proper town, trafficking in urgent business and important men. A boardinghouse and lawyers' offices joined the existing handful of structures near the steamboat landing: a store in which Calhoun owned a half interest with a minor white Republican; a school and antebellum warehouses; a stand of former slave cabins, the Smithfield Quarters, within view; the humble courthouse, shaded by a stately tree; and the road to Mirabeau Plantation, where the master of the old domain lived with his mixed-race wife in a reconstructed dwelling house.

Despite the obvious mark of the hunchback's unusual tastes, Colfax developed as a black man's town. According to area whites, in fact, "the Town of Colfax, or rather Colhoun's Negro Quarter of Colfax, was fast becoming "the Mecca of bad and desperate negroes from everywhere."[39] As they described it to a visitor in 1874:

> Calhoun, the proprietor, is humpbacked and eccentric to the point of mental aberration, was endeared to the negroes both by his peculiar habits and by the liaison he had formed with a yellow woman who had borne him several children. Therefore when he invited the blacks generally to come and set up their quarters on his plantation, some 17,000 acres in all, they flocked thither from all quarters.[40]

With Calhoun's sponsorship and the protection of the state militia, new arrivals and old-timers alike could hope to keep marriages sacred, to raise literate children, and to hold themselves as equals in the parish and the town. The transformation put to shame the more conventional associations of the concept of radical. Here, by careful husbandry, the blasted roots of chattel slavery gave bloom to a garden of unobstructed opportunity.

Eighteen seventy-two was an appalling year for agriculture. As described in the sugar planter's standby, Bouchereau's report on Louisiana crops, the season unfolded in a series of disasters: a cold, wet winter to rot the seed-cane followed by a drought so severe that farmhands had to haul water to the steam plants to process the cane that survived, a harvest-season hurricane, and late-breaking heat that dried the cane juice in the stalks. "To cap the climax of our misfortunes," Bouchereau recorded, "we had freezing weather on the 14th, 15th, and 16th of November, which proved a death blow to the crop and almost ruined many a planter."[41]

Cotton yields were similarly disastrous, but black residents of Colfax and environs did not mind. For the second time in their lives, they had witnessed the miraculous intervention of the government of the United States, first to make them free and more recently to secure their footing as free and equal, with help from Louisiana's born-again state apparatus. Eighteen seventy-two marked the jubilee year for this second coming. The procession toward elections in November displayed the solemnity of holy rites and the enthusiasm of a camp meeting.

The candidacy of Captain William Ward for a Grant Parish seat in the state legislature tapped into the flow of black exuberance. Tales of Ward's exploits in pursuit of the night riders had electrified the regional electorate, thrilling the radicals and prefiguring apocalypse for white conservatives. William Smith Calhoun offered Ward his personal support, supervising the transfer of the local party nomination from an incumbent to the black carpetbagger at a meeting of the Mirabeau Republican Club in July 1872. Ward's military reputation provided name recognition, while his comrades in the state militia ensured the candidate's safety and helped generate excitement.

Unlike 1868, when Republican office seekers took their lives into their own hands, the 1872 field benefited from enhanced security. In addition to the seven veterans and their companions in the local militia, Republicans received a show of support from federal troops, which visited Colfax briefly to investigate charges that white conservatives were using force. Anticipating violence, the commander of federal forces in the state, General William H. Emory, had gained explicit instructions allowing the dispatch of soldiers wherever needed to preserve order.[42]

Blacks in Colfax took matters into their own hands as well, convinced, in the words of Alexandria's short-lived Republican newspaper, that "opponents of Republicans are wide awake, cunning, and unscrupulous" in their determination to override the will of the majority. At a rally in Alexandria attended by the party hierarchy from New Orleans (including the man ridiculed in the conservative paper as "the late W. B. Phillips," in honor of his life-saving stunt the year before), local Republicans were urged to be vigilant. The band played the Irish folk song "Katie, Bar the Door," with its militant injunction to self-defense, before the interracial group sat down for a barbeque lunch.[43]

A split within the Republican Party complicated the contest for the most important offices. At the national level, "Liberal" Republicans led by newspaper editor Horace Greeley expressed revulsion at the cronyism and corruption on display in the Grant administration, and urged retreat from the aggressive federal prerogatives adopted in pursuit of southern justice. Louisiana's carpetbagger Governor Henry Clay Warmoth followed their lead, describing himself as uncomfortable with the effort to "Africanize" the state. The 1872 elections featured a united front between Warmoth's Liberal Republicans and conservative Democrats, united by their mistrust of the radical faith in black political participation. On the "Fusion" ticket, men who had voted and held office as Republicans joined cause with virulently antifederal Democrats and Klansmen. With John McEnery, a Confederate officer and Black-Code-era state legislator at the head of the ticket, the Fusionists nominated candidates for every local office on the ballot.

Louisiana radicals, for their part, nominated a white carpetbagger named William Pitt Kellogg for the governor's seat. Despite rumors that he preferred to wear gloves when shaking hands with African Americans on the campaign trail, Kellogg was committed to the national party platform of equality and suffrage.[44] Kellogg headed the pro–U. S. Grant Republican caucus based in the gargantuan U.S. Customhouse establishment in New Orleans, the nation's busiest port. The virulence and intrigue that made Louisiana the most dangerous terrain of the Reconstruction effort was mounting steadily toward its climax.

Election Day proceeded with deceptive serenity, as the forces of the internecine struggle gathered behind the scenes. Across the state, polls

opened with fanfare and little controversy, as both sides rallied voters for the end of the season. With support from Ward's militia and
local Republican clubs, black voters in Grant Parish and Alexandria
appeared in military formation, advanced under arms to polling places,
and departed as a unit.[45] Their raucous shouts and singing lay claim to
the victory of being counted and the certainty of superior numbers.
Sending William Ward to the statehouse—and delivering a landslide
for President Grant—Grant Parish radicals seemed to have secured victory and peace through strength.

SIX

Carnival of the Animals

THE CHAOS THAT ENSUED AFTER THE 1872 ELECTION derived in large part from the recent enlargement of the powers of the state government. Governor Warmoth's moves to invest electoral power in a Returning Board to which he alone appointed officers and an 1871 law requiring gubernatorial commissions for formerly elected offices at the parish level threw into question the legitimacy of every claim to victory in the state. The impeachment of Warmoth by his radical enemies in the outgoing legislature tremendously complicated the official tally of results. With the radical Customhouse faction's partisan, Lieutenant Governor P.B.S. Pinchback, serving in Warmoth's place (in a truncated term as the only African American governor in any state before the 1980s), the Returning Board split into rival versions, each certifying the victory of their favored slate of candidates. Both sides refused to back down, and Louisiana lurched dangerously toward dual government or civil war.[1] Warmouth himself survived an attempted assassination on Canal Street in New Orleans during broad daylight, escaping with his life after mortally wounding his assailant with a knife.[2]

Thanks to the quick work of Federal Circuit Court Judge Edward H. Durrell, who issued an injunction and secured the support of federal troops, William Pitt Kellogg and the radicals gained control of the statehouse in New Orleans. Undeterred, the McEnery ticket swore in its own officials and opened a rival session of the legislature at Odd Fellows Hall on Camp Street. Even President Grant admitted that the outcome of the election was "not altogether certain," though his administration recognized Kellogg's as the "de facto government" of the state. Under orders to avoid contact with McEnery supporters and to permit the Fusionists to proceed with his inauguration and the sessions at Odd Fellows Hall, the small contingent of federal troops in New Orleans observed the emergence of first dual governments in the Reconstruction era. With Metropolitan Police taking up defenses against rapidly organizing pro-McEnery gangs, the likelihood of a repeat of the 1866 New Orleans Riot loomed large in the city.[3]

On January 13, 1873—inauguration day for both Kellogg and McEnery—a third pretender to executive power made his stand. Unlike the rival governors, Rex, the King of Carnival and Lord of Misrule, made no claim to democratic election. Indeed, the secrecy surrounding his elevation and the identity of his core supporters was a critical wellspring of Rex's appeal. The King had made his first Mardi Gras appearance the previous year, requesting the compliance of the city and the state in the organizers' efforts to make the public celebration of Carnival safer, more accessible, and tourist-friendly. This year, his instructions appeared as edicts published in the local papers and in a series of wall posters bearing his royal crest. Rex demanded the obedience of police and armed forces in the city, issuing a specific summons for the services of the Metropolitan Police, who would guide the parades on Mardi Gras day, February 25. The authority of Rex's claim contrasted sharply with the crisis of legitimacy in the state government, compounding the confusion and heightening anxiety in the capital city.

The willingness of the carnival krewes to work with the Republican establishment showed the rising aspirations of the organizers of New Orleans's most distinctive cultural event. The newly established Pickwick Club provided the public face of the Mystick Krewe of Comus—like Rex, one of a handful of secret societies traditionally dedicated to the sponsorship of private balls during carnival season. Public parades promised to attract crowds, including celebrities such as Grand Duke Alexis of Russia, whose attendance in 1872 in the company of General George Armstrong Custer and other notables had inspired and delighted Mardi Gras elites. In honor of Alexis, for example, the colors of the House of Romanov—green, gold, and purple—were deemed the official colors of the season, and "If Ever I Cease to Love," a favorite song of the grand duke's American tour, became the unofficial anthem of Mardi Gras. Rex's summons to the Metropolitan Police for a military escort fit the organizers' purpose of establishing law and order on Mardi Gras Day, then as now the occasion for drunkenness and violence. A less imperious request from the Mystick Krewe of Comus engaged the services of the 19th U.S. Infantry's brass band in the Comus Mardi Gras parade on February 25, 1873. Union Army bands—the recipients of almost $20 million in wartime investments—were considered the best practitioners of the new style of brass music that the citizens of New Orleans had come to love. Thus the trumpets of the occupying force heralded the opening of the most celebrated and most infamous display in the tawdry history of Mardi Gras.[4]

The Mystick Krewe of Comus parade of 1873 signaled its theme in a puff of incense, the smoke from which illuminated the transparency of the title arch: "The Missing Links to Darwin's Origin of Species." The pageantry was overtly political, contradicting the spirit of cooperation invoked by the participation of Louisiana's besieged carpetbagger government in the festivities. This year's carnival would indulge the privilege to speak truth to power, or merely hold a scoffing mirror on the times, associated with the festival before Lent in Catholic communities around the world. Clothed in anonymity and satire, the members of the Mystick Krewe staged as puppetry the burning issues of New Orleans's crisis years.

The biological analogy established by Charles Darwin, the English naturalist, still in the early stages of his fame, provided a most perfect vehicle for social commentary, a strength the coming generation of scientific racists would exploit to the fullest. As inspiration for the Krewe of Comus, moreover, the merits of the theme as costume wear were plain to see. Animals of ingenious design and artful grouping conveyed a mostly ridiculous version of Darwinian evolution, to accompany the stanzas of an expository poem upon the romance of sexual selection.

> We, rich in faith and warm in strong affection,
> For thy great creed of "Natural Selection,"
> Convinced that man—the modern institution
> Owes his proud place to laws of "Evolution."
> Now come, great Sage, a living grand memorial
> Of Man's descent through lineage "Arboreal,"
> "The Missing Links"—those pre-historic sires
> Whose loves and lives a wondering race admires.[5]

The papier-mâché costumes, deemed to be too delicate to survive the crossing from Paris, were the first to be created in New Orleans, and set the standard to which every subsequent parade aspired. One hundred specimen types, including cheetahs, sea urchins, and even stray vegetables and plants, appeared in upper-body casts gently molded in the features and trappings of human shapes. The most striking (though not the most beautiful) presented caricatures of political types whom New Orleans audiences were certain to recognize as enemies of the native elite: carpetbaggers, scalawags, and "Negro politicians" satirized as lowly beasts. The serving president of the United States, for example, appeared with Comus in the guise of a tobacco grub, complete with general's blue cap and cigar.

Although the "Missing Link" himself (and his primate Queen) was portrayed in pure stereotype as a gorilla playing a banjo, other masquers represented figures close at hand in Reconstruction Louisiana.

> ...Chacma Monkeys fall liked ripened grapes
> Resistless victims of the Bearded Apes;
> That Mandrils, lost in soft voluptuous swoons,
> Should grace the nuptials of the bold Baboons
> And Chimpanzees, from waving tree tops hang,
> To court caresses from the fond Orang.
> Oh! rosy hues of Time's dim twilight morn!
> In such an hour the "Missing Link" was born;
> The great Gorilla, flinging wide the gate
> Of Darwin's Eden, and our high estate.

Among the black politicians depicted as monkeys, partygoers recognized Lieutenant Governor C. C. Antoine of Shreveport, mercilessly ridiculed that year in the Creole scandal sheets as "*ein vilain makak noir*"—a villainous black Macaca.[6] "Beast" Butler, the commander of the Union occupation force that took the city in 1862, paraded as a Hyena, while the New York-born governor of Louisiana, Henry Clay Warmoth, was the Snake, "the author of all our woes." Charles Darwin himself, done up as an ass, supervised the procession in the persons of the men who carried the transparency stanzas of the particular animal groups.

> Thus well endowed, ah! Darwin! Then—Alas!
> We trace his genius to the sapient Ass.[7]

The most irreverent costume, perhaps, mocked the white captain of the parade's own police escort, the New Orleans Metropolitan Police, here appearing as a dog. Accompanied somewhat incongruously by the Metropolitans and the 19th U.S. Infantry brass band, the Comus parade swung into motion uptown en route to its final destination in the French Quarter.

At Canal Street, then as now the threshold between business and culture in New Orleans, the "Missing Link" parade encountered crushing crowds that forced the early termination of the public festivities. The Metropolitan Police, serving as the butt of the joke, refused to push a passage into the narrow streets of the quarter, where some in the crowd did not seem to share the Krewe of Comus sense of humor. Music helped dissolve the tension, as the 19th Infantry band played the comical new Mardi Gras anthem, a rollicking coda to the Darwinian theme:

> If ever I cease to love
> If ever I cease to love
> May the fish get legs
> And cows lay eggs
> If ever I cease to love

After much shouting and dancing, the costume animals retired to the Varieties Theater, where their living tableaux climaxed the private Mystick Krewe of Comus Mardi Gras ball.

Nobody was killed, marking 1873 as the most orderly Mardi Gras to date. The Lenten season that would culminate in the Easter Sunday massacre at Colfax was off to a disarmingly peaceful start.[8]

Once the brief reign of the King of Carnival was over, the problems of dual government in Louisiana resumed with a vengeance. The 1871 law requiring the chief executive to commission local offices had drawn hundreds of candidates and their supporters to New Orleans during the carnival season. Vermont-born William Pitt Kellogg received candidates from both political camps in his makeshift governor's offices at the St. Charles Hotel, where rival delegations from Grant Parish made repeated visits in February and March.

Radicals, led by William Ward, now serving at Mechanics Hall Statehouse as a representative in the Republican-dominated legislature, sought Kellogg's support for the installation of a white sheriff, Daniel Shaw, and an African American parish judge, R. C. Register. Fusion conservatives from Grant Parish sent their own representative, James W. Hadnot, to the legislature convened at Odd Fellows Hall near Canal Street. Republican Fusionists set aside their complaints about the legitimacy of the Kellogg regime long enough to plead the case for their own sheriff and judge with the de facto governor. With control of the courthouse in Colfax subject to the authority of a divided state government, political leaders in Grant Parish remained in limbo, making periodic visits to the dueling executives and inviting the participation of any influential parties who would make the case.

The real struggle to control the courthouse would take place on the site, with physical force rather than legal and political maneuvering as its primary agent. Taking advantage of cozy relations with conservative incumbents elected in the repressive atmosphere of 1870, Fusionists took an early lead, installing Alphonse Cazabat as judge and Christopher Columbus Nash as sheriff. In January and February, Cazabat and Nash occupied the courthouse part of the time, as required by the part-time duties of each office. At the instigation of William Ward, however, radicals would make their own bid to control the courthouse in March 1873. Returning from New Orleans and summoning some members of his militia unit, Ward arrived to find the building unoccupied. The black men broke a window, opened the door, and took possession of the courthouse in the name of Judge Register and Sheriff Shaw.

By force of arms, they would control the building for the next six weeks—until the courthouse and the men who dared to claim it were destroyed.

SEVEN

Battle of the Colfax Courthouse

HE REPUBLICAN FACTION IN CONTROL OF THE courthouse was prepared for trouble, but Jesse McKinney was not. McKinney tried to stay out of trouble—a goal that required a black man to steer clear of politics in general and to keep away from the town of Colfax in particular, after the seizure of the courthouse initiated its militarization. In the two weeks before his death, McKinney had observed the passage of armed men of both races from his home near the ferry crossing on Bayou Darrow. He stuck close to his wife and six young children. The family was watching on April 5, 1873 when the white men shot him in the head. They heard him scream—"like a pig," as a black neighbor remembered it—and they heard some of the white men asking if McKinney was killed. "Yes," came the answer, "he is dead as hell."[1]

Republican commentators in Louisiana would later deplore the killing of a man at work, as they said, "peaceably building a fence around his property." In fact, in the charged environment of post–Civil War Louisiana, where black ownership seemed to threaten the social and economic order, the act of building a fence approximated a kind of defiance. McKinney had money. Like his father and brother, he acknowledged almost $500 in personal property in the 1870 census. Late in the season, his corn crib and pantries were fully stocked.

The white men who killed him were far from home. They needed food for their horses and water and provisions for their growing ranks.

After they shot McKinney, they dismounted and "danced like mad" for two hours, then settled in to feed their horses out of his supply.

Jesse McKinney did not die instantly, but lingered for six or eight hours. Assisted by another woman, Eliza Smith, his wife Laurinda loaded him and the children into a wagon while the whites in the yard mocked them, hooting lecherously and calling them "bad names."[2] Laurinda McKinney drove to her stepfather's house and laid her husband's body on the floor.

At sundown, when he died, his wife found her way to Mirabeau Plantation to ask for a coffin and a safe place to sleep. All of her neighbors had fled. The body remained unburied, attracting so many turkey vultures by the end of the week that the roof of the house was covered with birds.

The raiding party at McKinney's farm brought together an unlikely handful of area whites. Among participants later identified by the widow and other eyewitnesses, representatives from distant parishes made up the party that pulled the trigger. Denis Lemoine, a rollicking Creole from 60 miles away in Avoyelles Parish, joined his cousins from the extensive Natchitoches clan of Lemoines. On April 5, Lemoine was riding with Bill Irwin, a poor farmer from the Rapides section of Grant Parish. Their unlikely company suggested the reach and strategy of the white supremacist organizations that planned the attack on the Colfax courthouse. In fact, the Knights of the White Camellia and a group calling itself the "Old Time Ku Klux Klan" played a major organizational role. Acting as scouts, Lemoine, Irwin, and their associates secured a site to feed and water the horses of a growing contingent of armed men. They would visit the abandoned McKinney house on patrol and make liaisons there until supplies ran out.[3]

Like many who would join their ranks in the area around Colfax, Irwin and Lemoine were Confederate veterans. Apart from the killing of civilians and other excesses, white preparations betrayed a jaunty military spirit. Where former officers such as George Stafford and David Paul took the lead, volunteers formed "companies" and even designated ranks. Rapides Parishes offered three such units, under Captains Stafford, Paul, and Joseph W. Texada, all prominent planters and former slaveholders. Contingents from Catahoula, Concordia, and Winn Parishes traveled long distances under similar leadership. Others, such as Denis Lemoine, arrived as individuals or in small groups. Local residents offered directions and hospitality, putting up out-of-towners and providing meals as possible. Veterans figured prominently in the mix, but a significant number of young men joined in, including many, such as Stafford, who had lost older brothers and other relatives in the Civil War.

The talk around their campfires was of genocide. Many expressed the strong conviction that the seizure of the Colfax courthouse was the first step in a war of conquest to eradicate the white race.

> The Negroes at Colfax shouted daily across the river to our people that they intended killing every white man and boy, keeping only the young women to raise from them a new breed [explained the organizer of an elite Rapides Parish contingent]. On their part if ever successful, you may safely expect that neither age, nor sex, nor helpless infancy will be spared.[4]

"[T]he open threats of the negroes were to kill the white men and violate the white women," remembered one participant.[5] Another account suggested the participation of militant organizations in fanning the rumor.

> We were all startled and terrified at the news by a Courier who had just gotten in from our Parish Site, that the Negroes under the leadership of a few unprincipled white men had captured the Court House & driven all white inhabitants out of the Town, and were raiding stealing & driving the cattle out of the surrounding country. The Negro men making their brags that they would clean out the white men & then take their women folks for wifes.[6]

Another fragment of the rhetoric of such claims referred in Klan-style idiom to the way the "Tytanic Black Hand was sweeping over the Red River Valley in 1873," and to the urgent response of white manhood in the state.[7]

Their sojourn in the woods and swamps of Grant Parish produced both exhilaration and anxiety. For many of the poor men in the ranks, the muster provided the rare opportunity to ride on horseback, thanks to the generosity of men such as Christopher Columbus Dunn, who "hired out" the whole livery stable in Natchitoches to provide mounts for local volunteers. Those who walked, including Dunn's own son Milton, a newly graduated medical doctor, enjoyed the manly companionship and being outdoors in spring weather. The men established campsites in the woods at the McKinney farm and at the lumberyard on Rock Island, near the graves of Hal Frazier and Delos White. No small measure of nostalgia and sentiment warmed nights in camp, where the men sang old war songs including "Tenting on the Old Camp Ground," with its maudlin final chorus:

> Many are the hearts that are weary tonight,
> Wishing for the war to cease;
> Many are the hearts looking for the right
> To see the dawn of peace.
> Tenting tonight,
> Tenting tonight,
> Tenting tonight on the old camp ground.
> . . .
> Dying tonight,
> Dying tonight,
> Dying tonight on the old camp ground.

For most, the memory of war stirred associations with separation and the threat to families. In light of rumors about black conquest, white communities appointed home guards and prepared household defenses.[8]

White women and children made their own contributions to the coming fight, providing food, medical supplies, and even homemade ammunition. A local girl put in charge of preparing "blue whistlers" with buckshot and paper, for example, later recalled how her "young fingers eagerly wrapped these awful messengers of death." She also remembered the thrill of being guarded by her teenage sweetheart while her father was away: "What is sweeter than romance in the face of death?"[9]

Black citizens vacated their own homes with fewer romantic associations. The murder of McKinney—and the abduction of a second black man, Charles Harris, who was "carried off in the woods" the same day—rocked the confidence of black community of Grant Parish.[10] With partisans of the courthouse group sounding the alarm, word spread quickly of the threat to peaceable African Americans and their homes. An exodus from outlying households swelled the population of Colfax, with hundreds of new arrivals of all ages crowding the cabins at Smithfield Quarters and establishing campsites. A second large contingent fled to Mirabeau Plantation, where they joined Willie Calhoun as virtual captives of the fight.

Some of the arriving men were tapped to serve in Republican Sheriff Dan Shaw's *posse comitatus*, charged with apprehending the murderers of Jesse McKinney. In practice, the sheriff's posse operated as a militia under the command of William Ward. Prominent members of the 1871 militia unit took part in the defense of the Colfax courthouse: Eli Flowers, Peter Borland, O. J. Butler, Lev Allen, carpetbaggers and veterans; and local Union fighters Cuffy Gaines, Alabama Mitchell, and Edmund Dancer. R. C. Register, the Republican judge, urged the growing force to be courageous and keep possession of the courthouse until United States troops arrived.

Seeking strength in numbers in the meantime, Ward and his associates put out a call to black communities for additional men with guns. "We ask you in the name of [our] Liberty and [our] Children's [Rights]," Ward pleaded in a poorly spelled letter intercepted by his enemies, to "come to our sistence...as the whites does [for their own people]."[11] A rank-and-file recruiter named Bully Ellis was perhaps more eloquent. "He told me to come to Colfax and fight for the United States," a participant recalled.

Whites continued to visit and even live in the town of Colfax, where a few families occupied homes on town lots purchased from the Calhoun estate. On April 1, one week after the seizure of the courthouse, a party of 19 men led by a Fusion ticket state representative and reputed Klansman, James West Hadnot, made a show of strength in the town, riding fast and holding their rifles in sight. A smaller white reconnaissance party on April 4 discovered one of the white residents, W. L. Richardson, a former ally of Willie Calhoun, "under bars and lock and key—laying on fire arms" in anticipation of a black assault. Other whites at risk included the boardinghouse manager, George W. Scarborough, and a former parish judge, Jim Rutland. Rutland became so unnerved by the militarism of his black neighbors that he vacated his home and took up residence with friends on the opposite bank of the river.[12]

In an incident that became notorious, blacks in Colfax robbed Rutland's vacant house early in the month. The burglary provided the justification for a new push in New Orleans to get Governor Kellogg to recognize Nash and Cazabat and displace Shaw and Register as parish officers. After meeting with the governor, militia commander Longstreet, and U.S. district attorney J. R. Beckwith—who refused to invoke the federal Enforcement Acts against blacks in Colfax—Rutland and his conservative allies despaired of gaining assistance from the state government. "As he left the room," remembered Beckwith, "[Rutland] told me that...there would be hell in Grant Parish the next thing we heard from there."[13]

Armed confrontations on April 4 and 5 indicated the escalation of violence on both sides. The first occurred during a parley of major actors on both sides, including William Ward, Eli Flowers, and a black Republican serving as tax collector, Green Brantley. Meeting in a field to attempt a peaceful resolution, the conference broke up upon the arrival of a party of black riders bringing news of the shooting of Jesse McKinney. A white participant, John McCain of Montgomery, remembered that the "enraged Negroes ran up throwing their guns on the white men," and were restrained only when Ward and Flowers turned their own guns on the new arrivals.[14]

Ward assumed a more militant demeanor on the following day, when a black patrol near Smithfield Quarters encountered whites on horseback. As described by a white participant, Oscar Watson, the incident took place on Calhoun's property.

> We crossed 2 very mean boggy streams to get into the old sugar plantation on which this Parish site was located. We rode in the field about ¾ of a mile when one of the boys discovered a body of men about 40 or 50 strong ½ mile or such matter riding toward the bayou we had just crossed[. T]hey being on the opposite side from us and the banks grown up in willows we could only partially see them[. O]ne of the boys said to me they must be friends coming from our sister parish in answer to our call for help, so I immediately told the boys we we [sic] would go & meet them.

Riding close, someone in Watson's company identified the mounts of the larger group as mules.

> All at once when we had come to within about 500 yds of them one of the boys bellowed out [:] look out boys those are Negroes[!]

Captain Ward and his ride-out let fly with a round of gunfire, killing a horse and shooting off the thumb of a white participant before Watson and the other white "boys" turned and fled.

"You will most probably say why dident you fight it out but I assure you," wrote Watson, years later, "you would have been in the front rank making the mud fly just like I was." He had seen black power: "in front of us & on the side behind trees & logs were 50 negroes & behind us in the open field there seemed to me to be 4000 more coming our way."[15]

"I am in command," wrote Ward on April 5, describing the encounter on the Calhoun plantation as a battle, "all I Lack is help."

In another letter written April 5 or 6 (and since lost), Ward pleaded for assistance from Governor Kellogg. He entrusted its delivery to one of the few white men willing to take risks for the Radicals, the scalawag Willie Calhoun. Calhoun—whose term in the legislature had expired in 1870—remained heartily engaged in the political contest for his home parish, participating in the seizure of the courthouse and allegedly abetting or encouraging the attack on Judge Rutland's home.[16] He also had facilitated the exchange of a series of letters between Ward, Shaw, and Register and their counterparts on the Fusion side. He continued to participate at great personal risk, acting out of a sense of responsibility to protect his workers, political allies, and friends. "I tried to prevent bloodshed," he later explained.[17]

Placing the letter in his boot, Calhoun attempted to hail a steamboat at Calhoun's Landing, using the standard daytime procedure of hanging a flag on a post by the landing, but the first to pass refused to take on passengers at Colfax out of fear or hostility. Making his way to a little-used landing some distance below the town, he boarded the steamboat *LaBelle* on Monday, April 7. Calhoun declined the offer of his usual stateroom, finding his way to a nook deep in the hold of the boat. Despite his precautions, he was discovered before *LaBelle* reached Alexandria and removed from the boat by his old nemesis, J.G.P. Hooe.

Hooe delivered Calhoun to a large crowd of white men on the riverbank at Pineville—including James West Hadnot, Captains Dave Paul and Joe Texada, William Cruikshank, the Marsh brothers, and one of the Stafford boys—who seized Calhoun's personal documents and subjected him to an hour-long harangue on the dangers of friendship with Negroes.

"They told him no harm would come to him if he was innocent, as he said he was, of creating the riot," reported the steamboat captain, who contacted the Republican newspaper as soon as he arrived in New Orleans. It was all he could do. "The Belle was obliged to come down and leave Mr. Calhoun in their hands," he explained, "and it is feared he will suffer violence."[18]

Accompanied by an armed guard, who told him he ought to be hanged, Calhoun was forced to ride through the woods in the company of 40 or 50 white men. Reaching a secluded spot, the party suddenly

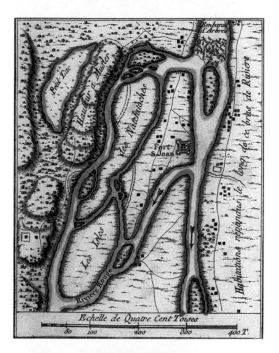

An 18th-century map
included a representation
of the Great Raft of the
Red River, an ancient
logjam stretching from
Natchitoches, Louisiana, to
Caddo Lake in Texas.
(Historic New Orleans
Collection)

Meredith Calhoun. He aspired
to what he called the
"sumptuous abundance of the
world." (Hemphill Collection)

Sugar and cotton on the wharves at
New Orleans. After three decades as a
captain of global commerce, Meredith
Calhoun chose to invest his personal
wealth in plantation slavery. (Historic
New Orleans Collection)

The retreat of the Union flotilla over falling waters, Red River Campaign, 1864. The officer who invented the removeable dams saved the fleet and won a battlefield promotion to the rank of brigadier general. (Historic New Orleans Collection)

A Calhoun family slave. (Hemphill Collection)

Ada Calhoun. While her brother William risked his life on behalf of black civil rights in Louisiana, Meredith Calhoun's daughter sat for a likeness in the Paris studio of Franz Xavier Winterhalter, portrait artist to Europe's royalty. (Hemphill Collection)

Watercolor of costume design for "The Missing Links to Darwin's Origin of Species," Mystick Krewe of Comus, Mardi Gras, 1873. President Ulysses S. Grant as a tobacco grub. (Tulane University Special Collections)

Watercolor of costume design for "The Missing Links to Darwin's Origin of Species," Mystick Krewe of Comus, Mardi Gras, 1873. Algernon S. Badger, superintendent of the New Orleans Metropolitan Police, depicted as a bloodhound. Badger would be seriously wounded at the White League "Battle of Liberty Place" in 1874. (Tulane University Special Collections)

Oh! rosy hues of Time's dim twilight morn!
In such an hour the "Missing Link" was born;
The great Gorilla, flinging wide the gate
Of Darwin's Eden, and our high estate.

"The Missing Link," the final illustration of the poem "The Missing Links to Darwin's Origin of Species," Mistick Krewe of Comus, Mardi Gras, 1873. The King of Carnival and his court advisers were satirical primate versions of black politicians.

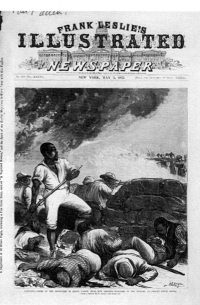

Christopher Columbus Nash. He led the white paramilitary force, claiming to have been elected sheriff of Grant Parish in the disputed elections of 1872. (Cammie G. Henry Research Center)

An engraving on the cover of a national magazine depicted the doomed black defenders of the Colfax Courthouse. (*Frank Leslie's Illustrated Weekly*)

Top: The Colfax pecan tree. Whatever happened in the vicinity of the "Riot Tree" remained a secret, even after the tree was featured in a Ku Klux Klan "Hall of Fame" and decorated with an American Forestry Association bronze medallion.

Right: A photo in a 1920s scrapbook. The inscription reads: "And to think the mayor of Colfax allow[ed] this sacred tree to be cut down for firewood for darkies! What a crime." (Cammie G. Henry Research Center)

The U.S.S. Ozark. Equipped with six cannons, including two swivel-mounted, 11-inch guns in its armored turret, it was perhaps the most formidable weapon ever put at the disposal of federal law enforcement. (Naval Historical Foundation)

Dr. Milton Dunn. A participant in the Colfax Massacre as a young man, Dunn became its leading local historian. (Cammie G. Henry Research Center)

The monument to the white heroes of Colfax. Its inscription reads "In loving remembrance, erected to the memory of Stephen Decatur Parrish, John West Hadnot, Sidney Harris, who fell in the Colfax Riot fighting for white supremacy." (Cammie G. Henry Research Center)

The Colfax historical marker, erected in 1951 by the Louisiana State Department of Commerce and Industry. (Cammie G. Henry Research Center)

halted, fired their weapons, and forced Calhoun to dismount. They stripped off his clothing, revealing the steel corset that helped him hold his torso upright. In his boot, they found the letter from William Ward to Governor Kellogg.

What happened next remains a mystery. Though he somehow survived, Calhoun could not remember what happened after he was stripped. According to the legend among local whites, the scalawag saved himself by giving the Masonic distress signal, asking, "Who will help the widow's son?" The large number of his brethren in the mob could not refuse the summons. Dressed and mounted once again, he rode with the group to Grant Parish, slept under armed guard on Bill Irwin's porch, and returned to the dwelling house at Mirabeau, where he would remain a prisoner, with a small contingent of armed whites, for the remainder of the week.[19]

Amid the excitement, Ward became seriously ill. Weakened by tuberculosis, he also suffered from severe rheumatism. He was seen in town using a walking cane and took to his bed early in the week. Sometime before Good Friday, April 11, Ward and Eli Flowers told their fellows they would "scout out" the next steamboat. Flowers had to lift his friend into the saddle and carry him in his arms up the gangplank of the *B. L. Hodge*. They departed for New Orleans, where Ward hoped to schedule a definitive interview with Governor Kellogg. His enemies suspected cowardice, and later claimed to hear that Flowers had admitted, on board the steamboat, that "it had become too hot for him in Colfax."[20] Neither Ward nor Flowers would be on the scene as tensions escalated toward the climax.

As Easter Sunday approached, the military character of the confrontation became increasingly pronounced. Blacks in Colfax drilled in formation and worked to stockpile ammunition, including homemade "blue whistlers" for bullets. With the assistance of the remaining Union veterans in the crowd—Mitchell, Gaines, Dancer, and a white man named James Terry (who departed before the fighting began), the men prepared three makeshift cannons using stovepipe and gunpowder and constructed shallow breastworks on two sides of the courthouse.

Ward and other allies of the Republican redoubt publicized the cause in New Orleans, making liberal use of bravado. "There is one thing apparent," observed an article published in the *New Orleans Republican* only 24 hours before the fighting began:

The local majority of Grant Parish is prepared to clean out the local minority of Grant in twenty-four hours or less if not prevented. In Grant Parish it seems there is a majority of colored men not only accustomed to the trade of war, but they keep arms of the most perfect character.

It was not only the Union veterans in the crowd who gave heart to the courthouse militants, however.

The colored population seemed to have reached a high height of exasperation and resolved to obtain a redress of the wrongs they had suffered, or believed they had suffered, and not to disband until they had obtained guarantees for the future. According to statements most worthy of belief, they are well armed, well disciplined, and confident of success.... The negroes, not even the field hands, are no longer the weak and simple creatures they were before the war. The years of freedom which they have enjoyed have had their effect on them, as well as the military education which many of them had received in the United States Army. The time is past, if ever it existed, when a handful of whites could frighten a regiment of colored men.[21]

Fortified by their faith in their rights as citizens, blacks in Colfax girded for the fight.

Whites made their own preparations, taking advantage of their control of the countryside surrounding Colfax to steal horses and mules from undefended black households. Creating army-style squadrons under the leadership of selected men, the whites assembled a version of a cavalry outfit. The white paramilitary patrolled constantly, assessing the strength of black defenses and scouting for the arrival of new recruits. During one such mission late in the week, Sam Shackleford, a former business partner of Calhoun, shot and killed Edward Dare, Calhoun's former slave, who was performing picket duty.[22] By Easter Sunday, according to their own estimate, the white line consisted of 140 men and teenage boys.

The arrival of a genuine artillery piece on Saturday night bolstered the preparedness of the white combatants. Captain C. C. Dunn of Natchitoches—who earlier had rented out the livery stable to provide mounts—coordinated the transfer of the 4-inch cannon from the deck of the steamship *John T. Moore,* a newly commissioned craft constructed in New Orleans by a wartime supplier for the United States

Navy. In subsequent court testimony, the captain of the *John T. Moore* would insist that the gun had been removed by force. In fact, Captain Billy Boardman's conservative politics were well-known on the Red River, where his was the only boat bold enough to fly the Confederate flag. Lashing the cannon to a wagon bed (from which the front wheels would later be removed for maneuverability), Dunn and his crew drove it 20 miles overland toward Colfax, somehow managing to cross Bayou Darrow, where white saboteurs had demolished the only bridge earlier in the week, and stashed it in the Calhoun sugar house. In the morning, a designated artillery crew would push the cannon to a hidden spot behind the dwelling house at Mirabeau, in readiness for battle.[23]

Despite the intensity of the buildup on both sides, Easter Sunday started slowly in Colfax. A handful of lost stalwarts departed the radical camp in the morning. A prominent African American from Rock Island came to town to implore the men to surrender the fight. No formal observance of the holiday could be discerned. A bustle of activity, in contrast, occupied the white force as it prepared to move in concert from its network of campsites around the town. Riding to a designated spot on Bayou Darrow, the white captains paused to review the plan of attack. Captain Dave Paul read the muster roll and made a final address to the men.

"I close my eyes [and] his face and form comes before my mind just as he was that morning," wrote a participant, 50 years afterward. "Boys," said Paul, "there are one hundred and sixty-five of us to go into Colfax this morning; God knows how many will come out of it alive."[24]

Upon the signal, the men swam their horses across the Bayou Darrow, crossing onto the Calhoun estate and initiating the hostile phase of their maneuvers. They rode in one company to the main road to Colfax and paused in battle formation where they could be seen from the courthouse and Smithfield Quarters. Christopher Columbus Nash—the former lieutenant—yielded military authority to Captains Paul, Stafford, and Wiggins but assumed formal responsibility for the fight as the Fusion ticket sheriff of the parish, acting as the head of a *posse comitatus* to redress the burglary of Rutland's home. As such, Nash rode forward, accompanied by two men, to issue a final order for the blacks to disperse.[25]

Bearing a white flag, Nash approached the Smithfield Quarters and asked for John Miles, a man later celebrated as a favorite of the white community. Miles would make the journey to the courthouse on Nash's behalf, walking out along the open road between the main positions of the armed rivals. Nash withdrew with his seconds to a point forward of the white line and observed as a black man exited the courthouse and mounted a dappled gray horse.

Benjamin L. Allen—known locally as Levy, Levin, or Lev—identified himself as the commander of the courthouse defense. Allen was one of two Buffalo Soldiers to remain in the radical camp after the departure of Flowers and Ward. Like the storekeeper, Peter Borland, who also chose to stay, Allen had long years of military experience, including the defense of stationary targets, such as garrisons and telegraph and railroad installations, against mounted Apaches on the Texas frontier. Though he never stood for office or played a visible role in Republican Party affairs, his commitment to preserving the possibility for black advancement in the parish was second to none. Allen had traveled the countryside during the buildup to the conflict, recruiting new men by appealing to the pride of their race. Even if he had no arms, he insisted, all black men should lend their hands to the defense. As for weapons, he said, "they could have his when he was killed."[26]

The interview between Allen and Nash was dignified and brief, despite the breach of protocol that placed the black military commander, not the sheriff, as the counterpart of the would-be white officeholder. In fact, Sheriff Dan Shaw, the last of the white men in the courthouse defense, had headed for Mirabeau Plantation just as Nash and the others rode into view. Lev Allen himself had given Sheriff Shaw the go-ahead. "Old man," said Allen, "go away and save yourself, if you can."[27]

White participants took grim delight in the fact that "not a single white Radical" remained with the ranks of black defenders. "Harvey, Payne, Shaw, Terry, and the other white wretches who had egged on the terrible combat between the two races took good care of their own bacon," they observed later in the *Colfax Chronicle*.[28] The foolish former master of the place watched helpless from his dwelling house, a prisoner, while even the black captains had left matters in the hands of a relative unknown.

"Lev, what do you negroes want there in Colfax?" asked Nash, "What do you depend on doing in there[?]"

"We are doing nothing more than we were before," Allen answered, "standing still, as we have been standing."

"We want that courthouse," said Nash.

"We sent an answer to Mr. Hadnot by Mr. Calhoun," said Allen. "Didn't you receive it?"

Nash explained that Hadnot did not "command this company," perhaps implying that the attacking party represented a more powerful coalition than the white supremacist organization "Old Man" Hadnot was thought to represent. Hadnot was not among the "captains" of the white squadrons, though he did distinguish his appearance in the ranks in a manner that may have evoked his status in the Klan or Knights of the White Camellia, carrying a sword and wearing a rosette medallion and red sash.

Allen observed the difference between the current standoff and the numerous recent occasions, "when they had killed several unoffending colored men at different times during their invasion." Now every black man in the town was carrying a weapon. He told Nash "that the defenders did not feel safe putting down their arms."

Having stated their cases, the two sides agreed to proceed with hostilities. Allen rode back to the courthouse redoubt, where he "received the approbation of the whole posse, the men all believing that the proposal of their assailants was a ruse to entrap them into disarming, that they might be incapable of resisting in case of a massacre."[29]

Nash had agreed to give Allen 30 minutes to remove the women and children from the line of fire. Most headed for Mirabeau Plantation on the open road. Stragglers, a group that included the elderly and mothers of small children, became reluctant to enter the line of fire as the deadline approached. Scaling the riverbank, six to eight feet to a narrow shore, a contingent waited out the battle from just below the action.[30]

A flanking maneuver brought one of the three white squadrons face to face with the noncombatants at the Red River shoreline, as a picked group of 30 men sought a new angle on the courthouse, some 75 yards from the riverbank. The encounter must have marked the interlude before the fighting with considerable tension down below, as the white men warned the gathering not to betray their location. No injuries or killings were reported, however, and the white squadron retained the element of surprise until the critical moment.

Up in the town, a kind of comic indolence set in as the warning period extended to about two hours. The improbability of the coming confrontation taxed the comprehension of men on both sides, the majority of whom knew one another by long acquaintance or at least reputation. In fact, the interlude of silence was repeatedly broken by shouted threats against specific individuals and their families, with most of the taunting emanating from the white side. Some of the white irregulars went into the Smithfield cabins, even helping themselves to hot lunches abandoned in haste. Another group played cards.[31]

Black defenders showed defiance and disbelief (except for Baptiste Elzie, one of three local brothers in the fight, who had fallen asleep in the trench). A sniper on the courthouse roof took potshots in the vicinity of the card game, causing the whites to reform their ranks around 2 P.M. As the white line moved forward, firing a few shots, one man jumped to the top of the courthouse earthworks in a dramatic show of begging and pleading, "bowing his head and throwing up his hands several times, adding some expression, the precise words not being understood," as a white eyewitness remembered it. By some gesture, the black supplicant made clear that he was mocking them. Then the firing began in earnest.

The white offensive proceeded in three parts. Wheeling the cannon into action, a crew of artillerymen led by a northern-born white Union veteran fired on the courthouse, using a supply of iron slugs cut from two-by-two-inch bars in lieu of cannonballs. To protect the artillery charge, a squadron of men dismounted, approaching on foot in infantry formation. A mounted component, essentially disengaged from the action, maintained the rear.

Cannon fire penetrated the line of defenders in the courthouse earthworks, claiming the first fatality of the fight. According to the account of Baptiste Elzie, who described it years afterward, a slug cut across the abdomen of Adam Kimball, who was standing. His bowels torn open, Kimball ran inside the courthouse, where his intestines fell out.[32]

A white participant would remark afterward on "the admirable manner in which the howitzer was handled by [Stephen] Parish and his mates." Parish was to be the first white casualty of the battle.

It has been said that he could have loaded his gun under cover at the Shackleford house, running it out when he wished to fire. This would have taken time and a few seconds sometimes in the critical period of a battle is like an eternity in its consequences.... I consider this brave and devoted man throwing aside all considerations but that of duty, [he] died at his post, and by his general conduct at the expense of his own life saved perhaps a score of our lives. Peace to his ashes! A religious man would ascribe it to the interposition of Providence in behalf of a sinful man engaged in a just cause![33]

While Parish was still firing, the unseen division of 30 under the riverbank opened fire from a cut in the soft earth. Scrambling up on horseback and making their way to the cover of trees, the men out-flanked the defenses, striking the radicals in their trenches and initiating their retreat. Meanwhile, the front division of the white force advanced into the main intersection of the town of Colfax:

> [W]e were within 50 feet of the breast works yelling shooting & charging around to beat the band. We kept straight on until we gained the shelter of 3 or 4 small houses just behind the intrenchments. There we all reloaded our old muzel loaders [sic] and cap & ball six shooters, and commenced a new battle [until] it got too hot for the Negroes, and they lit out for the court house some 100 yards distance.[34]

Some of the black defenders broke for the road, where they were shot. Others, such as Zach White, made their way to the river, where White swam a mile and a half to safety wearing clothes and carrying his shot pouch and powder horn. A white contingent led by Captain J.P.G. Hooe of Alexandria—who carried a sawed-off shotgun—awaited black militiamen who fled to the nearby black community of Cuny's Point. Those who ran for the woods—including Captain Lev Allen, who fled on horseback—fared best, capitalizing on the whites' uncertainty about black defenses that could not be seen. Allen freed his horse and found a hiding place with a view of the courthouse where he would remain until the fighting was done. Another handful of survivors spent the night up to their chins in a pond.[35]

The largest contingent—an estimated 65 men—retreated into the courthouse, where accommodations for a siege had been prepared. Only one of the 25th Infantry veterans, the storekeeper Peter Borland, remained with the defense, which also included the local Union soldiers Gaines, Mitchell, and Dancer. Shots from inside the courthouse felled the Yankee artilleryman, who survived, and fatally wounded a local man, Stephen Parish, also in the cannon crew. The black militia's jury-rigged artillery malfunctioned, but the brick walls and shuttered windows of the courthouse held firm against the last blasts of shrapnel. For the space of an hour, desultory gunshots (and the sound of shots fired in pursuit nearby) marked the standoff phase of the fight.

In their cleanup operations around town, the Fusionists and Klansmen had taken prisoner a handful of men in the warehouse and one hiding under a building nearby. From these, the captains chose a man named Pinkney Chambers and handed him a pole they had affixed to a saddle blanket doused in coal oil. "[Here's] a chance to save your life," they said; "we are going to light this and you must take it and put it on the roof." With "ten [double barrel] shotguns trained on him from his back, and I suppose 50 guns in front of him [in the courthouse]," as a white man remembered it, Chambers put the torch on the cypress shingles to start a lively fire.[36]

The men inside the courthouse observed as Pinkney Chambers set the roof on fire, but did not shoot him. Instead, they tried to knock the burning cypress shingles from the roof from the building's rough upper story. The cause was hopeless, and many of the men inside began to despair.

> I warned our people not to go into the courthouse [a black partici-
> pant told a reporter one month after the event]. I knowed it would be
> the end of 'em. But when the cannon went off we were all skeered,
> and huddled into the building like a herd of sheep. Then the burning
> roof began to fall on us, and every one was praying and shrieking and
> singing and calling on God to have mercy. The flesh of those further-
> est from the door began to roast. I could smell it. . . . The hair bunt off
> our heads, our clothes burn [ed] and our skin roast[ed].[37]

Among those fighting the fire on the second storey, a local man named Shack (or Jack or Jacques) White strayed too close to an open window. With the invaders deliberately shooting at the fire, providing cover as it grew, White took a bullet to the neck.

By this time, the white line had mostly dismounted and drawn close to the burning building. They were close enough for Shack White to recognize a friend among the men nearby. "Save me, Bill Irwin," he called from the window. Irwin replied that he owed him one, perhaps assuring him of the services of the surgeon and doctor in the company of whites. White tore the sleeve from his white shirt (some accounts say a large sheet of paper), put it out the window, and shouted, "We surrender!" Too late to save his life, he brought the courthouse siege to an unexpected halt.

Was he heard downstairs above the crackling of the fire on the roof? Could they know below about the improvised flag of truce? What they saw, within the incalculable space of time between two incidents, was the approach of armed white men to the door. The first, Sidney Harris, carrying a gun, opened the door. At his rear walked a man dressed in a sword and wearing the red rosette of his secret order, James West Hadnot.

Fast as thought, Harris was dead and Hadnot lay mortally wounded in the gut.

The black defenders of the courthouse had selected their targets with care. In more than two hours of fighting, they had scored only four major hits against their enemies: two on the artillery team and two against the men executing the abortive capture of the building. All represented strategic targets, designed to take out the threat of the cannon, in particular, and as such did credit to the marksmanship of those inside. Although whites made much of the defenders' superior, government-issue armament, the black riflemen fired infrequently. They lacked the taste for killing and its consequences, perhaps, and certainly made do with smaller lots and lesser quality of ammunition.

The shooting of Hadnot may be equally well attributed to confusion, to the spirit of last-ditch resistance, or to canny opportunism—the chance to eliminate a symbolic and powerful rival. If it was indeed a bloodthirsty act, it was the only one that the defenders had allowed themselves in the long bloody season of Easter 1873.

The horror that gripped the body of whites at the courthouse—a group that included "Old Man" Hadnot's three young adult sons—turned the momentum of the fighting as if on a switch. By this time, a handful of black men had emerged from the courthouse and begun to stack their arms. They were overwhelmed by a blast of gunfire from the white side. With men pressing out of the burning building amid continuing fire, bodies fell in a stack by the door, including several who were slightly injured or not hurt. Using pistols and Bowie knives, the whites killed several in close combat. The door slammed. Those afraid to surrender hid under the floorboards. The cinders crackled overhead, as white men sorted out the living from the dead at the doorway and just beyond.

"Get up, old man, you're not dead," said a man. Benjamin Brimm was 56 years old, the father of four girls, a former slave. He was directed to the base of a pecan tree some distance from the courthouse and made to wait with other prisoners. Fifteen minutes later, he was told to go inside the burning courthouse to retrieve the last of the holdouts before it collapsed.

"They was under the floor in the little back room," he later testified. "[Y]'all had better come," he called. They agreed, all but one. "I might just as well to be burned up as to be shot," said the man, who burned to death some time in the next hour. The others, including Alabama Mitchell, emerged safely and were taken prisoner. A few dozen—28 or 48, in typical accounts—waited under the pecan tree to learn the final resolution of the fight.[38]

After sunset it began to rain. The wounded blacks were moved to the porch of the nearby boardinghouse, while the remainder of the prisoners made do under the shelter of the tree. Black women, emboldened by the lack of gunfire, left their hiding places and moved within sight of the battlefield, staying well away from both the prisoners and the dead.

The armed force of whites was breaking up, with hungry men eager to make camp and others preparing for a long journey home. A young man of Montgomery would later recall his delight in camp on being provided with raw pork and cornbread by David Paul. After the physical vigor and wrenching emotions of the long day, and after nearly 24 hours without food, he said, "It was the best meal I ever ate." Others drank whiskey, some of it looted from the black cabins and the nearby store of Peter Boland, also one of the prisoners. The semblance of military discipline abated, as the remaining white chiefs discussed the fate of the last living black men in the town.

Nash wanted to set them free. "[N]ow boys," he asked Benjamin Brimm and the others, "if I take you all and send you home to your cotton, will you go to work?"

"I answered quick," remembered Brimm, "[as] I knowed Mr. Nash and he knowed me." Brimm promised he would.

A white man objected: "[B]y God, Nash…if you send these God Dam Negroes home you won't live to see two weeks." Having killed 50 or more in the courthouse fight and cleanup operations, many in the crowd may have feared reprisals, legal and personal, after the prisoners returned home. Others had personal scores to settle. The brother of Jeff Yawn—killed in 1871 by Ward's militiamen—wanted to kill a prisoner who may have played a role. Others sought vengeance for much less momentous grievances. "In 1870 you knocked me off a bale of cotton," said Clement Penn to Etienne Elzie, suggesting that the black man had made a fatal mistake. Liquor whetted the appetite for violence in the group. One man said that he had ridden 60 miles to kill niggers, and was not yet prepared to stop. Overriding Nash's objections, the remainder of the white force decided to execute the prisoners. "Unless these niggers are killed," a Grant Parish man, Thomas Hickman, told Nash, "we will kill you."[39]

"It was [George Scarborough] who gave the order to shoot us after dark," remembered a survivor. "He said, 'Kill the d—d niggers.'"[40]

Preparations for the execution were elaborate. It began on the gallery of George Scarborough's boardinghouse. Somewhat removed from the main conference of the white men, the wounded had been the first to attempt an escape. At least one man, Baptiste Elzie, succeeded in slipping away without being pursued—a significant feat in light of the fact that Elzie had been shot in seven places, and could hardly walk at the time of his escape. Alabama Mitchell was not so fortunate. Guarded by the young doctor, Milton Dunn, Mitchell was observed during his flight and took a bullet in his right leg. The wound was so severe that the muscles atrophied above and below the knee, leaving him partially disabled for life. The firing at the boardinghouse unnerved the main body of prisoners, still gathered beneath the pecan tree in the center of town.

"Don't worry, they are only shooting the wounded," they were told.[41]

The white men told the remaining prisoners to line up and prepare to be marched to the sugarhouse, where they would spend the night and be set free in the morning. Luke Hadnot, whose dying father had recently departed on a boat to Alexandria, called out the names of five men. The five stepped forward; Hadnot lined them up in close ranks, and killed all five with two gunshots. Others likewise identified their victims of choice. Clement Penn, for example, selected and killed Etienne Elzie while Elzie's wife, Annie, stood by only a few feet away. "I was looking directly at Penn when he shot my husband," Annie Elzie later testified. "I heard him beg for his life."[42]

Other whites betrayed more ambivalence toward the executions. "[G]o ahead, I am not going to shoot you," said the man assigned to escort Benjamin Brimm and a man named Baptiste White. "Come here old man I don't think I am going to shoot you. I am going to carry you to the sugar house." Moments later, the man shot Brimm and White, hitting Brimm in the back of the head. Neither of the black men died from their wounds. Meekin Jones had better luck:

> I asked a man if they were killing us; he answered that they were kill-
> ing the wounded; I was marched out with Levi Nelson; they called
> us beeves; one man said he was weary of guarding, and another said,
> "Shoot 'em down;" when a man pointed his gun at my head I raised
> my hands and told him that if he shot me he would kill an innocent
> man; then I broke and ran; I was shot at, but got over a fence and
> would not halt when called on; Judd Burrows got one of the bullets
> meant for me.[43]

Despite the large number of escapes and nonfatal injuries, however, the whites succeeded in executing most of the prisoners. An apparently successful strategy for overcoming moral scruples was to effectively dehumanize the black prisoners, whom their captors described repeatedly as "beeves," or cattle. "Have you got your beeves fixed?" asked a man, holding two prisoners in his gunsights. "[T]he white men said they had a good mess of beeves and would make a good time of it," one survivor remembered. Hearing the shrieks of the women nearby, one man found a source of amusement. "Listen at the cows bellowing over the dead bulls!" he laughed.[44]

One of the more hardened killers noticed that some of the wounded prisoners on the field remained alive. "[W]hat am I going to do with these damn niggers," he complained, "I cannot [kill] them all." Amid the general cleanup, Benjamin Brimm nearly lost his life. "The blood was in my nose and I could not fetch breath," he later testified. "I had to blow it out or I would be strangled to death." The gurgling sound brought two riders to his side. "[T]hey cocked the pistol and shot right down on me again," remembered Brimm. "God dam you," said one, "that will do you."[45]

About a mile upriver from the town of Colfax, the steamboat *Southwestern* answered the hail of "a young man armed to the teeth and very much excited," who asked that the boat land at Colfax to evacuate wounded white men to Alexandria. Asking "if we wanted to see dead niggers," the young man told the crew that "here was a chance, for there were a hundred or so scattered over the village and the adjacent fields," as the captain reported in the first eyewitness account to appear in the newspapers.

"On arriving at Colfax we found about a hundred armed men on the bank, and most of the passengers, myself among the number, went ashore to view the battle ground":

> Almost as soon as we got to the top of the landing, sure enough, we began to stumble on [bodies], most of them lying on their faces, and, as I could see in the dim light of the lanterns, riddled with bullets.
>
> One poor wretch, a stalwart looking fellow, had been in the burning courthouse, and as he ran out, with his clothes on fire, he had been shot. His clothes to the waist were all burnt off, and he was literally broiled.
>
> We came upon bodies every few steps, but the sight of this fellow, who was burned, added to the horrible smell of burning human flesh—the remains of those who were shot in the courthouse, which was still on fire—sickened most of us and caused a general cry of "Let's go back."

The captain continued in the company of the white militants.

> We came across one negro whose clothes were smoking, and who had probably been in the fire. Some of our party remarked that he was alive. Instantly one of our guides whipped out a six shooter, saying, "I'll finish the black dog." Of course we remonstrated, and he put away his weapon. Some one stooped down and turned the negro over. He was stiff and cold.
>
> A few minutes afterward we came on a big black fellow, who was reclining on his elbow, and, to all appearances, alive. The man with the six shooter hit him a fierce kick with his boot, and then stooped down and examined him, saying: "Oh, he's dead as h—l."
>
> When we came back near the landing, the boat's crew were carrying aboard the two wounded white men, a Mr. Hadnot and another, whose name I did not learn.[46]

The display of bloodlust would later be attributed to the white horror at Hadnot's death. "In regard to the ferocity displayed by some men, so commented on by the Northern press," explained George Stafford some weeks after the event: "I would say it happened after seeing the treacherous assassination of friends and near relations and before condemning [I would hope that critics would] say, 'put yourself in his place.'" He continued, however with a reference to the greater stakes.

> If you want a farther reason it means a "war of races." To the most observant mind it must be apparent that in a war of races under such circumstances, there can be *no quarter,* Vide Modoc war.

"Exceptions to this rule may be made by our race before being maddened by loss of friends or kinsmen," he continued, however, setting aside his comparison of Colfax to the contemporaneous massacre of Captain Jack and Modoc Indians by U.S. troops. "[A]fter that the black flag must prevail."[47]

During the night, the rain continued and the field of battle became quiet. Baptiste White and Baptiste Mills, injured only slightly, picked themselves up and stole away. Only Brimm continued to stir. Shot once in the head and once clear through the abdomen from side to side, the old man could not walk or stand. He was convinced, however, that his enemies would finish him off if they found him alive in the morning. Crawling twenty feet at a time, resting and perhaps losing consciousness along the way, Brimm made his way 300 yards to a cotton field before dawn. Sorely injured, playing dead, he remained virtually motionless on Monday, when the white veterans of the Colfax massacre returned to survey their bloody work.[48]

Chaos reigned in Colfax on Monday, when the excesses of the previous hours saw light of day. Scores of white men, including many who had not participated in the fight, came to town to witness the outcome of the struggle. The distribution of the bodies told much of the story. In the shallow breastworks around the courthouse, the bodies of the earliest victims could be seen. A significant number of corpses fanned out from the courthouse door, with piles on either side of the door in mute witness to the gunfire that greeted those trying to escape the fire. The ruins of the courthouse contained the smoldering remains of the man who feared to exit, and a few others were found killed beneath the warehouse and other buildings in the town.

Something special—still secret—could be found in the vicinity of the old pecan tree, which later became the object of special pride among area whites. According to some accounts, thirteen prisoners were hanged from its branches, and may have remained visible to visitors on April 14. By the time authorities arrived on Tuesday, however, the only bodies near the tree were the victims of gun violence. Most revealed gunshots to the head. One man's skull had been crushed. He had died with his hands still clasped in the act of begging for his life.[49]

Whites in Colfax Monday attempted to count the number of dead, a task complicated by the pursuit of some black participants by men on horseback. At least three of the identifiable victims on April 13 had been killed outside the town, one more than ten miles downriver in Cotile, Louisiana. The removal and burial of some of the bodies on Monday further disrupted the count.[50] Among those who attended to the numbers, the final tally varied on a wide range, with the most conservative reckoning the number of victims at 71. Whites may have indulged in exaggeration, but the most morbidly diligent white veteran historian of the massacre accepted the high number presented in Oscar Watson's reminiscences, "An Incident of My Boyhood Days":

> Next morning myself & 8 or 10 others went back to look and count the dead[. A]fter making the rounds of the town 165 dead was reported within the entrenchment [and] no one will ever know how many met their fate further out[,] as some 25 or 30 men scoured the Country for 4 or 5 miles [and] no report ever reached us of how many they killed in this raid.

The black men had brought it on themselves, he reasoned.

> [I]t was a sorry blunder the negroes made in [firing] on our men after surrender, for only their leaders would have been dealt with[. B]ut after their treachery the order went let none escape. The order was carried out.

Whether 70 or 165 or many more, the accepted number of victims was larger than any other incident of racial violence in American history (the only comparable number of casualties, the victims of the New York City Draft Riot of 1863, included large numbers of unfortunate whites). In surveying the damage, white men in Colfax were taking the measure of their terrible success.[51]

White men also took liberties with the bodies of dead men and the possessions of those displaced by the violence. They mutilated the bodies, most often by shooting the corpses. In one awful case, mischief-makers used gunpowder or some other means to blow up the corpse of a local man known as Big Frank. One widow reported finding her husband's corpse with the pockets ripped open and wallet missing.[52] Blacks in the area later complained about the theft of horses, mules, wagons, furniture, and money. "[Y]ea, even the clothes and shoes of the murdered men were taken and carried off," according to victims, "and this practice was being pursued for days after the massacre." W. R. Rutland, still aggrieved by his own loss of property in the burglary of his Colfax home, was seen riding a stolen horse around town.[53]

Whites in Colfax sought to publicize their victory on Monday while most of the bodies remained unburied, encouraging blacks they encountered to go view the dead. "Go to town, if you want to see a mess of dead beeves," said a man to a woman whose husband was killed in the fight. Others used bad language, forced strangers to bury bodies or cook food, and taunted the widows with references to sexual favors.[54]

Dorcas Pittman, the mother of one of the victims, arrived in Colfax on Monday to learn the fate of her son Lank, who had perished in the fight.

> When I went to Colfax the day after the fight I found my dead son's body; dogs were eating him; I took the remains home and buried them; I felt so bad that I didn't know what I did.[55]

Whites permitted the removal of Lank Pittman's body because of the extreme circumstances, and may have allowed other burials as well. On the whole, however, they were satisfied to leave the bodies where they fell.

Their pride in display revealed the symbolic significance of the white raid on the town. Conceived as a lesson to those who advanced the black cause in politics, the rout of the courthouse defense served notice of white determination. The white men of Louisiana would unite to defeat their enemies within, killing and dying for white supremacy and home rule.

EIGHT

Voyage of the *Ozark*

ℋELP HAD BEEN ON THE WAY. CONVINCED BY WEEKS of threats and counter-threats in his uptown office at the St. Charles Hotel, Governor William Pitt Kellogg had dispatched a militia force of two from New Orleans on Saturday night. Two colonels from the state militia, Theodore W. DeKlyne and William Whight, carried written instructions from Kellogg intended to resolve the standoff. They arrived at the scene of the fighting on Tuesday, April 15, 1873, to find the unburied bodies of 71 men. Too little and too late, the militia expedition served its most important purpose in bearing witness.

Colonel DeKlyne, the head of the mission, was another Radical Republican carpetbagger, Philadelphia-born and employed as a clerk in the U.S. Customhouse. Even though he and Whight had boarded their steamer in civilian clothes, DeKlyne could not conceal his identity as an interloper. News of his voyage up the Red River traveled faster than his boat. By Tuesday morning, a white delegation awaited his arrival at Cotile Landing, ten miles below Colfax, and escorted him peaceably to the scene of the battle.

DeKlyne's report on the number, distribution, and condition of the bodies became the key document in the campaign to bring the perpetrators of the massacre to justice. However, his accounting also served the interests of the whites themselves, who wished to publicize the terrible details for maximum political effect. With a candor that would never be repeated in subsequent incidents of racial violence in the United States, the organizers of the Colfax raid endorsed DeKlyne's official body count, conceding that additional victims had been buried or killed outside the confines of the little town.

The two militia colonels examined each of the bodies, recording the nature and distribution of the injuries. Though the victims had been exposed to the elements for two days, cool weather had delayed the progress of decay.

> Under the warehouse, between the courthouse and the river [DeKlyne reported], were the dead bodies of six colored men who had evidently crept under for concealment, and were there shot like dogs. Many were shot in the back of the head and neck; one man still lay with his hands clasped in supplication; the face of another was completely flattened by blows from a gun, the broken stock of a double-barreled shot-gun being on the ground near him; another had been cut across the stomach with a knife after being shot; and almost all of them had from three to a dozen wounds. Many of them had their brains literally blown out.

Black families, emboldened by arrival of the militia delegation, came forward to claim some of the remains and helped bury the remaining corpses within the trench around the courthouse.

Among the bodies, DeKlyne identified one that he recognized, Alex Tillman—"a dark black man though scarcely black," as he described him, perhaps in recognition of Tillman's refined deportment—whom he had met in New Orleans when Tillman was a delegate to the constitutional convention of 1867. Tillman lay outside the courthouse with his throat cut open, a range of scattered gunshots in his corpse.[1]

Though DeKlyne and Whight departed posthaste for New Orleans, the news of the Colfax Massacre preceded them. On the basis of reports from the civilian passengers and crew of the *Southwestern,* Governor Kellogg had declared Grant and the surrounding parishes to be in a state of insurrection. That Tuesday, Kellogg wrote to the commander of U.S. forces in Louisiana, General William H. Emory, requesting that a company of U.S. troops proceed to Colfax.[2] DeKlyne delivered his report on the killings on April 17. U.S. Marshal Samuel B. Packard, a major player in the Customhouse political faction, then named DeKlyne as his chief deputy for the investigation of events at Colfax, and ordered him to return to make arrests as soon as military escorts were provided. The U.S. attorney in New Orleans, New York–born James R. Beckwith, relayed DeKlyne's report and two urgent telegrams to the office of the Attorney General in Washington, D.C.[3]

U.S. Army officers in New Orleans did not require the Grant administration's prior authorization to act. President Grant himself had issued explicit orders in March 1873 instructing Emory to act to prevent attacks on the besieged state government. General Emory informed the General of the Army, William Tecumseh Sherman, of his plan to provide troops to act as *posse comitatus* to the U.S. marshal in his effort to arrest the perpetrators of the Colfax raid. Sherman telegraphed Washington's backing for the Grant Parish expedition, but delayed approving Governor Kellogg's request for additional troops in other troubled parishes. Like Kellogg, who chose not to send armed contingents of his own militia, Grant and the Department of War hesitated to intervene aggressively where white passions were already inflamed.[4]

General Emory acted fast, mobilizing a company of the 19th U.S. Infantry for Colfax on the evening of April 17. New Orleans agents of white supremacy, however, had already been at work to thwart his purposes. On the steamboat landing near the foot of Canal Street, captains had been advised to steer clear of the trouble at Colfax. The commanding officer of Emory's force discovered no one who was willing to transport the troops, "for the reason, as they aver, that it will ruin their trade." In addition to the stigma of abetting the invasion of the heartland of the state, the river captains feared violent reprisals on themselves and their crafts. Two days passed before the *B. L. Hodge* agreed to carry the men of the 19th Infantry to Grant Parish, and then only at an exorbitant price. On April 19, a force of 98, accompanied by Colonel DeKlyne, departed from New Orleans for the battle site.[5]

The soldiers arrived upon a scene of desolation. The fresh earth of the black men's fortifications—now serving as a mass grave—flanked the ruins of the burned-out courthouse. The houses and warehouses in the town were pocked by gunfire and the heavy shrapnel of the cannon blasts. Homes remained deserted, and for miles around weeds grew in fields abandoned during planting time. Large numbers of livestock had been slaughtered or driven away. Like a reprisal of the Civil War, replicating even the season of the year of the Red River offensive, the battle of the Colfax courthouse had introduced an era of privation for the residents of both races. "Imagine the worst conditions of anarchy and lawlessness," wrote a correspondent of the *New York Times* who visited the troops at Colfax about a week after their arrival, "and you will not come close to the truth of the situation in Grant Parish."[6]

A profound sense of insecurity compounded the hardship of the 19th's Colfax detail. Occupying the site where a force half again as large as their own had succumbed within a fortified building, they must have entertained the idea that the rebels would invade again. Indeed, after May 14, when a force of 600 McEnery whites occupied the parish seat in St. Martin Parish, soldiers reasonably may have feared that their post had fallen behind enemy lines. Their isolation in hostile territory was underscored by continuing problems with transportation. After pursuing a lead into faraway Franklin Parish, for example, Colonel DeKlyne found himself stranded when a boat hired by Marshal Packard failed to make an appointment.[7] When the company of soldiers relocated to the Louisiana State Seminary grounds in Pineville, they made their move under the cover of darkness. Removed from the scene of the Grant Parish horrors, they remained poised to absorb the unrepentant fury of the white community.

Indeed, the death of Hadnot had inflamed public opinion even among whites unsullied by participation in the massacre. Young E. R. Bossiat, editor of the leading conservative paper, Alexandria's *Louisiana Democrat,* spoke for the white establishment when he condemned the usurpation that resulted in the Klan leader's death.

"That J. W. Hadnot was one of the very best, honorable and purest of men, and a citizen favorably known and highly esteemed by the communities of Rapides and Grant, needs no recording in the Democrat," he wrote in an issue published on the first Wednesday after the killing. "[H]is death at this time, and under its peculiar circumstances, can but throw a pall of grief and regret over our whole people."

> Persecuted and hunted down, for the past three years by the barbarians who have murdered him at last, he...sleeps his last sleep amid the regrets and sorrows of a family and a people.

"The whites of Grant were driven in pure self defence to act the part they did," wrote Bossiat, "and in the eyes of God and man were justifiable in all and every particular. Let the awful and terrible responsibility fall on the guilty alone."[8]

Angry mourning gave way to threats after the appointment of a grand jury in the Colfax case late in April. Assisted by the state militia and U.S.

marshals, a courageous Republican district attorney in Natchitoches, Ernest J. Breda, had agreed to pursue indictments against white participants. Veterans of the killing publicly swore to disrupt proceedings, and established a campaign of intimidation. On the streets of Alexandria on April 22, J.G.P. Hooe and George R. Marsh, two of the first to be indicted, accosted a black man on the street, "drawing a dirk and a revolver," as the Republican newspaper reported, "accus[ing] him of testifying against them, and then knocked him down and beat him brutally." Lurid visions of what might actually happen appeared in a Democratic newspaper article about the fate of Grant Parish sheriff Dan Shaw, still living, but erroneously reported to have "broken his neck" while being transported during the riot. And the editor of the only Republican newspaper in the region, the *Rapides Gazette,* received daily and increasingly unsubtle suggestions to adopt the conservative line or else cease publication.

With homicides occurring "at intervals" after Easter Sunday, the newspaper editor and others in the white men's sights operated at significant risk. Blacks in particular were advised (in the conservative *Alexandria Democrat*) that they had "everything to lose." George Marsh, a river pilot rapidly acquiring a reputation as one of the most dangerous men in the area, stabbed to death a black father of three near his home in Pineville.[9]

Despite the risks, the grand jury proceedings soldiered on, relocating to Colfax early in May, where the pockmarked warehouse was refitted as a courtroom. The master of the ruined Calhoun estate was not available for playing host to the Radical prosecutor, Ernest Breda, having defected to New Orleans sometime after the arrival of the troops. Breda made the journey by horseback from his family's Cane River plantation house, a daily traverse over hostile ground that must have been only slightly less harrowing than the prospect of residing in the haunted boardinghouse. (Its owner, George Scarborough, was said to have initiated the execution of the black prisoners by shooting the wounded on the gallery of the building.) Jurors of undisclosed identity and undaunted courage came and served, surrendering their persons and their thoughts to the city of the dead.

Encouraged by the display of law enforcement, black families gradually abandoned their campsites on Mirabeau and in the nearby swamps. U.S. soldiers buried the remains of Jesse McKinney, opening for resettlement the row of black households on the Bayou Darrow where McKinney was murdered on April 6. The house where his body had been left to decompose was not reoccupied, as its occupant was killed on Easter Sunday. Adjusting to their losses—and caring for the large number of wounded men—black families haltingly resumed their work. They would not know the feel of normal life in the community for many months.

White participants confronted difficulties, too. Elites in Grant Parish pondered the prospects for commercial planting, now weeks beyond the seeding season for both cane and cotton. For white supremacist and Radical Republican landowners alike, the costs of terrorizing the labor force would continue all year; the New York Times reported that the projected losses due to death alone would cost 900 bales of the cotton crop.[10] Family farms, which fell behind schedule during the buildup to the fighting, had to make do afterward without the labor of men and boys who participated. With talk of conspiracy and treason coming out of the governor's office and grand jury proceedings, the Colfax dragnet threatened to catch up dozens, even hundreds, who had provided hospitality and rallied in support of the cause. An exodus of white men—continuing the pattern of the Colfax ride-out—disrupted ordinary life in white communities within a 100-mile radius.

Many of the men had anticipated a prolonged absence from home. For the young, in particular, the prospect of a season on the road contained as much appeal as the opportunity to fight for white supremacy. Texas was the premier destination for this kind, in keeping with a long tradition of ties between the neighboring valleys of the Red River. A group of young men from poor households in Grant, Natchitoches, and Claiborne parishes—brought together by the fight—secured saddle horses and a wagon for a journey of 450 miles. According to a participant, Oscar Watson, the Louisiana outlaws had a fine time in the Wild West, some even earning wages by working a cattle drive from Independence to Lampasas, Texas. Others took the opportunity to relocate permanently. The cracker carpetbagger Sidney Schumann, for example, who had been wounded commanding the artillery crew for the white force, departed for his native New York as soon as possible with his family in tow.[11]

Most stayed close to home. In a typical pattern, residents of Cheneyville in Rapides Parish (home to George Stafford and his conservative allies) established a camp in the wilderness near Bayou Boeuf.

Here the men resided part time, staying overnight and for nights on end when investigators drew near, and otherwise making furtive visits and sojourns in town. Women in Cheneyville devised a system of signals using white or red tablecloths displayed on a clothesline. Simply staying away from one's own home provided a measure of security. The most wanted man in Grant Parish, Christopher Columbus Nash, pitched his tent within the town limits of Colfax in a field belonging to James R. Williams. Others lived at home but slept in friends' houses and even public buildings. During a particularly hot time in Winn Parish, for example, a suspect changed his sleeping place from the Masonic Lodge to the Sardis church outside the hamlet of Atlanta.

Notes delivered on horseback or in caches of food and supplies apprised the roustabouts of enemy movements. "Darling," wrote Mrs. C. C. Dunn to her husband, in an undated letter delivered to some wild part of Natchitoches, "don't come home Saturday night—you will not be safe."[12]

Romance was in the air around the white towns and campsites, where "many love affairs blossomed that would otherwise have never come to bud," as a female participant recalled.[13] Sexually titillated by their own exploits, white fathers and brothers were vigilant in protecting their women from the sexual advances of black men. The prolonged absence from home exacerbated white concerns about the black threat to their households. A motivating factor for the onset of violence, sexual paranoia remained a simmering political concern.

Federal and state forces seemed possessed of the momentum in the conflict that spring. The story of the Colfax Massacre gripped the liberal imagination nationwide. *Harper's Weekly* and *Frank Leslie's Illustrated Weekly* featured profiles of the event, including original engravings that depicted black militiamen on the courthouse barricades, black families hauling off the dead and wounded, and a campsite of African American refugees hiding in the swamp.[14] The high echelons of the army, the Department of Justice, and Louisiana's carpetbagger elite had sworn to bring the perpetrators to justice, and had committed the muscle of the 19th Infantry and other resources to the campaign.

Many seemed to have responded to the massacre by redoubling their efforts to defend black prerogatives. A schoolteacher in a colored school in Union Parish north of Colfax, for example, had been whipped and ordered to leave the area. Instead, he bought a gun and kept it by his side in the classroom.[15]

On May 22, in light of turbulence in St. Martin Parish as well as the several parishes surrounding Colfax, President Grant declared parts of Louisiana to be in a state of insurrection. The declaration put into effect the martial law provisions of the 1870 and 1871 Enforcement Acts, in particular the clause suspending habeas corpus. Thus the suspects in the Colfax Massacre were stripped of the basic common-law right requiring authorities to "present the body" before a judge, to certify the legality of the detention and to initiate legal proceedings.[16] In other words, the accused stood at hazard of vanishing—unnamed and unrepresented by counsel—into the gulag of the government's choice.

Notwithstanding this privilege, the names of 50 suspected participants appeared shortly after Grant's speech in the indictment of the Grand Jury of the United States Court.[17]

The indictment on U.S. charges imposed a kind of double jeopardy on suspects in the Colfax case. Both the district attorney in Colfax, Ernest Breda, and the prosecutor in the federal court of Judge Edward H. Durrell, U.S. Attorney James R. Beckwith, relied on the investigation formally commanded by the U.S. Marshal, Samuel Packard, and conducted on the ground by Inspector DeKlyne and the 19th Infantry. Similar names appeared on the suspect lists in each case. With the grand jury proceedings in the Colfax case continuing amid great potential for violent disruption, the U.S. penalties provided a kind of insurance against the possibility of an abortion of justice at the state court level. On June 16, the federal grand jury extended its indictment to include 97 names. The investigation promised to yield dozens more. In New Orleans, Beckwith and the judge prepared one of the largest federal criminal cases in American history under the heading *United States v. Columbus Nash et al.* The powers of the state bore down on the Colfax environment with an intensity unsurpassed even in the era of the war.

Only 10 had been arrested. To say the least, the dragnet under Colonel DeKlyne's authority was proving ineffective against the organized resistance of the whites. The 10—whose names were not made public and may have later been released—remained in state custody, subject to the jurisdiction of the parish court in Colfax, though authorities arranged to detain them in New Orleans in light of the extreme difficulty of incarcerating them securely anywhere near the scene of the crime. None of the 10, apparently, proved willing to "puke," in the parlance used by 7th Cavalry investigators prosecuting Ku Klux Klan violence in South Carolina two years earlier: confessions and information leading to the apprehension of additional suspects were not forthcoming.[18] The slow pace of arrests and the withdrawal of federal troops to Pineville exacerbated the political ambiguity in and around Grant Parish—leading District Attorney Breda to complain that the uncertainty was costing lives. "These men are desperate," he wrote in early August, "and say that if they are going to be prosecuted for killing negroes on April 13, they might as well kill a few more negroes and radicals."[19]

Breda put his own life on the line every time that he appeared in the warehouse courtroom in Colfax. An armed mob of 60 or 70 disrupted the hearings of the parish court late in July and attempted to assassinate the African American judge, R. C. Register, whose disputed claim to office partially initiated the conflict in the town. The white riders referred specifically to the Colfax indictments, threatening to destroy the court if additional arrests were made. "What is to be done by those who have only a Kellogg commission for authority and no U.S. troops to protect them?" Breda asked, in a letter to Grant's attorney general, in which he speculated on the probability of his own death.[20]

The portentous, romantic, and mournful summer of 1873 held participants in limbo. Still, the Grant administration hesitated to present the grand jury indictments in the federal court. Attorney General George H. Williams was appalled by the large number of indictments and equally put off by Beckwith's estimate that a force of 150 troops would be required to make arrests. Confronting massive resistance in Central Louisiana, where households, communities, and church congregations successfully shielded the suspects, officials in Washington somberly pondered retreat.

At the heart of the matter within the federal government, the full-scale manhunt to deliver the 97 named conspirators divided the opinion of influential actors. Attorney General Williams spoke for those who shrank from the raw exercise of government power when he endorsed the prosecution of a limited number—6 to 12—of ringleaders of the violence. J. R. Beckwith, his subordinate, evoked the moral and practical urgency of holding the line against murderers and insurrectionists with grand ambitions. Both men considered the political consequences of the case. Beckwith's request for U.S. troops to aid in arrests of the Colfax offenders struck a sensitive point for the administration, which was fielding regular demands from Kellogg and other southern state governments to tranquilize active zones of insurrectionary violence. With the northern press fully exercised about extravagance and corruption in government programs, the assumption of additional responsibilities in Louisiana would certainly attract unfavorable attention. Beckwith, Breda, and others with their lives in the balance correctly viewed the political risks in reverse terms. They would raise the stakes or expect to abandon the game to the other side.[21]

What happened next is best described by a white woman who observed firsthand.

> Toward the latter part of summer a new song began to be heard—at first here and there—soon from every side. The words sounded senseless, but the air was throbbing, persistent, filled with jungle menace. It was sung everywhere, and each singer did his utmost to make it scary. The air was a throbbing, lilting melody that was enthralling, beautiful, and hideous, full of malice and hatred.

The witness, a teenage girl from Cheneyville named Dosia Williams, would never forget the song. Writing about it as an adult in the 1920s, she insisted, "I can still hear the wild exultant shouts" of "this throbbing, jouncing, rippling" song, which she described (not unfavorably) as "jungle music, pure and simple." Of course, the singers were black. The chorus on its own sounded nonsensical:

> De Ozark's a-comin,' move erlong chillum!
> De Ozark's a-comin,' move erlong chillum!
> De Ozark's a-comin,' move erlong chillum!
> De Ozark's a-comin,' move a-along!

In time, whites in the area would become familiar with the song's threatening lyrics, though only Dosia, later known as Dosia Williams Moore, would ever write about it. The song foretold the arrival of a gunship, the *Ozark,* its hold full of troops. Details that Moore did not record described the fearsome justice that would fall upon the guilty when the *Ozark* steamed their way.[22]

Blacks in Grant Parish, apparently, had inside information about the response of federal and state law enforcement to the Colfax killings. By September, the Justice Department had resolved on a course of action.

Beckwith acted on instructions to indict only the most important per-petrators, while Marshall Packard was empowered to cast his net broadly in a large-scale manhunt operation. Federal troops would serve as *posse comitatus,* working in conjunction with the U.S. marshal and officers of the state militia. Another six weeks would pass while the government and Kellogg resolved the terms of their cooperation, including the all-important matter of the distribution of the cost. With a push from an interested private citizen, who provided a hefty subsidy for the mission, the federal dragnet finally got under way in October 1873.[23]

The "generous friend of the state" who committed his own resources to the effort bought a boat.[24] Transportation had proved the weakest link in the chain of law enforcement in the Red River parishes, where steamboat captains and their crews were of a piece with the white com-munities making trouble. For years before the conflict at Colfax, the double-deckers that served as the vital link to commerce and civilization had also presented a range of hazards to men at odds with the conser-vative politics of the river valleys, who sometimes found themselves, as the displaced parish Radical William Phillips poignantly observed, at risk of falling under the paddlewheels. William Calhoun's kid-napping from the hold of *La Belle;* the army's difficulty in hiring the *B. L. Hodge;* Colonel DeKlyne's missed connection in Franklin Parish: all pointed to the need for dedicated, exclusive, and secure means of transport. The purchase of a boat resolved the problem of mobility and also offered a place to incarcerate and interrogate government detain-ees. Thus equipped, they could hope to bring law and order to the heart of the struggle.

Not just any boat would do. The waters of the Red River were notoriously fickle, a fact that the United States Navy had discovered the hard way during the abortive offensive of 1864. Falling waters, particu-larly in the spring, regularly brought a halt to the movement of ordinary craft, as the shifting loam of the riverbank unpredictably grounded their hulls. In 1864, the river had receded during the federal retreat, leaving the Union flotilla of 50 ships stranded at Alexandria. Only the timely invention of removeable "wing dams" permitted the accumulation of sufficient depth for the ships to escape. The *Ozark,* a river monitor, was the last gunship to pass over the falls created by the Union jetties, and took its place in the lineup on the basis of its state-of-the-art draft design. The naval commander of the Red River campaign, Admiral David

D. Porter, boasted that the class of ship that carried its name could maneuver "wherever the sand was damp."[25] Afloat on the *Ozark,* the Grant Parish posse would remain mobile longer than any other local vessel in a pinch.

The ship offered other advantages for a mission into hostile territory. Its ironclad hull was guaranteed to be impervious to all available fire. Should the going get tough, the *Ozark* could employ its battery of heavy artillery: three swivel-mounted 9-inch guns, a 10-incher, and two 11-inch cannon in the armored turret. It was fast, comfortable, and impressive to behold. Thanks to its armor-plated deckhouse, which served as a second cabin for the crew, the gunship resembled a traditional riverboat, only monstrously armed.[26]

Who purchased the *Ozark* and made it available to the Kellogg militia? Other than the reference to the generous friend of the state, no record of this seemingly momentous transaction has survived. Officially, the *Ozark* did not exist, having been decommissioned by the Navy and sold for scrap in 1865. Preserved illegally and made available to the men who would continue the fight against the rebels in 1873, the *Ozark* returned to the Red River, haunted its reaches for more than a year, and then vanished forever. The secret of its provenance and use would rust in peace in its ironclad hold.

Among the figures visible upon the deck, however, when the *Ozark* steamed into the Grant Parish region in late October 1873, was the twisted form of William Smith Calhoun.

The scalawag Willie Calhoun was deeply aggrieved and sorely hurt by the recent violence. His property had been destroyed, his political fortunes abused, his reputation as a patriarch of stature diminished by the slaughter of his keep. His captors had gone so far as to rob him of his personal dignity, stripping his clothes off and frightening him within an inch of his life. He remained defiant, returning home on the *Ozark* in the company of 35 soldiers of the 19th U.S. Infantry and 25 mounted Metropolitan Police.[27]

Calhoun had political and personal business to attend to at the scene of his recent losses. Calhoun had been the last white man standing with the courthouse, an unimpeachable eyewitness of the buildup to the violence, who almost certainly attained a direct view of the fighting by use of a spyglass. Who better to name and locate white acquaintances of long years for the government lineup? Like his fellow exile William

Phillips—also secured within the fortifications of the boat—Calhoun could appreciate a night's sleep on home turf. Even in New Orleans, where assassins had beset Governor Warmoth and Governor Kellogg, unsuccessfully, earlier that year, they were not as safe.

Traveling in the company of warriors, Calhoun may have also performed a labor of love. In July, Olivia Williams had given birth to the scalawag's second surviving son. Williams and young Eugene, the firstborn, had resided at Mirabeau in 1870, but their whereabouts during and after the massacre remain unknown. If they were in Colfax in autumn 1873, Calhoun would have paid them a visit. Even though they were mulattos (in the parlance of the day), he persisted in acknowledging Olivia and her children as his family. Bestowing his own name on the baby—William Smith Calhoun, Jr.—he served notice of his personal, political intention to persist in his unorthodox ways.[28]

The mission of the *Ozark* entailed significant risks despite its heavy armament. The very idea of "our [Louisiana] Navy in Buckram," the textile used to make clothing for slaves, elicited a "cackle" in New Orleans, even among sympathizers of the Kellogg government. Upstate, meanwhile, the state-based sailors steamed toward dangerous terrain. After six months on the lam, white participants in the Colfax fight had grown bolder, adjusting to their status as outlaws. Republican Sheriff Dan Shaw, who had remained in the ruins of the parish seat, occupying his office after the defeat, found the defiance of local whites "so flagrant, overt and violent" as to "render me powerless to do my duty." He submitted his resignation to Governor Kellogg on September 20—a concession to political violence also made by officials in Shreveport and nearby Franklin Parish that fall. The onset of the Panic of 1873 with nationwide bank failures in late September exacerbated the raw political and emotional tensions in Louisiana's heartland. Autumn itself invoked a range of emotions and stresses derived from the labor requirements of Louisiana's long harvest season, being the traditional time for African American workers to make demands on their employers. Since 1868, moreover, the election calendar had imposed its own violent rhythms on the season, marking the change of the weather every other year with the buildup to a battle for the ballot box.[29]

African Americans in Colfax, however, found cause for equanimity and even celebration that fall in the arrival of the *Ozark* and its cargo of troops. A series of parades—in answer to the white supremacist display six months earlier at Mardi Gras—set black communities all along the Red River into motion, as crowds turned out to cheer the Radical gunship. Unlike the "Missing Links of Darwin's Origin of Species," the November demonstrations would employ no elaborate costumery. Rough buckram abounded on shore, as well as numerous examples of clothing made from the industrial, washed-out fabric color known colloquially as "Negro pink." The simple poetry of hymns replaced the elaborate stanzas of the Krewe of Comus Mardi Gras theme. A favorite, remembered from the local Year of Jubilee, 1864, was "When the Lincoln Gunboats Come," the religious and triumphant anthem of the Union's unsuccessful Red River offensive. Its verses, lost to history, served perfectly to frame the joy of the crowd that gathered to witness the return of a flagship of that year's navy flotilla of fifty fighting ships.[30]

The return of the U.S.S. Ozark to the Red River valley during the bitter harvest months of 1873 resurrected a spirit of hope all but extinguished in the intervening decade. The gunboat arrived in defense of the same constituency that had greeted it the first time, when the riverbank parades had spoken truth to power as even carnival had never dared. Victims of the vicious hatred of area whites—now adapted to political killing instead of slaveholding—bore witness to their sufferings before an audience of armed avengers on the Ozark's armored deck. The Ozark served as base of operations for the arrest of perpetrators of the Colfax Massacre and their delivery to New Orleans on federal murder and conspiracy charges.

In striking contrast to the ragged appearance of the crowd, the uniformed armed forces on the Ozark paraded in style. Thirty-five fighting members the 19th U.S. Infantry, attired in Union blue, left the music to civilians on shore, some of whom toted brass instruments and drums of military vintage. A unit of 25 New Orleans Metropolitan Police occupied the center of attention, as organizers of the dragnet to arrest the 97 white men named in the government's indictment in the Colfax case. Metropolitans sported black-and-scarlet uniforms of conspicuously festive design and carried federal government-issue, state-of-the-art Enfield breech-loading rifles. More inspiring to the crowd, however, were the brown and black faces that appeared above the gilded epaulettes of the police uniforms. Stigmatized by southern conservatives as Louisiana's "Negro militia," the Metropolitans in fact included many officers whom contemporaries would have recognized as white. All embodied a figure of Justice that was blind to distinctions of color and caste.

To complete its mission, the *Ozark* would have to win the local war.

> What, we would ask [inquired the usually Republican *Rapides Gazette* of Alexandria] can a boat cruising up and down the river do against a body of men banded together or scattered about the country, watching or well informed of all her motions, or what could the force of mounted men she carries be they ever so brave, well armed, and well officered, do in pursuit of such a band, who not only out number them perhaps two or three to one, but have every other conceivable advantage?[31]

Memories of the Civil War retreat of Union gunboats fortified the courage of the Colfax unvanquished to resist arrest. They would greet the invaders with arms at hand, as they had in the spring of '64. The voyage of the *Ozark* stoked the smoldering murderousness of the site: "[S]uch a course in Rapides will simply organize a fresh hell here," wrote Edward Biossat, the editor of the conservative paper, "and on their heads be the fearful responsibility."[32]

The ritually invoked final phrase, delivered with lascivious menace in a series of *Alexandria Democrat* editorials that autumn, broadcast a fragment of Ku Klux Klan-style idiom that even uninitiated audiences could understand: the rich and powerful might intervene, but local African Americans would be made to pay the price.

Almost instantly, a Klan-type vigilante operation acted to realize the threat.

News of an "outrage" committed by the Metropolitan Police traveled fast—so fast, in fact, that local people up in arms about the crime could never successfully establish the exact date of its occurrence. On November 1, the *New York Times* reported the letter of an "Ex-Judge Merrill," probably Michael Ryan, describing the rape of two white women in the town of Colfax after dark on Saturday, October 25. The letter, dated October 28, appeared on the same day that Judge Ryan chaired a mass meeting of whites in Alexandria, one day after the first arrival of the *Ozark* "and its buzzard crew" at Colfax. In the letter, the "ex-judge" insisted that responsibility for the attack rested with the officers of the Metropolitan Police, who may have committed the crime in person, or else encouraged the credulous community of blacks in the area to act on a false promise of impunity from prosecution. The letter-writer claimed to have heard a black man say "that he had a right now, under the protection of the United States, to shoot any white man he wanted to shoot and to violate any woman he met."[33]

By the time the letter appeared in the paper in New York (under the headline "Reported Outrages by State Police in Louisiana"), the *Louisiana Democrat* in Alexandria had conceded that the "injurious rumors" about the involvement of the state police had "proved entirely unfounded," in light of the fact the *Ozark* and its crew had not arrived in the area until after the Saturday night in question. In subsequent reports, white accounts would de-emphasize the matter of the date of the attack, with some writers even suggesting that it happened before the Easter Sunday massacre.[34]

There was no uncertainty about the identity of the victims, Cordelia Lacour, age 33, and her teenage daughter Coralie, who appeared in accounts of the incident as the perfect epitome of defenseless southern womanhood. Cordelia Lacour, daughter of an old Rapides Parish planter family, the Layssards, had fallen into distress sometime well before the incident in October 1873. Having married into a tribe of poor Creoles from Natchitoches Parish, the lady had perhaps resigned herself to a life of genteel poverty early in life. Judging by the census, which shows the birth of her youngest child in 1863, Lacour lost her husband in the Civil War. Cordelia and her children lived in a house at the edge of her father's property, a location that came to abut the emerging town of Colfax in the early 1870s. The unmistakably African American character of the town—encouraged by the experimental thinking of its impresario, Calhoun—diminished the social standing of the few white residents, now subject to interracial interactions outside the boundaries of traditional roles. When the Lacour household was burglarized in the days leading up to the massacre in Colfax, some white residents may have anticipated further trouble.[35]

Mrs. Lacour and her daughter endured extraordinary risks in their Colfax home during the extended absence of white menfolk from the area. While the name of her 19-year-old son, John Lacour, did not appear in witness testimony among the identifiable participants, he was likely to have played a role in the Colfax fight. Young John was politically active—a fact that came to light during the pre-Easter robbery, which exposed his papier-mâché Mardi Gras costume amid the ransacked contents of the household.[36] In those days of Missing Links and Darwinian parades, membership in the Mardi Gras krewes denoted a species of political animal. Whatever the case, John Lacour was absent from home during the critical opening weeks of the government raid. His mother and sister, residing directly in harm's way, would be forced to bear the infamy that every white man in his campsite feared the most.

As recounted afterward by the "grand-father of the lady," the illustrious Captain Layssard, in a scandalously detailed letter to the editor of the *Louisiana Democrat,* the attack laid bare the essence of race hatred and black depravity. Having heard the approach of armed and drunken black men shortly after the landfall in Colfax of Metropolitan Police, Mrs. Lacour and her three teenaged children (plus an infant grandson of the scalawag governor Mad Wells) sought refuge in the cabin of "old confidential negroes" who soon became alarmed by the approach of the rowdy crew.

> [T]he armed negroes asked, "who do you have in there!" The negress replied "no one." The negroes said, "We know better! You have those white women in there [and] we want them out. If you don't drive them out we will burn your house up."
>
> "[D]o you hear that? Get out of here white women!" Mrs. Lacour said, "oh, no! let them burn it, I will build you a new house and replace everything you lose."
>
> The negress said, "oh, no! get out of here white women, I do not want any white women in my house." The negress then took Miss Lacour (the daughter) by the arm and forced her out of the back door [then] locked them [all] out.
>
> Mrs. Lacour entreated the negress to let her in. The negress replied, "go way! go way! white woman, I don't want any white women in my house!...I don't want any white children in my house!

Left to fend for themselves, the Lacours tried to placate the black ringleader, an allegedly notorious local scoundrel named Hampton Henderson, by asking him to hold the baby. "Hamp said, 'I will make your mother take the baby,' putting his hand on his knife." After a struggle, the grandfather reported, "he succeeded in violating her, in the presence of her mother and younger brother [while] the mother and son begged Hamp to desist." In case readers of the newspaper were in doubt about the awful responsibility for the attack, Layssard suggested a direct link between Henderson, his gang, and the recently arrived state militia: "After he satisfied his passion, he remarked, now I will go back to my company."[37]

In fact, as most whites would later concede, there was no link between Henderson and the Metropolitans. However, the voyage of the *Ozark* would still be judged the cause of the outrage. Without the agents of bayonet government on their heels, John Lacour and his white brethren would have been on hand to protect their women. And blacks in Colfax, still recovering from their defeat in April, would have never been so brazen. "[W]e make bold to assert," opined the *Democrat* on November 5, "that the presence of the Metropolitans was the cause of the perpetration of the diabolical outrage. To them and them alone belongs the fearful responsibility."[38]

The appearance of this "speck of war" in our community, complained a local voice, had so inflamed the raw emotions of the population as to practically ensure an outrage, and "even by the evidence of colored men themselves," the Lacour assault would merit the most severe reprisals. "[A] greater provocation to extreme violence," another editor complained, only six months after the massacre at Colfax, "could not possibly have been given."[39]

In the end, the bloodletting fell short of the Easter landmark. Two weeks into November, the name of the alleged rapist appeared in a series of newspaper accounts, which always also spoke of a coterie of unnamed accessories to the rape. Speculation on his motives focused on Henderson's ambiguous political associations, but a range of inconclusive other evidence, including the suggestion that he was a serial rapist, makes it hard to assess after the fact his personal innocence or guilt. Henderson and six to eight of his associates would never have their day in court. The white avengers would never name the men or even specify the number that they hanged and burned near Colfax on the night of November 11, 1873: to the scalawags, carpetbaggers, and jackbooted cops belonged the fearful responsibility.[40]

In case they failed to get the message, organized whites orchestrated the disappearance of a black U.S. marshal assigned to the Colfax detail. Like Hampton Henderson, Loyd Shorter had been a slave before the war, the property of Dr. Cruikshank, who purchased him from Landry Baillio of Alexandria. A house servant of mixed racial heritage whose unconventional name betrayed a connection to a local black sheep migrant from the Lloyd's of London clan, Shorter became active in politics after 1867, serving as president of the Phil Sheridan Radical Republican Club of Rapides Parish. Commissioned as a U.S. marshal by Colonel DeKlyne in the summer or fall of 1873, he received a certificate and a gun. On one fateful occasion, he was heard threatening to use his weapon against a white man whose bright yellow horse (called Punkin) had cut a prominent figure in the Easter Sunday fight.

> See this gun? Well, I'm savin' a bullet for Bob Whittington! And after I get him, I'm gona carry old Punkin' to Nyawleans for Kellogg to ride!

Like Willie Calhoun, Loyd Shorter worked as an informer for the Colfax investigation. Worst of all, he inspired the masses with his bad example. "When this man rode through the country, it was as if a magic wand had been passed over the colored population," remembered Dosia Williams Moore, the music lover. "[E]ven the tone of their songs changed."[41]

"The singular fact" about Loyd Shorter's example, another white observer recorded, was "that both he and his horse disappeared, and no trace of them has ever been found." Some time in November, during the early weeks of the *Ozark* campaign and the excitement about Hampton Henderson, Loyd Shorter was abducted to the wilderness near the Saline Bayou and Saline Lake in Winn Parish. His captors reportedly cut off his hands and feet, shot him, doused him in oil, set him on fire, and threw his body in the water. In the absence of physical evidence, no charges were ever investigated, but the example of the U.S. marshal was not forgotten. Editor Bossiat of the *Louisiana Democrat* added a line in Shorter's honor to his chorus of ritual warnings: a recalcitrant black, taught a lesson, would be said to have "gone up Salt River to hunt for Loyd Shorter."[42]

William Smith Calhoun would not be spared the murderous attentions of the local Klans. During his sojourn with the *Ozark,* a crowd of local whites, his associates of long years, boarded the gunship with the intention of throwing him overboard. According to the account of a self-described participant, the hunchback cunningly derailed the plot by getting friendly with the hoi polloi. "He set us up to champagne," remembered Jonas Rosenthal, an Alexandria merchant, who claimed to have overindulged. "We got tight and he got sober."[43]

In fact, a well-established taboo protected the scalawag from excessive force. Louisiana's white chivalry could scarcely stoop to conquer its asthmatic, deformed, and undersized bête noire. Even the *Democrat* had hastened to assure that Calhoun had been "in no wise ill treated or threatened" during his captivity in April.[44] Calhoun's apparently inexhaustible supply of money and panache must have helped smooth the rough edges, a capacity on lively display in his *Ozark* soirée. Some special quality had preserved his life again, against the odds. In the bosom of his battleship, Poor Willie must have hoped his luck would hold.

NINE

Getting Away
with Murder

On December 4, 1873, the state of Louisiana committed the seven suspects captured in the *Ozark* operation to the custody of the United States. The Grant administration was to realize its hope for a small, symbolic number of defendants in the Colfax case—though not on the terms they had envisioned during their discussions with U.S. Attorney J. R. Beckwith and others who had hoped to prosecute to the fullest extent of the law. Instead of a docket of the most prominent organizers of the violence, the United States would have to settle for prosecuting the small number of men that had been apprehended during the state and federal dragnet in November.[1] Wholesale resistance by white residents of the parishes surrounding Colfax had effectively shielded the vast majority of participants. Although law enforcement efforts continued into the New Year, officials would deliver only two additional suspects into custody. The improvident nine—most of whom were relatively minor players in the white conspiracy—would face the charges levied against 97 men in the original indictment. Dozens of others, including those whose names did not appear on the government's list, remained at large.

The absence of the lead defendant in the case of *United States v. Columbus Nash et al.* illustrated the failure of the government roundup. The would-be sheriff had managed to elude capture even as he remained in the vicinity of Colfax, camping in the pasture of James R. Williams.

When information on his whereabouts was leaked to investigators in November, Nash remained a step ahead, racing on the open road with the Metropolitan Police in hot pursuit. Overtaken at Aloha, a romantically named river landing eight miles north of town, Nash plunged his horse into the Red River, escaping to the other side in a hail of gunfire. According to the legend, the rebel leader paused to wave his slouch hat in defiance, spurred his horse, and made his getaway to Texas by an underground railroad of like-minded whites.[2]

Presented with a second string of white defendants, the prosecution mounted nonetheless a momentous case for conspiracy and murder. J. R. Beckwith, the U.S. attorney, had worked effectively with the grand jury to frame a sweeping set of charges against participants in the massacre. The indictment of 41 pages—which continued to carry the names of the outstanding suspects even as the case moved toward trial in early 1874—included 32 criminal counts. For the purpose of simplicity, the indictment specified only two African American men as victims: Alexander Tillman, the Republican activist and framer of Louisiana's 1868 Constitution, whose battered body had been identified by Colonel T. W. DeKlyne; and Levi Nelson, a Colfax blacksmith, who would later prove (in a blow to the prosecution) to be alive at the time of the trial. The defendants stood charged of conspiring to murder Tillman and Nelson and to deprive them of their legal and constitutional rights.

The charges in the Colfax case addressed the most fundamental issues of federalism and human rights. What were the privileges and immunities guaranteed by the Constitution? And which agency of government, federal or state, bore the chief responsibility to protect them? The Colfax indictment employed a comprehensive interpretation of the powers granted to the government of the United States by the Civil War amendments and by the Enforcement Act of 1870, which asserted the obligation of the federal government to protect the rights of citizens vis-à-vis states and individual lawbreakers.

Among the eight categories of crime specified in the indictment, the first two infringed upon Tillman and Nelson's privileges under the Bill of Rights—the 1st Amendment right to assembly and the 2nd Amendment right to bear arms. Three charges addressed rights guaranteed by the 14th Amendment, namely, Tillman and Nelson's claim to due process and equal protection under the law. The right to vote as guaranteed by the 15th Amendment had come under assault in the crimes identified in the sixth and seventh charges. Relying on the electoral protections of the 1870 Enforcement Act, the indictment charged the defendants with conspiring to deny Tillman and Nelson's right to vote and to punish them for having voted. The final charge asserted that the defendants had denied to Tillman and Nelson "the free exercise and enjoyment of every, each, all and singular several rights and privileges" secured by the Constitution of the United States, a sweeping guarantee granted in both the 1870 and 1871 Enforcement Acts.

The accused confronted four distinct sets of charges for each of the eight specific acts, giving the jury the option of finding them guilty of "banding together," "combining," "conspiring," or "confederating" for criminal purposes.

The motivating assumption behind the prosecution identified the federal government as the natural guardian of all rights granted by the Constitution and its enabling legislation. To the defense, of course, the claim seemed to trample on the traditional prerogatives of states, a sentiment vociferously seconded by white Louisianans and other southerners who had long denounced federal officials as usurpers. The trial promised an opportunity to vet the constitutionality of the Enforcement Acts and the theory that the Civil Rights Amendments transformed the relationship between the federal government and the states. These issues had been addressed before, in an 1871 and 1872 series of cases arising from Ku Klux Klan violence in South Carolina, but the issue of whether the Enforcement Acts were constitutional had not been definitively resolved. The case of the "Grant Parish prisoners," as it became known in the newspapers, offered an opportunity to revise the balance of power between the federal government and the as-yet-unvanquished southern states.

The assertion of enhanced federal powers in the Colfax case reflected the legal interpretation of J. R. Beckwith, the U.S. attorney. Like so many Louisiana officials in the Reconstruction era, Beckwith had arrived from out of state. Unlike most of the others, however, he arrived before the war—in 1860—in pursuit of some unrecorded dream or southern comfort. The occupation of New Orleans after 1862 provided ample opportunity to advance within the Unionist establishment, especially for a man of Republican political principles. Beckwith's hometown of Cazenovia, New York, outside Syracuse, appeared at the eastern edge of the region that had been most passionately committed to abolition and other liberal causes before the Civil War.[3] He kept his distance from the bare-knuckles fraternity of Republicans and radicals in New Orleans, but Beckwith's engagement in the Colfax case betrayed a deep humanitarian conviction. "It has never been my fortune to be connected with the prosecution of a case so revolting and horrible in the details of its perpetration and so burdened with atrocity and barbarity," he wrote to U.S. Attorney George Williams.[4] For more than a year after the massacre, the pursuit of justice for its victims would consume Beckwith's working hours and his personal strength.

Beckwith would wage the struggle almost alone. The immense show of government strength in the *Ozark* operation to apprehend the Colfax suspects belied a dearth of institutional support for the prosecution. In fact, the dragnet reflected the commitment of the state militia more than the federal government; Metropolitan Police rather than members of the 19th Infantry conducted the majority of operations. An individual benefactor, possibly Willie Calhoun, had provided the funds to purchase the gunship that came to symbolize the whole effort. Although the statutory prerogatives of the United States government provided legal cover for the operation, federal officials outside the state evinced little enthusiasm in their participation. For the Grant administration, the Louisiana troubles had come to represent the hazards of an activist policy in the South.

Louisiana had distinguished itself as the most difficult and disappointing state in the seething wreckage of the former Confederacy. As the object of the federal government's longest sustained intervention, its continuing recalcitrance appeared to rebuke the whole experiment of Reconstruction. Despite the tremendous commitment of attention and resources since 1862, when President Lincoln implemented his forgiving plan to reconstruct the state, the Louisiana example proved consistently damaging to federal goals: home to the deadliest political riots of the era, including the 1866 New Orleans riot as well as the Colfax Massacre; pioneer of "black code" legislation; and the first of several states to produce dual governments in disputed elections. For Ulysses Grant, newly embarked upon his second term but feeling the heat of corruption allegations in the Credit Mobilier and other scandals, problems in Louisiana were especially embarrassing in light of the high-profile role of his brother-in-law in state political affairs. As far back as 1870, the president's enemies in Congress had called for the removal of James F. Casey, the head of the powerful New Orleans Customhouse, whose partisan activities left Grant open to charges of nepotism and interference.[5] Anything that raised the specter of Louisiana in public discourse, including the appearance of intervention in political disputes, seemed to work to the disadvantage of the Grant administration.

The Justice Department, moreover, saw generally unfavorable prospects for prosecutions under the Enforcement Acts after the Supreme Court's decision in the *Slaughterhouse Cases,* a 14th Amendment ruling delivered on the Monday after the Easter Sunday massacre at Colfax. *Slaughterhouse,* which examined the case of New Orleans butchers disadvantaged by the carpetbagger state government's recent public health regulations, anticipated a narrow scope for federal action under the new constitutional amendments, which could not be employed to override what the court called the exercise of regular police power by the state. Grant's attorney general had called for a halt on related Ku Klux Klan prosecutions for most of 1872 and 1873, and only permitted the use of Enforcement Act authority in the Colfax case because of the extreme circumstances of the violence.

Attorney General George H. Williams had been emphatic in limiting the Colfax prosecution to a small number of perpetrators, in part because of the conspicuous expense of the investigation. The desire to control the cost of operations provided an additional incentive for caution in the employment of federal power for criminal matters. Especially after a scandal concerning Williams's purchase of a fancy carriage, a landaulet, for his use at government expense, the Justice Department operated under close budgetary scrutiny. "Landaulet" Williams, as he became known, refused to provide funds to hire additional lawyers and even balked at the expense of employing a court reporter in the proceedings.[6]

The cost of these constraints would be visible in the trial, most embarrassingly in the mistaken choice of Levi Nelson as one of the two named casualties of the violence. When Nelson took the stand to report that accounts of his death had been premature, conservative newspapers chortled with delight. "One main and choice negro swearer, Nelson by name, was actually killed in the fight," laughed editor Edward Biossat in the Alexandria *Democrat,* "but some stray Gabriel's last trumpet blew him alive again."[7]

The defense, in contrast, marshaled the flush resources of the Grant Parish prisoners and their supporters. The white community of the Colfax parishes—and indeed, of much of Louisiana—rallied to the defense of the nine men called to the bar by the United States. As a group, the nine represented varying economic backgrounds. The most affluent were Alfred Lewis, a 62-year-old Grant Parish planter worth more than $10,000, and William Cruikshank, descended from major slaveholders. Others were sons or cousins of families of significant means, such as J. P. Hadnot, the 18-year-old son of the "martyred" planter and Klansman, and Thomas Hickman, a lesser member of an old area family that included both august planters and minor criminals. Prudhomme Lemoine of distant Avoyelles Parish and Bill Irwin of Grant Parish represented the upper middle class. Two poor whites, the shoemaker Clement Penn of Grant Parish and Denis Lemoine of Avoyelles, completed the docket, which also included Oscar Givens, possibly of Bienville, Louisiana.[8] The nine presented a common defense, pooling their resources and benefiting from charitable contributions to the cause.

The affected communities of whites offered generous support to the Grant Parish prisoners, all of whom were loudly proclaimed to be innocent in the newspapers and other forums. The mayor of Alexandria opened a subscription fund for their relief to which prominent citizens of the surrounding parishes made donations. To sweeten the deal, a local man offered an elegant watch in a raffle, with proceeds from ticket sales dedicated to the defense. Ladies and young people did their part; J. P. Hadnot's classmates from the military academy in Pineville (later relocated and renamed Louisiana State University) mounted a benefit theatrical performance and women went door to door to solicit funds. Even white citizens of New Orleans made a show of support, organizing a gala benefit at the Opera House and circulating a petition for release signed by the most prominent members of the city's elite.[9]

Donations exceeded the prisoners' courtroom costs by a significant margin, and in practice served to offset income and opportunity lost by the individual suspects during their incarceration. In fact, lawyers representing the defense donated their own services *pro bono publicum,* only accepting nominal fees as a token of community appreciation.[10] A team led by prominent Democrats R. H. Marr and John Ellis represented the accused at the circuit court level, and additional counsel, including national heavyweights, joined in for the Supreme Court round. The defense prepared hundreds of witnesses—including some, such as former radical Sheriff Dan Shaw, who received cash payments for as much as $100 a day in exchange for their testimony.

To underscore the popular spirit, partisans of the defense appeared daily in the courtroom. Ladies of New Orleans (and probably the wives and daughters of the Red River parishes, visiting the city in the company of witnesses) piled fresh flowers on the defense table. A peanut gallery of whites cheered on the motions of defense attorneys, hissed at setbacks, and menaced witnesses and jury members on the streets. Exposed by the publication of their names and past political history, the district attorney and members of the jury endured regular intimidation in person and by mail. Beckwith received so many death threats in the form of letters, he said, that he ceased to pay them any mind, tossing them directly into the wastepaper basket. Accusations of partisanship and threats of reprisals against judges Woods and Durrell were so severe that friends of the court objected that "the officers of the court [had been] placed in the prisoners' box, with the accused turned prosecutors." Judge Edward Durrell, who had already earned the hatred of Louisiana conservatives for his role in the confirmation of Governor Kellogg, was publicly ridiculed as a drunkard and a party hack.[11]

Despite budgetary constraints, the prosecution mounted its own show of force, escorting witnesses to and from New Orleans on the *Ozark* with help from the U.S. marshals. U.S. marshals supervised the delivery of subpoenas and recruitment of voluntary witnesses during a visit to the affected parishes in February 1874, arranging for a single transport in time for the trial. The poor black people who provided the bulk of the testimony required transportation and probably a safe place to sleep during their extended stay in New Orleans. By providing a military escort of 70 armed militiamen, Beckwith and his allies could assure participants of at least temporary protection against enemy recriminations. The prosecution's strong-arm display produced good results: key participants, eyewitnesses, and others with firsthand experience had their day in court.

As events unfolded, government firepower proved necessary to protect the witnesses for the prosecution. A confrontation on the docks below Canal Street broke out during the departure of the *Ozark* and its cargo of participants after closing arguments in the second Colfax trial.

A mob of whites had turned out to harass the ship's captain and issue threats of reprisals against the witnesses. One agitator had been bold enough to mount the deck of the ship, where he engaged in a heated exchange with the captain. His action produced a sudden clatter of arms on the monitor's small upper deck. At the head of a clique of militia-men, gun-sights trained on the white offender, appeared the notorious dark-black visage of William Ward.

Ward had remained mostly aloof from the investigation and prosecu-tion of the Colfax case, a display of reserve that probably stemmed from the embarrassing circumstances of his timely departure from the scene of the conflict he had helped create. As a Grant Parish representative in Louisiana's House of Representatives, however, he had continued to advocate for the black citizens of his adopted home. While the Colfax trial was under way in February and March, Ward had been working to shepherd his special project, the reform of the state penitentiary sys-tem, through the legislature. Ward served as head of a committee that exposed inhumane conditions for the disproportionately black inmates of the state penitentiary in Baton Rouge. He also spoke out forcefully against the emerging convict leasing system, which, he argued, acted as an incentive for the arrest of African Americans for petty offenses.[12]

No longer a member of the state militia, Ward accompanied the Colfax transport for his own convenience. His old habit of command, however, and no small measure of his nerve, could be discerned in his instructions to the besieged *Ozark* captain. "Shoot the damn white hound," said Ward, holding a borrowed rifle to his cheek. "We'll see you through."[13]

Elaborate security requirements in New Orleans notwithstanding, blacks appearing for the prosecution assumed tremendous personal risk. One such witness, upon returning home, was accosted on the streets of Alexandria by the dastardly J.G.P. Hooe and George Marsh.

"O, you son of a bitch," cried Marsh, brandishing a dagger, "you sworn against me, did you?" In the presence of observers, the white men beat and kicked their victim mercilessly for several minutes, slash-ing him with the dagger and leaving him close to death.[14]

Putting their faith in the government, 140 citizens of the Colfax parishes appeared as witnesses for the prosecution.[15] Most of the tes-timony provided each witness's component of a straightforward nar-rative of events, beginning with the murder of Jessie McKinney and culminating in the forensic investigations of Colonels Whight and DeKlyne on the day after the battle. Whight and DeKlyne, along with William Smith Calhoun, appeared among the few white witnesses for the prosecution. The trial featured testimony from Colfax's black militiamen—Levi Allen, Peter Borland, and Alabama Mitchell. Along with other participants in the fighting, the black veterans explained how they came to be in Colfax in early April. Most claimed to have relocated to the town in fear after McKinney's death. Witnesses provided details about the fighting, identifying white participants by name and physical description. Although some testimony spoke directly to the roles of the accused—Bill Irwin and Denis Lemoine were particularly implicated in the McKinney killing—many whites who did not appear in the courtroom were also condemned.[16]

The testimony of female witnesses, many of whom observed the fighting and the execution of the prisoners at close range, proved especially poignant. The widows of Jessie McKinney and Etienne Elzie spoke movingly about their husbands' final moments. "The poor man was wet with the sweat of honest toil when he fell," said Laurinia McKinney. They definitively identified their husbands' killers. "Clement Penn is the man, and there he sits!" declared Annie Elzie, pointing her finger at the accused. Other women quoted verbatim from the white men's taunting and sexual innuendo, creating a sensation in the courtroom and adding to the judge's frustration with the stream of profanity emanating from the witness stand.[17]

The testimony of the widows and mothers against the Colfax defendants brought to life the human types described by W.E.B. DuBois later as the symbols of the Reconstruction era: "the one, a gray-haired gentleman...whose sons lay in nameless graves...who stood at last, in the evening of life, a blighted, ruined form, with hate in his eyes" and "the other, a form hovering dark and motherlike...[who] had aforetime quailed at that white master's command, had bent in love over the cradles of his sons and daughters, and closed in death the sunken eyes of his wife—aye, too, at his behest had laid herself low to his lust." The fraught juxtaposition of these men and women—"the saddest sights of that woeful day," according to DuBois—palpably transformed the courtroom drama into an allegory of the tragic era.[18]

Indeed, some of the most effective testimony in the prosecution's case was nonverbal. A large number of the black men on the stand had been injured in the fighting, and only one year later, some of the wounds remained visible. Benjamin Brimm had lost his left eye when he was shot in the head, and Alabama Mitchell was probably still using crutches to support his destroyed right leg. Describing the abduction and harassment of Willie Calhoun in his closing arguments, District Attorney Beckwith directed the jury's attention to the man's obvious physical disabilities, describing him as "an infirm man, who could not cope with a boy of fifteen." In another instance, Beckwith asked a man who had been injured to approach the docket of prisoners and identify the men he had seen at the fight. "The witness deliberately walked among them," reported the *New Orleans Republican*, "and confidently laid his hand on each. As he did a thrill ran through the entire courtroom, for the act declared the men murderers; even the attorneys for the accused looked on gravely."[19]

For all its power, the prosecution's case contained serious flaws. The 32 counts of the indictment notwithstanding, Beckwith concentrated on convincing the jury that the men were responsible for murder and conspiracy. Reference to the issue of electoral participation—a key premise of federal authority under the first Enforcement Act—was entirely omitted from witness testimony. Invoking the protections of the 14th and 15th Amendments, the indictment made repeated references to the victims as persons of color, and even specified that they had been victimized "by reason of and for, and on account of [their] race and color."[20] In the presentation of evidence, however, the matter of racial motivation had been muted, in part because Beckwith failed to establish the link between the violence on April 6 and April 13 and the goals, membership, and tactics of white supremacist organizations. These flaws would be particularly consequential in the second of two trials in the Colfax case, after the proceedings of February and May 1874 concluded in a mistrial. Sitting alongside Judge Woods in his capacity as a judge of the 5th Judicial Circuit, Supreme Court Justice Stephen J. Bradley would form judgments on the merits of the case that informed his later deliberations for the high court. In his subsequent rulings, Justice Bradley seemed to lose sight of the race war in the prosecution's tangled recreation of individual acts of violence.

The defense strategy was more complex. Aiming for the gut instincts of the seven white members of the jury, a major line of argument depicted the assembly of blacks at the courthouse as threatening, provocative, and illegal. The lawyers played on fears of black militia-men, inviting testimony on the armament and drilling procedures of the black ranks. The robbery of William Rutland's Colfax home and other excesses served to illustrate the overall propriety and necessity of the white raid.

The defense presented some evidence of the innocence of individual defendants. No one tried to deny that Denis Lemoine, J. P. Hadnot, and Bill Irwin participated in the fight, and witnesses ventured only the most tentative alibis for William Cruikshank and Oscar Givens. One witness claimed to have seen Tom Hickman at home on Easter Sunday, while another claimed to have seen Hickman at another man's home. A. C. Lewis was said to be at home near Colfax and also reported to have visited a Grant Parish blacksmith shop. A man from Avoyelles Parish claimed to have seen Prudhomme Lemoine at church that morning, a common defense, although unlike some of the suspects who were not apprehended, Lemoine did not offer the sworn affidavits of his whole congregation to his participation in Easter services.[21]

The most sustained campaign to establish an alibi concerned the whereabouts of Clement Penn, the poor shoemaker. Several people were willing to swear that they saw him at the Cane River home of Narcisse Fredieu, observing the fight with Fredieu and others from a vantage point in the branches of a tree. The claim may well have been true. Fredieu, one of the few white men from the area who dared to appear as a witness for the prosecution, was no friend of the KKK, having been subjected to persecution himself for his refusal to disavow his mixed-race wife and children. Being two and a half miles away during the fight, however, did not exonerate Penn from the main murder charge against him, levied by the widow of Etienne Elzie. Penn's presence at the Fredieu home around noon in no way precluded his participation in the execution of the prisoners, which took place sometime after 8 P.M.[22] Some white observers, however, subscribed wholeheartedly to the theory that Penn (and possibly Cruikshank) had been wrongfully charged. For John McCain, a white participant who managed to avoid being prosecuted, the misplaced blame would be "enough to make hot blood flow with leaps and bounds," even half a century afterward, when McCain wrote his memoirs.[23]

After the February and March proceedings ended in a mistrial (with a single African American juror insisting on conviction and the remainder in favor of exonerating some or all of the defendants), defense attorneys began in earnest to challenge the constitutional authority of the ongoing prosecution. Substituting the names of other black victims for those of Tillman and Nelson, the district attorney brought the same charges against the same defendants (minus Alfred Lewis, acquitted in the first trial) under the new case name *U.S. v. Cruikshank et al.*[24] The defense team immediately filed a motion in arrest of judgment, asking the presiding judge to dismiss the charges on the grounds that the Enforcement Acts that empowered the prosecution had been rendered void by the recent Supreme Court decision in the 1873 *Slaughterhouse Cases*. As part of this strategy, the defense requested the attendance in court of Justice Joseph Bradley of the United States Supreme Court. Much to the chagrin of the D.A., the Supreme Court justice agreed to preside alongside Judge Woods in the Circuit Court, an arrangement consistent with his routine responsibilities to "ride the circuit" in the southern states. Bradley delayed his ruling on the motion in arrest of judgment, promising to rule on the constitutional issues at stake in the event of convictions.[25]

The presence of Justice Bradley encouraged and even emboldened partisans of the defense. In a prank that must have delighted the gallery of their supporters, attorneys placed the operator of a Pineville bordello on the stand to rebut the testimony of William Smith Calhoun, who frequently attended the proceedings. The man insisted that the scalawag had been at his house for half an hour, "transacting private business," instead of in the custody of the mob that removed him from the steamboat *La Belle.*[26] More seriously (but also in a breach of normal procedures), the defense devoted three days to closing arguments in which they made the case that the Enforcement Acts overstepped the boundaries of federal power as defined in the *Slaughterhouse* precedent.[27]

The trial concluded amid widespread speculation that the prosecution had failed. As if to celebrate the pending victory, a group of about 30 Grant Parish whites donned Klan-type disguises and removed two black prisoners from a jail cell in Winnsboro. The prisoners, A. B. and Tom Norris, accused of robbing and murdering a flatboatman on Bayou Macon, received summary justice at the end of a rope.[28]

On June 10, after three days of deliberation, the jury delivered a verdict of not guilty for all parties on the counts alleging murder. Only three of the eight defendants—William Cruikshank, J. P. Hadnot, and

Bill Irwin—were convicted of conspiracy. The results convinced the heartbroken district attorney that the jury had been intimidated by threats of violence—a possibility he understood from personal experience. Conditions in the state, complained Beckwith, made it impossible to convene a jury "with courage enough to convict under any pressure of proof."[29]

The defense filed again their motion in arrest of judgment, which Justice Bradley packed into his carpetbag for a hurried trip to Washington. The judge promised to return promptly and deliver his ruling on the constitutional questions in the case.

Bradley returned to New Orleans overland and by steamboat in the most stifling heat of the summer. "This was the hottest day I have known," he wrote in his diary on June 24. The document in his possession was hotter still: an opinion that vacated the three convictions in the Colfax case, voiding Beckwith's indictment and declaring key sections of the U.S. Enforcement Acts to be unconstitutional. Delivered from the bench of the circuit court, the opinion carried much of the authority of the high court. Bradley openly implied that he had secured the approval of his Supreme Court colleagues during his visit to Washington. Moreover, the New York–born Bradley, whose circuit included most of the states of the former Confederacy, was widely regarded as the court's leading expert on the Civil War and Reconstruction-era amendments. Bradley chose to uphold the motion to dismiss that Judge Woods had decided to reject, splitting the decision of the circuit court and ensuring that *U.S. v. Cruikshank* would be certified to the Supreme Court level. The result, in the mind of observers and participants, was to give an air of final judgment to the critical issues at stake in the Colfax case.[30]

Justice Bradley rejected the counts in the Colfax indictment that aimed to protect the victims' rights as specified in the 14th Amendment. Bradley's reasoning was constrained by the narrow interpretation of the court's ruling in the *Slaughterhouse* decision (handed down on April 14, 1873, one day after the Colfax Massacre), in which he and three other justices had submitted a dissenting opinion. Like *Slaughterhouse,* the circuit court ruling in *Cruikshank* denied sovereignty to the government of the United States over the rights of citizens traditionally associated with the common law and Bill of Rights, including the right to assemble and to bear arms as cited in the Colfax indictment. The protection of these privileges and immunities was deemed to be the exclusive province of state government. Guarantees against the denial of due process and equal protection under the law—likewise cited in the counts of the *Cruikshank* indictment—were also deemed to be beyond the scope of federal action except insofar as state laws or the action of agents of the state abridged these rights (a limitation made notorious later in the Supreme Court's verdict in the *Civil Rights Cases* of 1883, in which *Cruikshank* was cited as precedent).[31] Where acts of individuals threatened the enjoyment of the rights of citizens, according to the Bradley verdict, the federal government was helpless to interfere:

> The affirmative enforcement of the rights and privileges themselves, unless something more is expressed, does not devolve upon [the federal government], but belongs to the state government as part of its residuary sovereignty. For example, when it is declared that no state shall deprive any person of life, liberty, or property without due process of law, this declaration was not intended as a guaranty against the commission of murder, false imprisonment, robbery, or any other crime committed by individual malefactors....

In other words, as the judge restated the matter, "the power of congress...does not extend to the passage of laws for the suppression of ordinary crime within the states."[32]

According to Bradley, the law did extend to Congress the right to prosecute "offenses which aim at the colored citizen's enjoyment and exercise of his rights of citizenship of equal protection of the laws because of his race, color, or previous condition of servitude." The indictments in *Cruikshank,* however, were judged to fall short of that standard.

The guarantees of the 15th Amendment invoked by the prosecution likewise failed to find justification in the *Cruikshank* indictments. Contrary to the interpretation of the authors of the voting rights enforcement legislation, Bradley ruled in favor of a narrow interpretation of the rights secured under the revised version of the Constitution.

> Congress has not acquired any additional right to regulate...elections, or the right of voting therein, which it did not possess before, except the power to enforce the prohibition [of race-specific legislation] imposed on the states, and the equal right acquired by all races and colors to vote.

Unconstrained by the judicial precedent of the *Slaughterhouse* deci-sion, which limited his commentary on the 14th Amendment, Bradley acknowledged that the power to protect black voters against dis-crimination extended to congressional oversight of nonstate actors. "[N]otwithstanding its negative form, [the Amendment] substantially guarantees the equal right to vote to citizens of every race and color," Bradley wrote. He continued:

> I am inclined to the opinion that congress has the power to secure that right not only as against outrage, violence, and combinations on the part of individuals, irrespective of state laws. Such was the opin-ion of congress itself in passing the [1870 Enforcement Act] at a time when many of its members were the same who had consulted upon the original form of the amendment in proposing it to the states.

In the *Cruikshank* case, however, Bradley was convinced that the indictment "does not contain any allegation that the defendants com-mitted the acts complained of with a design to deprive the injured per-sons of their rights on account of their race, color, or previous condition of servitude. This, as we have seen, is an essential ingredient in the crime to bring it within the cognizance of the United Stats authorities."[33]

The ruling delivered a crushing rebuke to prosecutor James Beckwith. Though each of the 32 counts in the indictment made ref-erence to the race of Colfax victims, the relationship between racial conflict and the Easter Sunday violence remained unspecified.

> Perhaps such a design may be inferred from the allegation that the persons injured were of the African race, and that the intent was to deprive them of the exercise and enjoyment of the rights enjoyed by white citizens. But it ought not to have been left to inference; it should have been alleged. On this ground, therefore [the major counts of the indictment are] defective and cannot be sustained.

Disregarding at least one specific reference to race as the cause of the dilemma, Bradley reproached the indictment for "vagueness and generality" of its usage of federal guarantees under the Constitution. In fact, the defects of the prosecution arose from its presentation of the merits of the case. By neglecting to delineate the ideology and mechan-ics of Louisiana's white supremacy conspiracy, Beckwith had botched the opportunity to invoke the special prerogatives of the 14th and 15th Amendments. "It should, at least, have been shown," the judge complained, "that the conspiracy was entered into to deprive the injured persons of their right to vote by reason of their race, color, or previous condition of servitude."[34]

As a Republican and radical himself, perhaps, Beckwith failed to see the political contest as a matter of race. Indeed, the concept that the Civil Rights Amendments applied only to African Americans, first articulated in the *Slaughterhouse* decision, was unexpected and terrible news for white Republicans in the South. Like native-born southerners of both races, the Supreme Court came to see the two-party rivalry in the South in the context of white versus black. The scalawags and carpetbaggers who played such a prominent role in the struggle for control of Grant Parish did not benefit from the specific protections extended to blacks in the 14th and 15th Amendments. The *Cruikshank* decision gave momentum to the abandonment and unlamented disappearance of white dissidents from the political landscape of the South.

The prosecution had also failed to make an explicit case for a white conspiracy targeting the political assets of African Americans. The omission derived in part from Beckwith's failure of imagination, a reflection of his professional isolation and unsustainable personal burden in the case. Caught up in the horror of the details of the massacre, the district attorney neglected to develop the mechanics of the conspiracy and banding alleged in various counts of the indictment. In practical terms, however, Beckwith would have approached the task of reconstructing this conspiracy with meager resources. With no cooperating white participants, prospects for the government inquiry were dim. Even in the 21st century, after two lifetimes of confessions and remembrances by white participants, the contours of white supremacy organizations in the crisis remain partially in shadow. The old secret societies—especially the Knights of the White Camellia, if indeed they did participate—managed to guard their membership and tactics in the Colfax fight.

Even as the trial was under way, however, the Knights and Klans were stepping out of the shadows to lay claim to a public identity for Louisiana's white supremacy movement. The Louisiana White League, a statewide paramilitary organization, had initiated its bid for recognition in February and March 1874. Growing out of that year's Mardi

Gras celebrations—which featured a reprise of the racist Darwinian parody staged by a new secret carnival krewe, the Knights of Momus, as well as costumed Ku Klux Klansmen in the Rex procession, serving on the "staff" of the King of Carnival—the White League membership list came to include many of the most illustrious names in the state.[35] The opening of first Grant Parish trial just after the holiday emboldened the planners by displaying the weak hand of law enforcement, with its beggarly selection of defendants and overworked prosecutor. Around the state, militants set aside their cloaks and hoods to advocate openly for white man's government and home rule.

In the area around Grant Parish, the emergence of the White League was signaled by the March 1874 launch of a new conservative newspaper in Alexandria. Its title, *The Caucasian,* left little ambiguity about its political bent. The three-man masthead of the *Caucasian* revealed a direct link to the violence at Colfax, including two names from U.S. Attorney Beckwith's original indictment. George Stafford, a financial backer of the project, was the planter and Confederate officer who had served as the captain of Rapides Parish participants in the fight. Robert P. Hunter, a self-described "last-ditcher" who would later be identified as one of the few "organizational Klansmen" in the area, assumed editorial responsibilities. *The Caucasian* would advocate openly for the Democratic Party and serve to coordinate the activities of white militants. In its inaugural edition, the paper promised "no security, no peace, and no prosperity for Louisiana" until "the superiority of the Caucasian over the African, in all affairs pertaining to government is acknowledged and established."[36]

Despite the bluster, the first six months of 1874 passed without incident. Governor Kellogg would later comment on the incongruous peacefulness of the interlude. "During the imprisonment and trial of the Grant Parish prisoners," he testified to a committee of Congress in 1875, "the laws were enforced, taxes were collected with unusual regularity, and the constituted authorities were respected and obeyed."

With the announcement of Justice Bradley's verdict in the *Cruikshank* trial, however, Kellogg said, "the aspect of affairs at once changed." The decision "was hailed with the wildest demonstrations of approval." Not only were the celebrated Colfax prisoners to be set at liberty, but the opinion "was regarded as establishing the principle that hereafter no white man could be punished for killing a negro."[37]

In fact, the Bradley opinion delivered only a partial blow to the federal criminal statutes outlined in the Enforcement Acts. With attention to its detailed instructions on framing the racial animus of political attacks, revised indictments in the Colfax case and similar crimes could have hoped to succeed. District Attorney Beckwith, mortified by Bradley's judgment of his errors, was eager to continue the prosecution, which continued to enjoy the support of the state militia, U.S. marshals, and army operations to arrest the suspects who remained at large. His superiors at the Justice Department, however, were fundamentally opposed, in keeping with the long-standing reluctance to bring Enforcement Act proceedings during the tenure of Attorney General George Williams. "I do not think it advisable to take any further steps in this matter," wrote Williams on July 17, "until the question shall be decided by the Supreme Court."[38] Months or years before the conclusive adjudication of the case, *U.S. v. Cruikshank* had made dead letters of the federal Klan laws.

The resounding chorus of celebration that greeted Bradley's opinion in Louisiana drowned out the objections of Beckwith and others who saw a future for federal law enforcement under the acts. The release of the remaining Colfax prisoners provided the occasion for strident boasts and gala celebrations. "All hail to the judge," wrote the Alexandria *Caucasian,* for when the prisoners emerged, "free and unfettered, we felt that *their release was our release* from a thralldom worse than death."[39]

Music and cannon fire saluted the passage of the prisoners' steamboat up the Red River. Bypassing Alexandria, home to Cruikshank and Hadnot, the party disembarked at Calhoun's Landing in Colfax, where they were met by the largest crowd ever convened in the parish. According to a U.S. army officer, who had the misfortune to be traveling on the same boat (after an unsuccessful bid to be relieved of his detachment's hardship duties at the Colfax post), the meeting was attended by most of the local white participants in the Easter Sunday fight. The chivalry of the Red River parishes relished the opportunity to appear in public without fear of arrest.

Armed with this sense of impunity, a group thought to include one of the newly released prisoners indulged a craving for revenge on their way home. They fired their pistols and trampled on the garden plots of black households nearby. Two black men were killed that night, and both in a manner to send a message. The first would be found in the open road, a dagger sticking out of his throat. The other had been practically decapitated while standing in the threshold of his own home.[40]

Two days later, on June 27, Christopher Columbus Nash appeared in Natchitoches at the head of an armed force said to number a thousand men. The mob forced the resignation of five Republican parish officials, whose lives were spared in exchange for their agreement to leave the town on the first available boat. The incident was the first in an escalating series of paramilitary attacks on the political enemies of the White League.[41]

Nash allegedly also participated in the infamous murder of blacks and Republican officials in Red River Parish, 50 miles upriver from Colfax. Acting on the heels of a disorganized raid (in the spirit of the June 25 killings in Grant Parish) in which a black victim had killed one of the white attackers before he died, the White League convened in the parish seat of Coushatta, where they imprisoned and demanded the resignations of six white Republicans associated with Marshall Twitchell, a carpetbagger political boss. After four days of white power demonstrations, during which organizers hanged two black men and tortured another to death in sight of the crowd, the Coushatta Republicans were released to the company of an armed escort, to be delivered across the state line into Texas. A second party on horseback rode down the group in broad daylight, killing all six and grotesquely abusing the bodies. Sheriff Frank Edgerton, one of the victims, had anticipated his own death, and warned Twitchell of the dangers of armed resistance to the White League. To defy them, he wrote, less than two weeks before his death, "would only be a second Colfax, thanks to Justice Bradley.... I am certain we are on the verge of civil war."[42]

In its next incarnation, the White League insurgency would assume the guise of outright war. Convening 8,000 troops in New Orleans under the leadership of "Major General" Frederick N. Ogden, head of "Governor" McEnery's Louisiana State Militia, white militants staged a coup d'état on September 14, 1874. The Battle of Canal Street, as it became known, featured a pitched confrontation with Longstreet's militia and the New Orleans Metropolitan Police under the Henry Clay statue in the heart of the business district. Business leaders, including all 113 city fathers and part-time Mardi Gras revelers in the Pickwick Club, lent a hand. Conservatives seized control of city hall, the statehouse, and facilities where weapons were stored around town, cutting telegraph wires and calling for the resignation of Governor Kellogg and the Republican legislature. More than 30 people died before six regiments of federal troops arrived in New Orleans to restore order.[43]

Despite the presence of the army, the mobilization of the White League continued at full throttle as elections approached. Around Grant Parish, a company of the 7th U.S. Cavalry accompanied U.S. Marshal J. B. Stockton (whose former partner Theodore DeKlyne had died under obscure circumstances on August 4, 1874). Stockton reported the "greatest reign of terror and intimidation" in the vicinity of Natchitoches. "These people swear," he reported, that "as soon as I go away with the cavalry they intend to kill all the prominent black and white republicans in the parish."[44] Sometime after this complaint, Stockton was "grossly insulted" by James Cosgrove, editor of the Natchitoches People's Vindicator, who spit a plug of tobacco into Stockton's face. "This man, Cosgrove," complained Donald McIntosh, the first lieutenant of the 7th Cavalry detachment, "while drunk, made threats against me, and in a violent and defiant manner used indecent and insulting language in the full hearing of the guard and enlisted men of my command."[45] The commander of the 7th Cavalry detachment became so uneasy about the likelihood of an attack that he asked the company drummer to sleep in his tent, "ready to give the alarm."[46]

McIntosh, who would be killed along with every member of his company 18 months later at the Battle of Little Bighorn, took pity on blacks and Republicans of the region, as did the commanding officer of the 7th Cavalry's Red River division, Lewis Merrill, who survived the Indian wars. "There is absolutely no hope for them from the enforcement of any local law," Merrill wrote in November 1874, and yet "in many cases no United States statute covers the wrong done to them." In light of this impunity from prosecution, Merrill was filled with foreboding. "I much fear, too, that this is only the beginning."[47]

"I have never seen in my life a condition of society similar to that in Grant Parish," reported another U.S. officer. "I was amazed and astonished. It is a community that cannot be judged by any other."[48]

As Election Day approached, threats against Republican officeholders and aspirants became more explicit. John DeLacy, the African American sheriff of Rapides Parish, ran into trouble at the store operated by A. M. Rosenthal (who later claimed to have become intoxicated while trying to assassinate William Smith Calhoun). "A man told me there that me, Mr. Connoughton, and Mr. [Kelso]," the three African American officeholders in Rapides, "would be obliged to leave the parish or be killed." Captain Stafford of *The Caucasian* and the Stafford Guards, DeLacy swore, "told me in the State house it was death or war if I went back."[49]

A white man named Moss shot William Ward three times on the day after election returns showed him winning by a majority of 184 votes. Assisted by friends and transported by soldiers to New Orleans, the old soldier survived to fight another day.[50]

By January 1875, as yet another battle for control of the statehouse in New Orleans got under way, the state of quasi-war in Louisiana would tax the patience of the nation for the last time. Dispatching General Philip Sheridan to investigate the flood of violence in the state, President Grant made a final personal effort to determine the politically astute course of action. Congress sent its own delegation to New Orleans, conducting hearings chaired by Massachusetts Senator George Hoar. After a brief inquiry, Sheridan reported that conservatives had perpetrated no fewer than 2,500 political murders in the state since the end of the Civil War. The general characterized the leadership of the white community in Louisiana as "banditti."

In a move that would forever blacken his reputation in the Pelican State, Sheridan imposed a curfew and suspended the public observances of the Mardi Gras holiday. He would have liked to do more. "What you want to do," Sheridan informed Senator Hoar over breakfast at the St. Charles Hotel (during which native patrons openly groaned and hissed at their table), "is to suspend the what-do-you-call it."[51]

The writ of habeas corpus—notwithstanding President Grant's recognition of a state of insurrection in Louisiana—now provided a bulwark beyond which the enemies of white supremacy would not dare to venture. The president remained personally appalled by the violence in Louisiana, citing specifics of the Colfax case in a message to Congress in January 1875.[52] In the aftermath of the *Cruikshank* decision in the circuit court, however, his administration felt compelled to forfeit its prerogatives under the Enforcement Acts of 1870 and 1871, most of all the extreme provisions of the Ku Klux Klan legislation that permitted incarceration without representation. The show of federal force in the Colfax prosecutions had resulted in setbacks to the project of pacification and reconciliation that would last for generations. "They thought to 'fire the northern heart'" in the *Cruikshank* prosecution, "but it wouldn't fire at all," a Democrat exulted just after the New Year. "The North is becoming tired of the eternal nigger, to whom the greatness, glory, and prosperity of this country has been sacrificed."[53] Rather than pursue the maximalist solutions advocated by Sheridan and other radicals, the country as a whole would direct its attention elsewhere in 1875 and afterward. Republicans of either race would be required to fend for themselves.

The Legacy
of *Cruikshank*

THE PHILANTHROPIST PAUL TULANE, WHOSE 1882 bequest established the New Orleans university that bears his name, traveled to Europe in the 1840s in the company of his French-born father. Louis Tulane had made his fortune in the jewel of the Americas, St. Domingue, during the decades when sugar was made with blood and worth its weight in gold in the Atlantic markets. As a refugee from revolutionary Haiti in the twilight of his life, he led his grown-up son on a tour of France dimmed by nostalgia and regret. While the likes of Paul Tulane's contemporary, Meredith Calhoun, enjoyed the elegant society of Paris and its old-regime suburbs, the Tulanes haunted the half-abandoned seaboard towns that had served as the trade and transit terminals of the West Indies boom. Like the merchant mariner Calhoun and his erstwhile sponsor, Stephen Girard, the elder Tulane had once heard the clink of money in the very syllables of Nantes and Bordeaux.

In contrast, on their journey 20 years before the Civil War, they saw the rusted gates of warehouses hanging on a single hinge. Sounds emanating from a street-side room of "a noble mansion—almost a palace," Paul remembered, proved to be the hammer of a cobbler patching shoes amid the humble trappings of his trade. Heading home to New Orleans, he learned the purpose of his father's somber itinerary. "Nantes and Bordeaux were built up on the West Indies trade," Tulane declared.

The abolition of slavery in the dominion of France after the Haitian Revolution and the termination of the transatlantic slave trade by the British Navy in the 1830s had destroyed them. "You will see New Orleans," he predicted, "which, like them, is dependent on slavery fall into like circumstances." Deprived of the illicit foundations of its bounty, the Haitian exile said, "New Orleans will be ruined."[1]

As evidenced by their historic gift, the lessons of the Haitian Revolution safeguarded the Tulane family fortune against the perils of Emancipation. Civil War and Reconstruction notwithstanding, Paul Tulane contributed nearly $400,000 to improve education in New Orleans before his death in the 1890s. Around him, the business capital of the Old South had eased into genteel disintegration, disguising its distress behind a mask of revelry in bygone ways. Stranded on low ground by the historic cataclysm of slavery, the black population of New Orleans remained even as the demand for its labor ebbed away. The elements themselves conspired to uproot all the artifacts of New Orleans's golden age.

The site of the 1873 bloodshed likewise passed into an era of increasing irrelevance. Once a rampart of global commerce, the town of Colfax gradually surrendered to its ghosts. Its capitalist dynasty hobbled forward in the new era in the person of the disgraced hunchback. Meredith Calhoun's legacy proved to be enduringly poisonous for Poor Willie and his artificially extended Louisiana household, now consigned to subordinate political and economic status in the old domain. With the force of original sin, the devastation willed into the world by the seizure of free people into slavery continued in the successive generations. Colfax became a town where even the new white masters subsisted in perpetual dearth of prosperity. Its tribute to its past was inscribed upon a roadside marker that few outsiders would pass.

A late victory for the cause of white supremacy in Colfax, the Supreme Court decision in *U.S. v. Cruikshank,* arrived without fanfare on March 28, 1876. Louisianans had contributed their share to the high court proceedings of the state's most notorious criminal case. The chief counsel for the original bench of Grant Parish prisoners, New Orleans attorney R. H. Marr, continued to represent William Cruikshank, J. P. Hadnot, and William Irwin during the appeal of their conviction. For the white citizens of Colfax and its environment, however, the urgency of the case had receded when the circuit court set all the men

at liberty pending their appeal. Acting on the promise of impunity in
Justice Bradley's opinion of 1874, White Leaguers on the Red River and
elsewhere saw the outcome of the high court case as the likely restate-
ment of a foregone conclusion.

A counterpart to the ennui of Louisiana racists could be found
among their erstwhile rivals in the Grant administration, which devoted
minimal resources to the *Cruikshank* case. The government's man in
Louisiana, by the time of the hearings in Washington, had long since
quit the case. Within months of the Bradley verdict, Attorney General
Beckwith had resigned his post under pressure from the murderous
White League.[2] For his part, Attorney General George Williams, who
had promptly instructed U.S. lawyers across the South to curtail prosecutions under the Enforcement Acts, took charge of *Cruikshank* with
the detachment of a mortuary aide. The Justice Department's brief to the
Supreme Court summarized the infamous facts of the case in bloodless
prose and all but ignored the legislation that had enabled the federal
charges against the perpetrators. Incredibly, the government chose to
omit any reference to the racial identity or political rights of the Colfax
victims, including the relevant protections of the 15th Amendment.[3]

The defense, in contrast, mounted a first-rate case. Informed by
Marr's knowledge of the Louisiana trials and verdicts, august names of
the federal bar coalesced around the cause of Cruikshank, Hadnot, and
the unnamed Klansmen who might share their fate. Two of the eight
members of the all-star team had served in Congress; an Alabamian
who had resigned from the Supreme Court in 1861, Justice John A.
Campbell, lent additional prestige. Reverdy Johnson, who died shortly
before the final verdict, had been Attorney General of the United States
and a participant in the first Enforcement Acts prosecutions in South
Carolina in 1871. Including the Californian David Dudley Field, whose
brother and long-time law partner Stephen sat in judgment with the
current Court, the defense team spoke with the authority of broad credentials and overwhelming political clout. Their fervent dedication to
the *Cruikshank* cause deluged the bench with documents and impas-
sioned courtroom oratory.[4]

More than simple prejudice inspired the rally in defense of the
Colfax killers. In the first centennial celebration year 1876, the defense
of the Colfax killers invoked a fundamental premise of the American
experiment, that the government that governs best, governs least. In the

emergency of war and Reconstruction, the characteristically American suspicion of authority had not abated. Peace, in fact, required the relaxation of the armored grip. Force, as conceived in the legislation condemned with that term, threatened basic privileges of free citizens, including the right of rebellious, dissident intent, made sacred in 1776.

Their claims as Sons of Liberty notwithstanding, however, the enemies of *Cruikshank* served the counterrevolution. Holding Justice by the sword-arm, the conservatives sacrificed a vibrant minority to the unhidden agents of terrorism.

The Supreme Court's decision was unanimous. Delivered on the same day as the unanimous verdict in *U.S. v. Reese,* another Enforcement Acts and 15th Amendment case, *U.S. v. Cruikshank* defined the legal standing of experimental federal electoral politics in the South. *Reese* was a poll tax and ballot box case, arising from maneuvers at the county level in Kentucky to disqualify black voters by bureaucratic obfuscation. Dismissing the charges in the indictment, the author of the majority opinion, Chief Justice Morrison Waite, directly invalidated sections 3 and 4 of the 1870 Enforcement Act, specifically the power to prosecute and fine electoral officials who placed barriers on voting.[5] The blunt rebuke to overreaching in the congressional branch represented a rare exercise of the power of judicial review, in an era when the Supreme Court was moving into a new era of assertive participation in political checks and balances.[6]

Cruikshank, in legal terms, struck a more glancing blow to voting rights enforcement. In considering the case, which was certified to the court upon Justice Bradley's objection to the convictions in the circuit court, the nine justices of the Supreme Court took up the defense motion in arrest of judgment, its original claim against the charges in the U.S. indictment. Its ruling merely dismissed Attorney Beckwith's 41-page indictment as insufficient, leaving open the possibility that prosecutors could and should have drawn appropriate criminal charges under the Enforcement Acts.

The problem, according to Chief Justice Waite, who wrote the opinion, stemmed from the prosecution's failure to sufficiently describe the racial dynamics of the crimes at Colfax. The text of the indictment omitted what Waite called "a description of the substance of the offence." In fact, the district attorney had presented the facts of the case in the indictment in terms explicitly linked to offenses under the Enforcement Acts without attempting to establish a narrative of the events that culminated in the Easter Sunday massacre. Without reference to the political context of the struggle, the charges led Waite to "suspect that race was the cause of the hostility." But as it "was not so averred," he insisted that the court could scarcely apply the protections of the 14th and 15th Amendments, which the *Slaughterhouse* and other decisions had declared to apply exclusively to African Americans. "The defect here is not in form," wrote the chief justice, "but in substance." Only the most narrowly defined charges of racial discrimination in politics could invoke the special protections of the Civil War amendments.[7]

The ruling dismissed the *Cruikshank* prosecution on technical grounds, but Waite's opinion ventured deeper, addressing the fundamental political issues raised by the case. Government exists, wrote the chief justice, to protect the rights of citizens; and yet the "duty of government to afford protection is limited always by the power it possesses for that purpose."[8] Life, liberty, and property—despite the guarantees of the 14th Amendment, represented the "very highest duty of the States, when they entered into the Union under the Constitution." Thus, "[s]overeignty, for this purpose, rests alone with the States." The 14th Amendment's guarantees of these "inalienable rights" in its due process clause, following Waite's reasoning, were extraneous and "add[ed] nothing to the rights of one citizen as against another." The 15th Amendment, likewise, did not confer a positive right of suffrage on African American men, but merely secured them against discrimination based on color. "The right to vote in the States comes from the States," wrote the chief justice, where the United States could protect "no voters of their own creation."

The legal outcome of the *Cruikshank* decision was minimal: Congress was asked to revise the Enforcement Acts to ensure that their provisions applied exclusively to acts that prejudiced the civil and political rights of African Americans as guaranteed in the 14th and 15th Amendments. In political terms, however, the court's instructions spelled the end of federal intervention in southern civil rights and voting rights abuses. The Congress charged with the task of engineering sustainable federal prerogatives had little interest in the problem. Indeed, since the 1874 elections the conservative Democratic Party had control of the House of Representatives. The Republicans—once passionately committed to its emerging rank and file in the South—had largely turned its back on the Reconstruction-era, black-and-white North-South coalition and come to concentrate on building bridges between the interests of white men in the North and the West.[9] The age of revolution had abated.

The reaction moved forward with historic and sustained political momentum. The campaign to redeem the South channeled all the strong emotions of secession and defeat. In 1876, white Louisianans continued to groan under the heel of those they viewed as black and federal usurpers. More than half of the registered voters in the state that year were African American men, most of whom refused to be intimidated by the victory of white supremacy in *Cruikshank* and *Reese*. With black voter turnout over 75 percent in the fall elections, White Leaguers were required to engage in furious and scurrilous maneuvers to suppress the ballots.[10] Bald-faced fraud and mass confusion in Louisiana (along with two other southern states) compromised the credentials of electors in the presidential contest, leaving the outcome of the 1876 election in the hands of Congress. Thus the lawlessness inspired in part by the Colfax Massacre and *Cruikshank* came to play a role in the electoral compromise that ended Reconstruction, formally and permanently, and recognized the moderate Republican presidency of Rutherford B. Hayes.

In another politically potent parade, U.S. Army troops took their final leave of Louisiana in April 1877, marching ceremonially before packed crowds in the French Quarter of New Orleans. The sounds of military brass echoed through its narrow streets one final time, punctuated continually by triumphant rebel yells.[11]

The campaign to reduce black political participation proceeded fitfully and painfully in the coming years. The decisions in the voting rights cases, *Cruikshank* and *Reese,* had not disavowed black enfranchisement, or even the federal obligation to prevent its obstruction. The rulings only limited the likelihood of intervention to prevent systematic abuses. In combination with the withdrawal of troops stipulated in the 1876 agreement, this bar to oversight empowered mass intimidations and manipulations at the polls. Democrats in the South accepted this obligation without shame, as expressed in the words of a song circulated to the faithful in advance of the 1880 contest.

> Just one ballot to each man—
> That is, one to each Caucasian.

We are getting shet of niggers
And, without the soldiers' aid,
We can fix the 'lection figgers.
March 'em off, for we're afraid.[12]

Eighteen seventy-nine, the year that self-styled "Bourbons" chanted the doggerel from "We're Afraid," saw the heavily Democratic new state legislature in Louisiana vote to hold a new constitutional convention to replace the hated Reconstruction-era document. Legislators borrowed directly from Justice Waite's opinion in *U.S. v. Cruikshank* when they demanded relief from the burdens of black enfranchisement, asserting that "the Constitution of the United States has not conferred the right of suffrage upon anyone."[13] The 1879 Louisiana Constitution did not fulfill the worst expectations of African Americans in Louisiana, who feared they would not only lose the right to vote but would also be confined upon plantations in a reprisal of the Black Codes and conditions of slavery. However, they would surrender much of their political power to gerrymandered congressional and legislative redistricting. Most important, the Constitution chose to schedule future state and local elections in odd-numbered years, separating them from congressional and presidential contests, and thus precluding additional federal oversight.[14] In the ten years after the ratification of the new constitution, the black electorate in Louisiana contracted by more than 30 percent.[15]

Colfax and its surrounding parishes would be "redeemed" by Democrats in keeping with the larger state and sectional momentum. A black political organizer based in Shreveport, Henry Adams, observed a range of electoral manipulations in the Red River country between 1876 and 1879. Technically color-blind accommodations, including the last-minute relocation of polling sites and the use of multiple ballot boxes, suppressed and discounted the African American vote. Registrars insisted that names did not appear on lists of voters, mocking blacks as illiterates and accusing them of identity fraud. As experts of a practice known as "counting out," white electoral officials ensured that voting tallies in white precincts sufficed to overwhelm the voices of blacks who managed to cast their ballots. Force remained a ready resort. Throughout the election season, White Leaguers and their allies mounted militant displays that terrified Republican organizers and intimidated would-be candidates and voters.[16]

A grand jury investigating electoral misconduct after 1878 concluded without indictments after two black witnesses were murdered on their way to testify in New Orleans.[17]

The piney-woods country of Central Louisiana emerged as the political stronghold of white supremacy in the state. Organizers of the Colfax Massacre stood as Democratic candidates in Grant Parish in the 1876 and 1878 elections and were elected. C. C. Dunn, who had purchased horses for participants from Natchitoches and coordinated the acquisition of the little cannon, became president of the Grant Parish police jury, the sole agency of local government. Alphonse Cazabat became parish attorney. The would-be sheriff Columbus Nash was content to serve as parish tax collector in 1877; his efforts resulted in $7,307 in tax payments, in contrast to $863 collected by his Republican predecessor. In subsequent years, Nash opened a prosperous store in the town, serving on the police jury, the school board, and every important committee of public interest. After the second courthouse and all the records of the parish burned in 1878, for example, Nash served on the committee that considered a petition to relocate the parish seat closer to the whites-only community of Montgomery. The intervention of Ada Calhoun (now married to George W. Lane of Huntsville and New Orleans) saved the day for the town of Colfax when Nash and company accepted her donation of a 21-acre plot (including the unmarked grave of Colfax victims) to serve as the future courthouse site.[18]

The notorious Calhouns remained active in community affairs despite the changing political character of Grant Parish. Their persistence is hard to explain, and particularly anomalous in the case of the worldly Miss Ada, who apparently spent little time on the family plantations prior to the late 1870s. As Mrs. Lane, Ada took an activist role in the management of what remained of her father's estate, spending many months in residence amid the ruins of the family plantations. Business was not booming. As recorded in the annual reports of yields from sugar plantations, the great mill at Firenze fired irregularly, producing a dozen or so hogsheads every two or three years, and ceasing forever after a catastrophic boiler explosion in 1889, which claimed the lives of eight attendants.[19] Annual yields in cotton—largely collected from sharecroppers—and the sale of lands in private deals and sheriffs' auctions now served as the mainstay of Meredith Calhoun's posterity in Colfax.

Ada Lane also took a firm hand in the management of Calhoun family affairs. With her encouragement, perhaps, and certainly with the endorsement of the white community around Colfax, William Smith Calhoun was persuaded to be married to a white woman, Cora Purvis of Mobile, Alabama, with whom he eloped some time around 1880. Within a year or two of the ceremony, Olivia Williams, who had given birth to Calhoun's two mixed-race sons, was dead. According to the family legend, the scalawag's cast-off mulatto bride met her end at the hand of Ada Calhoun Lane, who took advantage of an epidemic of yellow fever in 1878 to eliminate the stain on the family's reputation. Conscious but delirious with fever (or in the suspended state said to be characteristic of the disease), Olivia Williams was allegedly buried alive, begging Ada for mercy until the final shovelful of dirt.[20]

The children of Olivia Williams were likewise removed from the scene, appearing on the census in New Orleans in the household of a mulatto freedwoman named P. Williams. William Calhoun, Jr., who supposedly witnessed his mother's premature interment, would later renounce all connection with the family and refuse his aunt's offer of a share of inheritance.[21]

His older brother, Eugene, found his way into the household of railroad financier Jay Gould, whose interest in the New Orleans Pacific Railroad brought him briefly to Central Louisiana in the late 1880s. William Smith Calhoun, who served as a director of the line, known locally as the Backbone, must have made Gould's acquaintance at this time and sought accommodations for his son. As a servant in the Gould mansion at 579 Fifth Avenue in New York, where elaborate security measures were employed to protect the family of the self-described "most hated man in America," Eugene apparently found a kind of sanctuary. He would remain there as head butler, passing as white, until the death of the robber baron's straightlaced philanthropist daughter, Helen Gould Shepard, in 1938.[22]

Others on the losing side of the racial divide in Colfax adjusted with more difficulty. Between 1875 and 1879, African Americans in the area participated in a campaign to vacate the scene of their recent distress and establish an autonomous community of blacks in an unspoiled location. The Exodusters, as they called themselves, had their origins in a Shreveport-based freedmen's organization known only as "the Committee," led by a dynamic former slave named Henry Adams. The climax of the Exoduster movement unfolded in the spring of 1879, when some 6,000 African Americans, including many from the

Red River valley, migrated en masse to found a settlement in Kansas. "Kansas Fever" inspired harsh reprisals on the part of white elites, who had already taken steps to halt the disappearance of their disappointed workforce. As late as 1916, long after the collapse of the Kansas community had put an end to the Committee's utopian schemes, outmigration remained an attractive option for Louisiana's disaffected African Americans. That year, the mayor of New Orleans petitioned unsuccessfully for local railroads to refuse to carry local blacks out of state toward the Promised Land.[23]

Black survivors of the courthouse defense and massacre tended to stay close to home. Militia captain William Ward, who won another term in the Louisiana Senate in the deal that settled the contested election of 1876, severed his ties to Grant Parish after his summary ejection from the legislature in an incident involving his use of a gun in the Senate chamber. "This is the kind of disturbance that they have in the Louisiana legislature," began an unsympathetic account in a national political journal:

> a fellow named Ward, representative from Grant Parish, was ruled out of order. Thereupon he took possession of the floor. The chair, he said, paid no attention to him. "I will be heard," "I will be heard," he repeated again and again, with domineering voice and manner and ferocious gestures. Every time he uttered this sentence he brought his fist down flat upon his desk, producing a sound like the discharge of a musket. The chair ordered the sergeant-at-arms to seat him, but as soon as the sergeant-at-arms approached him he drew a revolver and dared the officer to touch him. The sergeant-at-arms then called to his aid the metropolitan police [*sic*] stationed in the building....By the call of the bugle the Captain summoned his men to arms and the excitement was intense. He was taken out of the building amid cries of "bring him back," "expel him," "he's a damn scoundrel," "let's get rid of him." Then the colored members got the floor and denounced him most vigorously (we forgot to say that Ward is colored), as having caused the death of those who fell in the Grant Parish massacre, and one of them offered a resolution of expulsion. Indeed, he had no friends; as he deserved none [and] he was expelled by a vote of 49 to 9.[24]

Still disabled by tuberculosis and rheumatism, Ward lived out the remainder of his life in an apartment on Rampart Street in New Orleans, collecting a soldier's pension from the U.S. government.[25]

THE LEGACY OF CRUIKSHANK   163

Alabama Mitchell and Cuffy Gaines remained in Colfax as share-croppers, residing with their families on a plantation owned by William Smith Calhoun. By 1900, both men had found their way into the federal army pension system, with the liberal assistance of members of the white establishment. Mitchell, for example, received an early disability pension with the aid of his old nemesis Dr. Milton Dunn, who provided sworn testimony about Mitchell's identity and medical reports about the lasting effects of the gunshot wound to the leg that Dunn himself had almost certainly inflicted. Surrounded by family (including a son named after William Calhoun), Mitchell died in 1924 at age 78.[26]

For the few effective radicals and blacks remaining in the national Republican coalition, the plight of southern migrants and tenants signaled the premature loss of faith in the success of the democratic experiment. "[The Negro] has a standing in the supreme law of the land," the old survivor Frederick Douglass urged against the momentum of despair, "[t]he permanent powers of the government are all on his side." Notwithstanding the surrender of federal prerogatives in *Cruikshank* and the groundswell of white militancy, Douglass exhorted, Reconstruction's promise of racial equality could not be overcome by killing and hate. "What though for the moment the hand of violence strikes down the negro's rights in the South," he wrote, at the dawn of the Jim Crow era in the 1880s, "those rights will revive, survive, and flourish again."[27]

Poor Willie, the hunchback, died in 1891 at the age of 55, survived by Cora and their young white daughter. His obituary, in the recently established, conservative *Colfax Chronicle,* provides one of the few reflections on his character that survives in print. Its revealing and poignant assessment of his life is worthy of an extended quotation:

> The deceased has been a remarkably eccentric and noted character in this region for years. Indeed, he was well known throughout the entire state, from his connection with public affairs at and subsequent to the creation of Grant Parish....He was of a taciturn and cynical disposition, but with it all never refused to secretly bestow liberal charity whenever he thought it deserved. Many believed him to be heartless and unsympathetic, still it is a fact that he did hundreds of kindly acts but seemed through some inconsistent perverseness to delight in being thought otherwise than liberal and humane. In his

time he had the control of great wealth, but his management was always marked by strangeness and eccentricity of careless lavishness that was altogether unaccountable. His death was sudden and unexpected, the result of cold combined with longstanding asthmatic affliction. He was buried...in the yard of his residence on the bank of the Red River, near the graves of his children.

Very gently, in light of the tumult that surrounded Calhoun's life in the town he established, the editor of the *Chronicle* gave voice to a spirit of conciliation. "May the sod conceal all his faults from human eyes," he wrote, "and only his kindly deeds be remembered."[28]

By the time of Calhoun's death, a gauze of sentiment had come to cover the prevailing white remembrance of the Colfax Massacre. The first retrospective of the event appeared in an inaugural edition of the *Colfax Chronicle* and retained a measure of the old spirit of finger-pointing and defensiveness.[29] By the early 20th century, however, when the son of "Captain" C. C. Dunn began collecting the reminiscences of his fellow participants, a tone of filial reverence and homage to the passing generation had been established. This spirit reached an early high point three years later, in an obituary for Dunn clipped from the *Shreveport Journal:* "Captain C. C. Dunn was of that stalwart crew...who have made the 'new south,' and to his name, an old friend subscribes: 'The passing tribute of a sigh.'"[30] Dr. Milton Dunn of Natchitoches, the captain's son, emerged as the most visible "veteran" of the violence and dedicated long hours to the preservation of its memory.

The era of commemoration of the "riot" moved toward its climax amid another striking realignment of Louisiana's political caste. White supremacists had grown tired of election season violence and manipulations. In particular, they shrank from the ongoing need to falsify electoral returns in a state where 44 percent of registered voters were black. "It is true that we win these elections," an editor of the conservative *New Orleans Times-Democrat* wrote in the 1890s, "but at a heavy cost, and by the use of methods repugnant to our idea of political honesty and which must, in time, demoralize the people of Louisiana." With populist candidates speaking ominously about building a political alliance between blacks and poor whites, Louisiana's Democratic majority sought to erect insuperable obstacles to black participation and convened a constitutional convention for that specific purpose in 1898.[31]

The president of the 1898 convention acknowledged from the podium that they met "principally to deal with one question"—black disenfranchisement. The solution would be far from straightforward, owing to the difficulty of keeping the door open to poor and illiterate whites while avoiding reference to color, which would activate the protections of the 15th Amendment. The authors of the new constitution would ultimately congratulate themselves on developing "an *elastic* test—that is, a test which could be interpreted by registration or election officials" to achieve the necessary effect. Its primary mechanism was a complex voter registration form, asking voters to account for their age in years, months, and days; to correctly identify their ward and precinct numbers; and to swear that they have not lived in a "common law" marriage or fathered an illegitimate child. Any errors or false statements became grounds for rejection. To reinforce the wide authority invested in registrars by the form, the 1898 constitution also imposed the first "grandfather clause" in the history of the South. Its provisions permitted illiterates and others who could not complete the registration form correctly to vote if their ancestors had been eligible to vote before the Reconstruction Act of 1867 had initiated the failed experiment with black suffrage.[32]

Louisiana's ruling class was ecstatic. "The white supremacy for which we have so long struggled at the cost of so much blood," wrote the governor, "is now crystallized into the Constitution as a fundamental part and parcel."[33]

The results were immediate and dramatic. Whereas 130,444 African American men had been registered to vote in the 1896 elections, only 5,320 remained eligible in 1900, a loss of more than 95 percent. African Americans now constituted only 4 percent of registered voters in the state. By 1904, the number of voters had dropped to just over 1,000, representing less than 2 percent of age-eligible black men. Black-majority parishes, including those in the vicinity of Colfax, returned large majorities for white supremacist candidates, who committed their offices to the legal and official subjugation of the black community.[34]

Segregation was the most visible component of the white supremacist agenda. Louisiana took the lead in denying equal access to public spaces as decisively as it had in the political arena. Even before the disenfranchising constitution of 1898, the state's pioneering segregation laws had produced another chilling pronouncement from the Supreme Court of the United States. The landmark decision in *Plessy v. Ferguson* in 1896 legitimated Louisiana laws, such as the state's railroad-car statutes, that reserved public accommodations for whites. Similar laws erected a host of quotidian humiliations for African Americans in Louisiana and the South. Designating separate and unequal facilities for whites and "coloreds," segregation emerged as the most notorious example of Southern excesses in the twentieth century.

For all its sting, however, segregation merely symbolized the subordinate status guaranteed by more invidiously devastating public policy. Economic subjugation persisted in the twentieth century as the *raison d'être* of white supremacy. Whites in government ensured the relative prosperity of the master race by unequal distribution of the public wealth. In 1920, for example, the Louisiana state government provided up to $37 per pupil to educate white students in the public schools, but only $3.49 for each black pupil.[35] Similar disparities prevailed in sanitation, agricultural, and health services. Starved for education and other assistance, black communities sank deeper into poverty and dependency in rural communities and in cities such as Shreveport and New Orleans. White employers exploited this distress with low wages and abysmal working conditions.

The practice of convict leasing showed the system of repression at its worst. As early as 1883, the critic and muckraker George Washington Cable decried the abuse of Louisiana's courts and prisons on behalf of white employers. "What shall we say to such sentences inflicted for larceny as 12, 14, 15, 20, and in one case 40 years of a penal service whose brutal tasks and whippings kill in an average of five years?" he asked. Cable's investigation revealed the wholesale abuse of prisoners by leaseholders, whose contracts for farm laborers and other projects absorbed the whole expense of incarcerating prisoners. Echoing the protests of William Ward, who made convict-leasing and prison reform the focus of his short career as Grant Parish's representative in the state legislature, Cable described the penal system in the state as a "field of blood," in which 14 percent of inmates lost their lives each year to brutal working and living conditions.[36]

Violence and the threat of violence provided the structural underpinnings of white supremacy and black subordination, and yet Louisiana's experience of the Jim Crow century proved remarkably quiet. Across the South, racial tension and competition erupted in periodic bloodletting.

Lynch law claimed the lives of thousands of individual blacks on spe-
cious claims of sexual improprieties and other charges. A handful of
confrontations escalated into full-blown "riots" that resulted in dozens
or hundreds of black deaths. In Wilmington, North Carolina in 1898,
in Rosewood, Florida in 1921, and in Tulsa, Oklahoma in 1922, white
marauders in command of government and the press would be spared
the indignity of any public inquiry into their crimes.

White Louisiana had known riots and had unflinchingly stared
down the scrutiny of outraged observers. It would brook no challenge
in the aftermath of Colfax and Redemption. While their counterparts
in other states struggled to assert their supremacy, white supremacists in
Louisiana could enjoy a measure of security on the basis of their fearsome and enduring victory. They would gratefully acknowledge this
advantage in a series of reverent commemorations of the massacre
of 1873.

The occasion of the next great war produced a flood of emotion for
veterans of the Confederacy and the Colfax Massacre. In September
1914, white participants in the raid met in the reconstructed courthouse
to pray for the United States and to raise a glass or two in remembrance
of old times. All but five of the surviving members of the old-time Klan
participated in a ceremony in which the names of all participants were
read aloud to an assembly of citizens of Colfax. "When Roll Call came
it was [as] solemn as much as anything [you] ever saw," wrote Milton
Dunn to an absent comrade. "It was a dead hush for some time but what
with the sighs [of] weeping women broke forth the most tumultuous
cheering ever heard." Dunn and others in the line of veterans com-
ported themselves with manly dignity. "Somehow I stood firm [and]
did not give way—not that emotions did not move my heart for my
beloved comrades."[37]

By 1920, sentiment had given way to decisive action to commemo-
rate the victory of white supremacy at Colfax. The Ku Klux Klan,
reborn amid a national firestorm of negativity and prejudice, burnished
the bloody history of Colfax as a triumph for the righteous. The Grant
Parish Police Jury voted to honor the grave of Sidney Harris, one of
the three white men killed during the attack, and the only one who
was buried in the little graveyard adjacent to the courthouse in the
center of town. Within a year, the initiative resulted in the erection
of a monument to all three of the white "victims" of the massacre.

The monument, unveiled in a public ceremony on April 13, 1921, featured a white obelisk about eleven feet high, which bore the following inscription:

> In Loving Remembrance
> Erected to the Memory of the Heroes
> Stephen Decatur Parish
> James West Hadnot
> Sidney Harris
> Who fell in the Colfax Riot fighting
> for White Supremacy
> April 13, 1873

A soaking rain fell on the day of the dedication, but the white community for miles around turned out in force. Led by a marching band, the veterans of the fight marched under umbrellas to the cemetery, where the students of the all-white Colfax High School processed around the little monument to music, dropping flowers. The widows and daughters of the fallen men unveiled the obelisk, and the assembled crowd sang "Tenting on the Old Camp Ground."

With old age diminishing their numbers and their glory—a tragedy epitomized by the absence of the ailing C. C. Nash—the final stanza of the song assumed a special poignancy for the crowd.

> Many are the hearts that are weary tonight,
> Wishing for the war to cease;
> Many are the hearts looking for the right
> To see the dawn of peace.
> Dying tonight,
> Dying tonight,
> Dying on the old Camp ground.

Nonetheless they proceeded resolutely through the rain once more toward the center of the town. There, they stopped to designate as a memorial the old pecan tree where the Colfax stalwarts had murdered their black prisoners on Easter Sunday night. A copper plaque provided by the American Forestry Association was affixed near the spot where the earth had been darkened with black men's blood.[38]

Within a few years of the dedication of the monument, white Colfax residents began to promote the thesis that the 1873 "riot" had effectively terminated the national experiment with Reconstruction in the South. Citing the importance of *U.S. v. Cruikshank* in facilitating the reassertion of southern political will, the editor of the *Colfax Chronicle* established the small town's claim to fame in a 1926 article. "The decision of the Supreme Court destroyed Reconstruction and all of its works and the national government was compelled to abandon a policy of force towards the South and adopt a policy that might conform to the requirements of civilization and the rights of man," he wrote.[39] A local booster, writing for a national trade journal, was bold enough to call the massacre "the most important event in the life of the nation after Appomattox."[40]

This inflated opinion of the significance of the event came to dominate what passed for the full spectrum of political and cultural opinion in Louisiana. White progressives, embodied in the person of Cammie G. Henry, embraced the preservation of its memory in the overlapping enterprises of Melrose Place, the Natchitoches plantation house where Henry assembled scrapbooks and patronized folk arts and Creole literature. Conservatives in the Louisiana legislature and in the highway department chose to recognize the Colfax Riot with the historical marker celebrating the demise of "carpetbag misrule in the South."

Professional historians maintained a dignified silence about claims for the glory of Colfax. In an era when sympathy for southern nationalism dominated the study of the Reconstruction era in American universities, the bloody excesses of provincial Democrats found few enthusiasts among professors out of state. Reflecting their distaste for its gory backstory, perhaps, the decision in *U.S. v. Cruikshank* appeared near the bottom of the list of landmark cases in Reconstruction jurisprudence. Half-remembered, the history of the Colfax Massacre remained a subject for the citizens of Colfax, whose pride in the era of war and Reconstruction came to substitute for prosperity and wholesome community in the 20th century.

In Colfax and Louisiana as a whole, the boisterous energy and murderous drive of the past subsided as the great engines of capitalism shuddered and slowed. The golden age of cotton and the sugar plantations gave way to an era of tourism and small business. New Orleans, once a crucible of global interests, maintained a foothold with its modernized port facilities and petroleum refineries. Swelled with refugees of the growing rural underclass, however, the city surrendered its low-lying districts to despair.

Good government went the way of booming business, as the state became infamous for demagoguery and corruption in politics. President Lyndon Johnson, stopping in New Orleans during his triumphant reelection campaign in 1964, acknowledged that his advocacy of racial equality made him unlikely to win votes in segregationist Louisiana. For the same reason, however, he suggested that the people of Louisiana had paid a high price for the victory of white supremacy. "I'm going to give you a good Democratic speech," the president announced, identifying his party with the liberal values that had shaped its national policies since the 1930s. "The poor old State," he jibed, drawling, in an anecdote about Mississippi, "they haven't heard a Democratic speech in 30 years. All they ever hear at election time is nigra, nigra, nigra."[41]

Johnson's plain talk about the crippling legacy of racial subjugation in the South was paired with decisive action in the Civil Rights Act of 1964 and the Voting Rights Act of 1965, arguably the most sweeping acts of Congress since Reconstruction. Revisiting the prerogatives assigned to government in the defunct Ku Klux Klan and Enforcement Acts of the 1870s, the legislation wielded the 14th and 15th Amendments on behalf of a crusade to enlarge the sphere of privileges of citizenship.

Louisiana, the dark and bloody ground of the First Reconstruction, would assume a more moderate face in the second, staying out of the headlines in the 1960s while neighboring Deep South states shocked respectable opinion. Many of its parishes, however, including Grant, qualified as Voting Rights Act "specially covered areas" by virtue of low rates of black voter participation and were subjected to federal oversight. Prompted by the federal government, registration of African Americans in the Red River parishes increased as much as 1,000 percent. In the first 20 years of enforcement, the Voting Rights Act enlarged Louisiana's total electorate by one quarter and resulted in the election of hundreds of African American officials, including long-serving sheriffs and police jurors in the parish of Grant.[42]

Along with voting rights, African Americans insisted on recognition in the decades after 1965. The demand for black history—presented in force on university campuses far from Grant Parish—mobilized scholars and students in pursuit of suppressed and forgotten truths. For John Hope Franklin, a leader in the new field who was himself a survivor of the Tulsa race riot of 1923, the scholarship of the late 1960s conveyed "an exhilarating sense of discovery...not unlike that conveyed by Ripley's 'Believe It or Not.' "[43] Franklin and his students, for example, in seeking to reconstruct the history of the Tulsa Riot, were forced by the silence of published sources to rely on the memory and oral history of black survivors. Such revelations confirmed and explained the subjugation that African Americans in the South and elsewhere still struggled to overcome.

The untold story of the Colfax Massacre takes its place among the tragedies and curiosities of Believe-It-or-Not black history. Developed late, in the light of the 21st century, its story must yet be reconciled into the broader narrative of American history. At the end of the inquiry, the effect that strains credulity most remains the novelty of its details and sweep: old times such as these were painful to remember, but best not forgotten. Overlooked but under close consideration at last, the hidden history of the Colfax Massacre tells a story of its own time as well, and of the ongoing, engaging process of overcoming.

Acknowledgments

LIBERAL WHITE SOUTHERNERS SUCH AS THOSE IN MY FAMILY ARE uncomfortable with the politics and logic of the saying, "Southern by the Grace of God." And yet I must credit my Alabama upbringing for expediting my process of research and discovery. The serendipity that placed the origins of the story of the Colfax Massacre in my north Alabama hometown mobilized the great expertise of a family friend—Tom Carney of *Old Huntsville Magazine*—on my behalf. Tom's early contributions saved numerous steps and enriched the content of the whole.

Other writers and hobbyists with an interest in southern and Louisiana history also lent their aid. I am indebted to J. Greggory Davies, Bill and Charlotte Horacek, Don Maher, Glynn Maxwell, Charles Stansell, Lalita Tademy, and Stefanie Troup for documents, articles, readings, and encouragement. Tybring Hemphill, who traced his Calhoun family roots from Louisiana to British Columbia, generously copied and mailed the results of years of genealogical inquiry.

Professional historians played a key role in shaping and steering the project. I turned first to my former graduate instructor, R. Kent Newmyer, professor of law and history at the University of Connecticut. I also worked closely with Robert Kaczorowski of Fordham University, who loaned primary documents and made helpful comments on early versions of the legal analysis. I am grateful to Ryland Clarke, J. Garry Clifford, Stephen P. Halbrook, Sarah Heard, Tod Houghtlin, Massimo Maglione,

Thomas G. Paterson, and Joel Sipress. Jon Deiss, a professional researcher, expertly reviewed military records at the National Archives. Thanks also to Nandini Roy.

This work would not have been possible without the immense resources of the New York Public Library and its magnificent branches on Fifth Avenue at 42nd Street and at the Schomberg Center for Research in Black Culture in Harlem. I also had the advantage of working with Mary Linn Wernet and Sonny Carter at the Cammie G. Henry Research Center at Northwestern State University in Natchitoches, Louisiana— probably one of the best small archives in the country—which provided reams of customized materials online and by mail. Special thanks to John Magill, Sally Stassi, and Mary Lou Eichhorn of the Historic New Orleans Collection, to Melissa Smith at the Tulane University Archives, and to Becky Nugent, Doris Lively, and Denise Pearson at the Grant Parish Library in Colfax.

Andrew Stuart, David Callahan, and Dominique D'Anna Stanley encouraged me to think of myself as an author and helped to bring my dreams to life. Special thanks to Andrew for his leap of faith. I am grateful to Dedi Fellman, who opened the door for me at Oxford University Press, and to Tim Bent, whose editorial contributions and encouragement helped shape my musings into a book.

My parents—Sam Keith, Janet Watson, and Don and Rosemary Plane—assisted with research and read early versions of the project. I am indebted to Buck Watson for a lifetime of love and inspiration.

I am thankful for the hardworking boys of Collegiate School, who dutifully engaged with me in aspects of this study, and for Marshall Plane, whose energy, curiosity, and faith sustained his mother's.

Brian Plane is the author of so much happiness in my life, including the opportunity to write this book. I will always be grateful for his loving and scholarly contributions.

Notes

INTRODUCTION

1. Ron Wikberg, E. J. Carter, and Floyd Webb, "Tragedy at Colfax," *The Angolite: The Prison Magazine* 14 (November/December 1989), 51; A. R. Baker, "Reminiscences of Natural Gas in the Oil Country," *Magazine of Western History* 7 (February 1888), 454; "The Great South," *Scribner's Monthly* VII (December 1873), 158.

2. "Skull of Human Is Excavated at Colfax" [newspaper clipping, circa October 1927], Melrose Scrapbook 67, Cammie G. Henry Research Center, Northwestern State University, Natchitoches, LA.

3. "Did You Know," *Alexandria Town Talk,* February 28, 2005; "Colfax Has Rich, Storied History," *Alexandria Town Talk,* July 8, 2002.

4. Wikberg, Carter, and Webb, "Tragedy at Colfax," 51. See also "The Curious Fountain of Colfax," *Progress,* June 17, 1938, and "The Flaming Fountain," *Alexandria Town Talk,* February 17, 1949.

5. James W. Loewen, *Lies Across America: What Our Historic Sites Get Wrong* (New York: New Press, 1999), 36, 210. See also W. Fitzhugh Brundage, *The Southern Past: A Clash of Race and Memory* (Cambridge: Harvard University Press, 2005), 5.

6. Mark T. Carleton, "The Politics of the Convict Lease System in Louisiana, 1868–1901," *Louisiana History* 8 (Winter 1967), 6–7.

7. William A. Dunning, *Reconstruction, Political and Economic* (New York: Harper and Brothers, 1907), 219.

8. Katherine S. Mangan, "Portrait: The History, Routine, and Terror of a Prison System," *Chronicle of Higher Education* 38 (June 3, 1992), 38–39; John Masterson, "Few Holds Barred for Prison Publication," *Folio: The Magazine for Magazine Management* 19 (July 1990), 41.

9. Francis X. Clines, "Remembering the Murderer Who Did Good," *New York Times*, October 9, 1994; "Tossing Away the Keys," Radio Documentary by Sound Portraits, transcript available online at http://soundportraits.org/on-air/tossing_away_the_keys/transcript.php3; Amy Bach, "The Unforgiven," *The Nation*, January 21, 2002, available online at http://thenation.com/docprint.mhtml?i=20020121&s=bach. For incarcerations and other statistics, see State of Louisiana, Department of Human Health, "Community Safety: Grant Parish Health Profile," report online at http://www.dhh.louisiana.gov/OPH/PHP%202005/PDF/Grant/Safety%20Grant.pdf.

10. Eric Foner, *Reconstruction: America's Unfinished Revolution, 1863–1877* (New York: HarperCollins, 1988), 437.

11. Lalita Tademy, *Cane River* (New York: Warner Books, 2002), 510–517.

12. Lalita Tademy to the author, April 6, 2007. See also Lalita Tademy, *Red River* (New York: Warner Books, 2007), 417.

13. Tademy, *Red River*, 3.

CHAPTER 1

1. Louis C. Hunter, "The Invention of the Western Steamboat," *Journal of Economic History* 3 (November 1943), 201–220; James Mak and Gary M. Walton, "Steamboats and the Great Productivity Surge in River Transportation," *Journal of Economic History* 32 (September 1972), 620, 624; Ralph D. Gray, "Review of *Conquering the Rivers: Henry Miller Shreve and the Navigation of America's Inland Waterways* by Edith McCall," *Journal of American History* 71 (December 1984), 624.

2. Todd Shallat, "Engineering Policy: The U.S. Army Corps of Engineers and the Historical Foundation of Power," *The Public Historian* 11 (Summer 1989), 11; Hunter, "Invention of the Western Steamboat," 219.

3. Michael Grunwald, "A River in the Red," *Washington Post* (January 9, 2000), A1; Joe Angert, "Old River Control," *Mighty Mississippi Website* (Spring 2000), http://users.stlcc.edu/jangert/index.html; Rita Robison, "Taming the Red River," *Civil Engineering* 65 (June 1995), 64–65.

4. "History of Colfax Lodge No. 259, F.&A.M.," Lucille Carnahan Collection, Folder 4, Cammie G. Henry Research Center, Watson Memorial Library, Northwest State University, Natchitoches, LA.

5. Caroline Patricia Smith, "Jacksonian Conservative: The Late Years of William Smith, 1826–1840," (Ph.D. diss., Auburn University, 1977), 26; Milton Dunn notes on pages 19 and 20, Melrose Scrapbook Number 67, Cammie G. Henry Research Center, Watson Memorial Library, Northwestern State University of Louisiana, Natchitoches, LA; Mabel Fletcher Harrison and Lavinia McGuire McNeely, *Grant Parish: A History* (Baton Rouge: Claitor's Publishing Division, 1969), 49.

6. "Judge Smith," *Huntsville Democrat*, September 6, 1836.

7. William Smith, "To 'A Citizen,'" *Huntsville Democrat,* November 1, 1836; Shallat, "Engineering Policy," 11.

8. Quoted in Smith, "Jacksonian Conservative," 279.

9. Quoted in Sean Wilenz, *The Rise of American Democracy, Jefferson to Lincoln* (New York: W. W. Norton & Co., 2005), 230; and Nancy M. Rohr, *An Alabama School Girl in Paris, 1842–1844: The Letters of Mary Fenwick Lewis and Her Family* (Huntsville, AL: Silver Threads Publishing, 2001), 22; Clement Eaton, *History of the Old South* (New York: Macmillan, 1949), 385.

10. 1820 *United States Federal Census* [database online at Ancestry.com], M33, Roll 121, 164.

11. Smith, "Jacksonian Conservative," 201; Alan L. Olmstead and Paul W. Rhode, " 'Wait a Cotton-Pickin' Minute!' A New View of Slave Productivity": Working Paper, April 2005, University of California at Davis, Department of Economics, and University of North Carolina, Department of Economics, http: /www.econ.yale.edu/seminars/echist/ eh04–05/olmstead042005.pdf.

12. Probate Record Number 416 1/2: William Smith, Madison County Record Office, Huntsville, AL.

13. Paula Mitchell Marks, *In a Barren Land: American Indian Dispossession and Survival* (New York: William Morrow and Company, Inc., 1998), 49–52; James Wilson, *The Earth Shall Weep: A History of Native America* (New York: Grove Press, 1998), 156.

14. Quoted in Smith, "Jacksonian Conservative," 64.

15. "The Richest of the Rich, Proud of a New Gilded Age," *New York Times,* July 16, 2007.

16. Girard to Calhoun, January 19, 1830, Stephen Girard Papers, Girard College and American Philosophical Society, Philadelphia, PA.

17. Murphy D. Smith, "The Stephen Girard Papers," *Manuscripts* (Winter 1977), 17–19.

18. Henry Atlee Ingram, *The Life and Character of Stephen Girard, Mariner and Merchant* (Philadelphia: Private Edition, 1892), 130–131.

19. Calhoun to Girard [dateline St. Petersburg], July 6, 1827; Harry Wildes, *Lonely Midas: The Story of Stephen Girard* (New York: Farrar and Reinhart, 1943), 169–174.

20. Quoted in ibid., 170–171.

21. Frederick Law Olmsted, "The South: Letters on the Productions, Industry, and Resources of the Slave States," originally published serially in the *New York Daily Times,* reprinted in Charles E. Beveridge, Charles Capen McLaughlin, eds., *The Papers of Frederick Law Olmsted, Volume 2: Slavery and the South, 1852–1857* (Baltimore: Johns Hopkins University Press, 1981), 220.

22. 1850 *U.S. Federal Census Slave Schedule* [database online at Ancestry.com], M432, 1009 rolls, National Archives and Record Administration, 1860 *U.S. Federal Census Slave Schedule* [database online at Ancestry.com], M653, 1438 rolls, NARA.

23. During the 1832 Senate election in South Carolina, the disclosure of the movement of slaves from Smith's local property to Alabama created a small controversy. Smith, "Jacksonian Conservative," 256.

24. "Negroes," *Huntsville Southern Advocate,* November 1, 1836; "The Present High Prices," *Huntsville Southern Advocate,* December 20, 1836.

25. Peter Kolchin, *American Slavery, 1619–1877* (New York: Hill and Wang, 1993), 9.

26. Marks, *In a Barren Land,* 91–96; Anthony F. C. Wallace, *The Long Bitter Trail: Andrew Jackson and the Indians* (New York: Hill and Wang, 1993), 80–86, 94; Francis Paul Prucha, *The Great Father: The United States Government and the American Indians* (Lincoln: University of Nebraska Press, 1984), 82; Alexis de Tocqueville, *Democracy in America, Volume I* (New York: Vintage Classics, 1990), 340.

27. Wallace, *Long, Bitter Trail,* 81, 86.

28. Kolchin, *American Slavery,* 125–126; Alrutheus A. Taylor, "The Movement of Negroes from the East to the Gulf States from 1830 to 1850," *Journal of Negro History* 8 (October 1923), 379.

29. Taylor, "Movement of Negroes," 380.

30. *1850 U.S. Federal Census Slave Schedules.*

31. Sarah Thomas Interview, *Slave Narratives,* Federal Writers Project, Works Progress Administration [database online at Ancestry.com] (Provo, UT: Ancestry.com, 2000).

32. Herman Freudenberger and Jonathan B. Pritchett, "The Domestic United States Slave Trade: New Evidence," *Journal of Interdisciplinary History* 21 (Winter 1991), 457, 474; Probate Record Number 416 1/2, William Smith: Madison County Record Office, Huntsville, AL; American Press Institute, "Journalists' Toolbox Update [Currency Converter]," *Columbia Journalism Review,* http://www.cjr.org/tools/.

33. Mabel Fletcher Harrison and Lavinia McGuire McNeely, *Grant Parish: A History* (Baton Rouge: Claitor's Publishing Division, 1969), 103–105; Donald D. Cameron Oral History, Grant Parish Library, Colfax, LA.

34. Richard J. Follett, "The Sugar Masters: Slavery, Economic Development, and Modernization on Louisiana Sugar Plantations, 1820–1860" (Ph.D. diss., Louisiana State University and Agricultural and Mechanical College, 1997), 99.

35. Rick Halpern, Richard Follett, et al., "Documenting the Louisiana Sugar Harvest: Antebellum Information, Rapides Parish, 1844–1914," A Joint Project between the University of Toronto and Sussex University, 2004, http://www.utoronto.ca/csus/sugar/index.htm.

36. Joseph Karl Menn, *The Large Slaveholders of Louisiana, 1860* (New Orleans: Pelican Publishing Company, 1964), 104, 110; American Press Institute, "Journalists' Toolbox Update [Currency Converter]," *Columbia Journalism Review,* http://www.cjr.org/tools/.

37. Probate Record Number 416 1/2, William Smith: Madison County Record Office, Huntsville, AL.

38. Henry C. Lay Collection, File 418, Huntsville Public Library, Huntsville, AL.

CHAPTER 2

1. "Annotated Itineraries of Olmsted's Southern Journeys," in *Papers of Frederick Law Olmsted,* Beveridge and McLaughlin, eds., 465 (see chap. 1, n. 20).

2. John B. Rehder, *Delta Sugar: Louisiana's Vanishing Plantation Landscape* (Baltimore: John Hopkins University Press, 1999), 90.

3. Olmsted, "The South," 217; "Colfax Fight" [unattributed notes collected by Milton Dunn], Melrose Scrapbook #67, CGH (see intro. 1, n. 2); Cameron OH, GPL (see chap. 1, n. 32).

4. Olmsted, "The South," 217.

5. *Antoinette Boulard v. Meredith Calhoun* [no number in original], 13 La. Ann. 445; 1858 La. LEXIS 22 [database online at LexisNexis Scholastic Edition]. See also A. J. A. [author], "The Doctrine of Exemplary Damages in Its Application to Corporations," *Michigan Law Review* 9 (February 1911), 340.

6. Cameron OH, GPL.

7. Olmsted, "The South," 218–219.

8. Ibid., 219.

9. Ibid., 219.

10. Cameron OH, GPL.

11. "Model for Mrs. Stowe: Meredith Calhoun Was the Original Simon Legree," *Washington Post,* July 19, 1896.

12. Olmsted, "The South," 220–221. See also slightly differing accounts of the same incident in drafts and the public version of Olmsted's *Back Country,* described in annotations to the previous account in ibid., 223.

13. Frederick Law Olmsted, *The Cotton Kingdom: A Traveller's Observations on Cotton and Slavery in the Southern States* (New York: Knopf, 1953), 270, 277.

14. "About Uncle Tom's Cabin," *Washington Post* (August 31, 1896), 7; D. B. Corley, *A Visit to Uncle Tom's Cabin* (Chicago: Laird & Lee, Publishers, 1892), 4–5.

15. "Model for Mrs. Stowe: Meredith Calhoun Was the Original Simon Legree," *Washington Post,* July 19, 1896.

16. "Merideth Colhoun Esq.," *Red River Republican,* April 6, 1847; "The Last Cargo of Slaves," *Morning Oregonian,* July 24, 1875.

17. G. M. G. Stafford, *The Wells Family of Louisiana, and Allied Families* (Alexandria, LA: Standard Printing Company, Inc., 1941), 106.

18. Charles Edward Stowe and Lyman Beecher Stowe, *Harriet Beecher Stowe: The Story of Her Life* (Boston: Houghton Mifflin Company, 1911), 125; Barbara A. White, *The Beecher Sisters* (New Haven: Yale University Press, 2003), 30, 208.

19. Harriet Beecher Stowe, *Key to Uncle Tom's Cabin* (Cincinnati: American Reform Tract and Book Society, 1856), 41–43.

20. Ibid., 41.

21. Quoted in Ibid., 230; Olmsted, *Cotton Kingdom,* 457.

22. G. P. Whittington, "Rapides Parish, Louisiana—A History [Part V]," *Louisiana Historical Quarterly* 18 (January 1935), 630.

23. "The Last Cargo of Slaves," *Morning Oregonian,* July 24, 1875.

24. Rohr, *Alabama Schoolgirl,* 122.

25. Le Petit Homme Rouge [Ernrest Alfred Vizetelles], *The Court of the Tuileries,* 1852–1870 (London: Chatto & Windus, 1912), 71, 261–262; "Art Treasures Sent from This City to Chicago" [newspaper clipping] *Huntsville Times,* n.d. [circa May 1911], Hemphill Collection.

26. Ibid., 121.

CHAPTER 3

1. Rohr, *Alabama Schoolgirl,* 25–26 (see chap. 1, n. 9); "Model for Mrs. Stowe: Meredith Calhoun Was the Original Simon Legree," *Washington Post,* July 19, 1896.

2. Inventory of the Estate of William Smith, April 27, 1841, Hemphill Collection; Rohr, *Alabama Schoolgirl,* 24–26, 216.

3. Richard O. Nahrendorf, "Review of *Sozialer Wandel und Krankheit* by Manfred Pflanz, *American Sociological Review,* 28 (August 1963), 681; "Jules René Guerin," *Who Named It* [website], http://www.whonamedit.com/doctor/cfm/1321.html; Kathleen Wellman, "Book Review: *Constructing Paris Medicine,*" *Isis* 92 (March 2001), 195–196.

4. Ibid., 59; [Testimony before U.S. Claims Commission, House of Representatives, circa 1866], Calhoun Family Vertical File, FF Calhoun #47, Huntsville Public Library, Huntsville, AL.

5. Ann Elizabeth Fowler LaBerge, "Debate as Scientific Practice in Nineteenth-Century Paris: The Controversy over the Microscope," *Perspectives on Science* 12 (Winter 2004), 424.

6. Rohr, *Alabama Schoolgirl,* 155; Francis E. Anstie, "Over-Eating and Under-Eating," *Cornhill Magazine* 8 (1863), 35–47.

7. Rohr, *Alabama Schoolgirl,* 105, 155, 170.

8. Olmsted, *Cotton Kingdom,* 456–457 (see chap. 2, n. 13).

9. "Passengers Sailed," *New York Times,* July 21, 1859, 8.

10. Rohr, *Alabama Schoolgirl,* 221.

11. "History of Colfax Lodge No. 259," Carnahan Collection, Folder 4, CGH (see chap. 1, n. 4).

12. John D. Winters, *The Civil War in Louisiana* (Baton Rouge: Louisiana State University Press, 1963), 83, 164–165.

13. Sue Eakin, *Rapides Parish History* (Alexandria: Historical Association of Central Louisiana, 1976), Reprinted on RootsWeb.com, http://www.rootsweb.com/~larapide/history/eakin/index.htm.

14. "American Civil War General Officers Record: Leroy Augustus Stafford" [database online at Ancestry.com]; Clement A. Evans, ed., *Confederate Military History* XII (Wilmington: Broadfoot, 1987), 317.

15. Winters, *Civil War in Louisiana,* 35; Milton Dunn notes, Melrose Scrapbook No. 67, CGH (see intro., n. 2).

16. 1860 *United States Federal Census* [database online at Ancestry.com], M653–423, 445, NARA; Booth, *Louisiana Confederate Soldier,* II:725.

17. 1860 *United States Federal Census* [database online at Ancestry.com], M653–423, 109, 118, NARA; Andrew B. Booth, *Records of Louisiana Confederate Soldiers and Louisiana Confederate Commands* (Spartanburg, SC: Reprint Co., 1984), 1:545, 3:102.

18. G. P. Whittington, "Rapides Parish—A History [Part IV]," *Louisiana Historical Quarterly* 17 (October 1934), 744.

19. Booth, *Louisiana Confederate Soldiers,* II:1253; Milton Dunn, "Christopher Columbus Nash, A Tribute," (Colfax, La.: Colfax Chronicle, n.d.), 4; James M. McPherson, *Battle Cry of Freedom: The Civil War Era* (New York: Ballantine Books, 1988), 460, 527–532, 640–642.

20. Ted Tunnell, *Crucible of Reconstruction: War, Radicalism, and Race in Louisiana, 1862–1877* (Baton Rouge: Louisiana State University Press, 1984), 23.

21. National Cemetery Administration. *U.S. Veterans Cemeteries, ca.*1800–2004 [database online]. Provo, Utah: MyFamily.com, Inc., 2005. Original data: National Cemetery Administration. *Nationwide Gravesite Locator.*

22. Stafford, *Wells Family,* 106 (see chap. 2, n. 17).

23. Walter McGeehee Lowrey, "The Political Career of James Madison Wells," *Louisiana Historical Quarterly* 31 (October 1948), 1008–1009.

24. For an example of the masthead, see *Red River Republican,* January 30, 1847. See also Testimony of J. M. Wells in "United States Election Committee, Fourth District of Louisiana, *J. P. Newsham v. Michael Ryan,* Statement of Ryan with Brief" [pamphlet reprint, n.p., n.d.], Bound Pamphlet Volume, New York Public Library Pamphlet Collection (NYPL), 11.

25. Mary Calhoun to Meredith Calhoun, January 28, 1861, Hemphill Collection; Mary Ann Cruse letter, April 3, 1861 [notes on archival research at Duke University by author Nancy M. Rohr], Huntsville Public Library, Huntsville, AL.

26. Receipts of Sales of Public Lands, Department of the Interior, Hemphill Collection.

27. *Huntsville Democrat,* September 11, 1861; *Passenger Lists of Vessels Arriving at New York,* 1820–1897 [database online at Ancestry.com], Micropublication M237, Rolls 95–580, NARA.

28. Whittington, "Rapides Parish [Part V]," 8.

29. "Jubilee Songs," *The American Experience* [database online at the Public Broadcasting Service], http://www.pbs.org/wgbh/amex/singers/sfeature/songs_swing_l.html; "Great Day" [from *American Negro Songs* by J. W. Work, 1940], http://negrospirituals.com/news-song/great_day.htm.

30. W.E.B. DuBois, *Black Reconstruction in America* (New York: Oxford University Press, 2007), 112.

31. U.S. Army Pension File: Alabama Mitchell, NARA.

32. General Affadavit: Loyal Gaines, August 8, 1901, Alabama Mitchell Pension File.

33. Freedman's Bank Records, 1865–1874 [database online at Ancestry.com] Provo, Utah: MyFamily.com, Inc., 2005. Original data: *Registers of Signatures of Depositors in Branches of the Freedman's Savings and Trust Company, 1865–1874*. Micropublication M816, 27 rolls, NARA.

34. Robin Miller, "Unknown Hero," *Alexandria Town Talk,* February 16, 2003.

35. [Admiral David Porter's report to Gideon Welles] Quoted in Thomas Ayers, *Dark and Bloody Ground: The Battle of Mansfield and the Forgotten Civil War in Louisiana* (Dallas: Taylor Trade Publishing, 2001), 251.

36. Joseph L. Brent, "Operations of the Army of Western Louisiana, after the Battle of Pleasant Hill," *Southern Historical Society Papers* 9 (June 1881), 257.

37. Ayers, *Dark and Bloody Ground,* 250; Curt Anders, *Disaster in Damp Sand: The Red River Expedition* (Carmel, ID: Guild Press of Indiana); Chester G. Hearn, *Admiral David Dixon Porter* (Annapolis: Naval Institute Press) 256; [Cover illustration: *Champion No.* 3] *Harper's Weekly* (April 4, 1863) [reprinted online at http://www.sonofthesouth.net/leefoundation/civil-war/1863/ september/vicksburg-canal-dam.htm]; "Report of Pilot William Maitland, June 25, 1864," in *Report of the Joint Committee on the Conduct of the War,* Thirty-Eighty Congress, Second Session [electronic version online at Googlebooks. com, http://books.google.com/books? vid=OCLCo 2048818 &id=iyqɪjrmuT 3MC&pg=PA269&lpg.htm]; "History of Colfax Lodge.," Folder 4, Carnahan Collection, CGH.

38. J. B. T. Marsh, *The Story of the Jubilee Singers* (London: Hodder & Stoughton, 1875), 152.

39. Herbert Aptheker, "Negro Casualties in the Civil War," *Journal of Negro History* 32 (January 1947), 76.

40. James McPherson, ed., *The Atlas of the Civil War* (New York: Macmillan, 1994), 148–149; Nathaniel Cheairs Hughes, Jr., ed., *Liddell's Record: St. John Richardson Liddell* (Baton Rouge: Louisiana State University Press, 1997), 182.

41. Quoted in Winters, *Civil War in Louisiana,* 365.

42. "Concerning the Loyalty of Slaves in North Louisiana in 1863 [*sic*], Letters from John H. Ransdell to Governor Thomas O. Moore, dated 1863, with an Introduction by G. P. Whittington," *Louisiana Historical Quarterly* 14 (October 1931), 492–493.

CHAPTER 4

1. William E. Highsmith, "Some Aspects of Reconstruction in the Heart of Louisiana," *Journal of Southern History* 13 (November 1947), 464.

2. John C. Rodrigue, *Reconstruction in the Cane Fields: From Slavery to Freedom in Louisiana's Sugar Parishes, 1862–1880* (Baton Rouge: Louisiana State University Press, 2001), 57.

3. J. W. Alvord, *Third Semi-Annual Report on Schools for Freedmen, January 1, 1867* (Washington: Bureau of Freedmen, Refugees, and Abandoned Lands, 1867), 2; "Louisiana," *New York Times,* May 19, 1866.

4. Ibid., 467–468; "Louisiana," *New York Times,* August 25, 1866.

5. Alcée Bouchereau, *Statement of the Sugar and Rice Crops Made in Louisiana, 1874–1875, with an Appendix* (New Orleans: Pelican Book and Job Printing, 1875), v; Howard A. White, *The Freedmen's Bureau in Louisiana* (Baton Rouge: Louisiana State University Press, 1970), 67.

6. Highsmith, "Reconstruction in the Heart of Louisiana," 468.

7. "No More Auction Block for Me" [from *The Jubilee Singers* by Gustavus D. Pike, 1873], http://www.negrospirituals.com/news-song/no_more_auction_block_for_me.htm.

8. Rodrigue, *Reconstruction in the Cane Fields,* 44–45.

9. Highsmith, "Reconstruction in the Heart of Louisiana," 464.

10. Rodrigue, *Reconstruction in the Cane Fields,* 82–84.

11. Highsmith, "Reconstruction in the Heart of Louisiana," 469.

12. H. P. Hathaway, "Monthly Report of the Assistant Inspector, October 1868," Records of the Assistant Commissioner for the State of Louisiana, Bureau of Refugees, Freedmen, and Abandoned Lands, M1027, Roll 31, NARA.

13. Ibid; *Calhoun v. Fletcher,* n.1, Supreme Court of Alabama, 63 Ala. 574; 1879 Ala. LEXIS 120 [database online, Lexis-Nexis Scholastic Edition].

14. *Biographical and Historical Memoirs of Grant, Red River, Sabine & Winn Parishes, Louisiana* (Shreveport: J & W Enterprises, 1889), 8.

15. Ibid.

16. DuBois, *Black Reconstruction,* 664 (see chap. 3, n. 29).

17. J. W. Alvord, *Seventh Semi-Annual Report on Schools for Freedmen, January 1, 1869* (Washington: Bureau of Freedmen, Refugees, and Abandoned Lands, 1869), 6–7; J. W. Alvord, *Eighth Semi-Annual Report on Schools for Freedmen, July 1, 1869* (Washington: Bureau of Freedmen, Refugees, and Abandoned Lands, 1869), 48; Foner, *Reconstruction,* 98 (see intro., n. 10).

18. Alvord, *Seventh Report on Schools for Freedmen,* 38.

19. Mrs. R. S. Cameron and Miss Isabella Dean, "Early History of Colfax and Its School," *Colfax Chronicle,* March 22, 1935.

20. Alvord, *Seventh Report on Schools for Freedmen,* 37.

21. Alvord, *Third Report on Schools for Freedmen,* 23–24.

22. Quoted in DuBois, *Black Reconstruction,* 647.

23. J. W. Alvord, *Ninth Semi-Annual Report on Schools for Freedmen, January 1, 1870* (Washington: Bureau of Refugees, Freedmen, and Abandoned Lands), 41; Alvord, *Eighth Report on Schools for Freedmen,* 40.

24. Rohr, *Alabama Schoolgirl,* 116.

25. F. X. Winterhalter to M. Calhoun, January 20, 1867 [note included with family papers], Tybring Hemphill Collection.

26. Quoted in Walter Lowery, "The Political Career of James Madison Wells," *Journal of Southern History* 15 (November 1949), 1090.

27. Foner, *Reconstruction,* 279.

28. Richard M. Valelly, *The Two Reconstructions: The Struggle for Black Enfranchisement* (Chicago: University of Chicago Press, 2004), 31–32; DuBois, *Black Reconstruction,* 466.

29. Charles Vincent, "Black Louisianans During the Civil War and Reconstruction," in *Louisiana's Black Heritage,* Robert R. McDonald, John R. Kemp, and Edward F. Haas, eds. (New Orleans: Louisiana State Museum, 1979), 95; Eric Foner, *Freedom's Lawmakers: A Directory of Black Officeholders during Reconstruction* (Baton Rouge: Louisiana State University Press, 1996), 55, 59, 442.

30. DuBois, *Black Reconstruction,* 466.

31. Allen W. Trelease, "Who Were the Scalawags?" *Journal of Southern History* 4 (November 1963), 23.

32. Valelly, *Two Reconstructions,* 23–45; Steven Hahn, *A Nation Under Our Feet: Black Political Struggles in the Rural South, from Slavery to the Great Migration* (Cambridge, MA: Harvard University Press, 2003), 177–178.

33. Highsmith, "Reconstruction in the Heart of Louisiana," 482.

34. W. B. Phillips Affadavit, January 14, 1875 in *Use of the Army,* 401.

35. Milton Dunn, *C. C. Nash: A Tribute,* 5; *Ninth Census of the United States,* 1870 [database online at Ancestry.com].

36. William B. Phillips affidavit in *Report of the Joint Committee on Elections,* New York Public Library Pamphlet Collection, NYPL.

37. *Military Records of Individual Civil War Soldiers* [database online at Ancestry.com], data compiled by Historical Data Systems, Kingston, MA.

38. D. W. White to Charles Bromie, June 27, 1867, Records of Field Offices for the State of Louisiana, Bureau of Freedmen, Refugees, and Abandoned Lands, Roll 13, M1905, NARA.

39. Highsmith, "Reconstruction in the Heart of Louisiana," 483.

40. Louis R. Nardini, Sr., "A Grant Parish History," *Colfax Chronicle,* August 24, 1962.

41. J. W. Alvord, *Sixth Semi-Annual Report on Schools for Freedmen, July 1,* 1868 (Washington: Bureau of Refugees, Freedmen, and Abandoned Lands, 1868), 1.

42. *The Grant and Colfax Songster: Comprising a Choice Selection of New and Popular Songs and Ballads for the Campaign* (New York: Beadle and Company,1868), 5.

43. "Testimony of George Buttrick," in *Report of the Select Committee on That Portion of the President's Message Relating to the Condition of the South,* January 15, 1875, Congressional Serial Set v. 1657, House of Representatives, 43rd Congress, 2nd Session (Washington: Government Printing Office, 1875), 340–341, 343.

44. Allen W. Trelease, *White Terror: The Ku Klux Klan Conspiracy and Southern Reconstruction* (NY: Harper & Row, 1971), 129.

45. *Report of the Joint Committee, Louiisiana Elections Committee, Hugh J. Campbell, Chairman* [reprint of 1868 report], Bound Pamphlets, IL p.v. 14 no. 4, New York Public Library Pamphlet Collection, NYPL, 25.

46. "Testimony of W. S. Calhoun, August 1868," in House Reports, No. 101, Serial 1657, *Condition of the South: Report of the Committee Chaired by George F. Hoar* (Washington, D.C.: Government Printing Office, 1875), 338; W. B. Phillips, "A Little History of Grant Parish," *New Orleans Republican,* January 3, 1874; Phillips affidavit, January 14, 1875, and "1868—Political," in House of Representatives, 44th Congress, 2nd Session, *Use of the Army in Certain of the Southern States,* Executive Document No. 30 (January 24, 1877), Congressional Serial Set v. 1755 (Washington, D.C.: Government Printing Office, 1877), 170, 401.

47. "1868—Political," in *Use of the Army in Southern States,* 170.

48. W. S. Calhoun affidavit in *Supplemental Report of the Joint Commission of the General Assembly of Louisiana on the Conduct of the Late Elections* (New Orleans: A. L. Lee, State Printer, 1869), 250–251.

49. W. B. Phillips affidavit, in *Report of the Joint Committee of the General Assembly of Louisiana on the Conduct of the Late Elections and the Condition of Peace and Order in the State* (New Orleans: A. L. Lee, State Printer, 1868).

50. "The Presidential Election," in ibid.

51. "Testimony of W. S. Calhoun, August 1868," 338; Vincent, "Black Louisianans," 94.

52. Tunnell, *Crucible of Reconstruction,* 157 (see chap. 3, n. 20); DuBois, *Black Reconstruction,* 337.

53. Tunnell, *Crucible of Reconstruction,* 157; Phillips, "Little History of Grant Parish."

CHAPTER 5

1. "Monthly Report of H. P. Hathaway, Assistant Inspector of Freedmen for the Parish of Rapides, State of Louisiana," *Records of the Assistant Commissioner for the State of Louisiana, Bureau of Refugees, Freedmen, and Abandoned Lands,* 1868–1869, NARA Microfilm Publication M1027, NARA.

2. D. M. White [sic] affidavit, W. S. Calhoun to W. B. Phillips, December 12, 1868, and D. W. White to General A. L. Lee, in *Report on the Conduct of Late Elections* (see chap. 4, n. 52); D. W. White, "Monthly Report of the Assistant Inspector, October 1868," Records of the Assistant Commissioner for the State of Louisiana, Bureau of Refugees, Freedmen, and Abandoned Lands, M1027, Roll 31, NARA.

3. John I. McCain, "Reconstruction Days in Colfax," Judge Jones Collection, Folder 33, CGH; Carl A. Brasseaux, Glenn R. Conrad, and R. Warren Robison, *The Courthouses of Louisiana* (Lafayette: Center for Louisiana Studies, 1977), 81.

4. Nathan Newman and J. J. Gass, "A New Birth of Freedom: The Forgotten History of the 13th, 14th, and 15th Amendments," Judicial Independence Series, Brennan Center for Justice at NYU School of Law, www.brennancenter.org, 11.

5. W. S. Calhoun to W. B. Phillips, December 12, 1868, in *Report on the Conduct of Late Elections.*

6. Captain N. B. McLaughlin, 4th U.S. Cavalry, to General Thomas H. Neill, Adjutant General, Department of Louisiana, January 21, 1869 [document reproduced on LAGenWeb Archives], http://ftp.rootsweb.com/pub/usgenweb/la/winn/newspapers/recon/reckwwkc69.txt; Richard Briley, *Nightriders: Inside Story of the West and Kimbrell Clan* (Montgomery: Mid-South Publishing, 1963), 5.

7. "Washington," *New York Times* (December 18, 1866), 1.

8. Brooks D. Simpson, *Let Us Have Peace: Ulysses S. Grant and the Politics of War & Reconstruction, 1861–1868* (Chapel Hill: University of North Carolina Press, 1991), 173; "Thirty-Ninth Congress, Second Session," *New York Times* (February 27, 1867), 1; "Closing Up of the Thirty-Ninth Congress," *New York Times* (March 5, 1867), 1.

9. Tunnell, *Crucible of Reconstruction,* 157–158 (see chap. 3, n. 20).

10. Ibid., 159–160.

11. Valelly, *Two Reconstructions,* 102–103 (see chap. 4, n. 20); Foner, *Reconstruction,* 446–447 (see intro., n. 10).

12. *Report on the Conduct of Late Elections.*

13. "United States Election Committee, Fourth District of Louisiana, *J. P. Newsham v. Michael Ryan,* Statement of Ryan with Brief [pamphlet reprint, n.p., n.d.], Bound Pamphlet Volume, New York Public Library Pamphlet Collection, NYPL, 12, 19–20.

14. "J. P. Newsham v. Michael Ryan" [Pamphlet provided to the House of Representatives Election Committee in the matter of the Fourth Congressional District of Louisiana] (New Orleans: n.p., n.d.), New York Public Library Pamphlet Collection, 10–28; "Forty-First United States Congress—Membership Changes" [article online at Answers.com], http://answers.com/topic.forty-first-united-states-congress-membership-changes; "Congress," *New York Times* (May 24, 1870), 5.

15. Foner, *Reconstruction,* 424–431 (see intro., n. 10).

16. Valelly, *Two Reconstructions,* 94–95.

17. Octavia Myers testimony, January 30, 1875 in House of Representatives, 43rd Congress, 2nd Session, *Report on the Condition of the South,* Serial No. 261 (Washington: Government Printing Office, 1875), 302.

18. McCain, "Reconstruction Days in Colfax"; "David Lee Shaw: Noted Pioneer Dies in Winnfield" [newspaper clipping, n.p., n.d], Melrose Scrapbook 67, CGH (see intro., n. 2); McLaughlen to Neill, January 21, 1869.

19. J. W. Alvord, *Tenth Semi-Annual Report on Schools for Freedmen* (Washington: Bureau of Refugees, Freedmen, and Abandoned Lands, 1870), 33.

20. W. B. Phillips affidavit in *Use of the Army in Southern States,* 402–403.

21. Dunn, *C. C. Nash: A Tribute,* 5.

22. Joel M. Sipress, *The Triumph of Reaction: Political Struggle in a New South Community, 1865–1898* (Ph.D. dissertation, University of North Carolina at Chapel Hill, 1993) 80–81; "Arrest of Alleged Kuklux in Louisiana on the Charge of Murdering a Native of New York," *New York Times,* November 6, 1871.

23. Milton Dunn, "Some Notes about Ex-Sheriff Shelby of Grant Parish" [newspaper clipping, *Colfax Chronicle* n.d.], Melrose Scrapbook 67, CGH (see intro., n. 2); Gary Schreckengost, "First Battle of Manassas: 1st Louisiana Special Battalion," *America's Civil War Magazine* [article archived online at History.net], http://historynet.com/acw/articlearchive/

24. *Calhoun v. Fletcher,* Supreme Court of Alabama, 63 Ala. 574, December 1879, decided [document online at LexisNexis.com] LEXIS 120; Appointment of Postmasters: Louisiana—Grant Parish, M841, Roll 50, NARA; Statement of Disability, Bureau of Pensions, Department of the Interior, January 15, 1898 and December 6, 1898, Peter Borland Pension File, NARA.

25. Muster Rolls, 92nd U.S. Colored Infantry, Registers of Enlistment in the United States Army, 1789–1914, Record Group M233, NARA.

26. *Annual Report of the Adjutant General of the State of Louisiana for the year ending December 31, 1871* (New Orleans: n.p., 1872), 22; Committee of Seventy, *History of the Riot at Colfax* (New Orleans: Clark and Hofeline, 1874), 1; Otis A. Singletary, *Negro Militia and Reconstruction* (Austin: University of Texas Press, 1957), 66–67.

27. Nathan and Gass, "New Birth of Freedom," 6.

28. Sipress, *Triumph of Reaction,* 81–82; Robert P. Hunter testimony, *Condition of the South,* 514.

29. Eric Foner, *Forever Free: The Story of Emancipation and Reconstruction* (New York: Knopf, 2005), 175–176.

30. Newman and Gass, "New Birth of Freedom," 6.

31. George P. Sanger, ed., *The Statutes at Large and Proclamations of the United States of America, from December 1870 to March 1871* (Boston: Little, Brown, and Company, 1871), 141–142.

32. Ibid., 13–15; Du Bois, *Black Reconstruction,* 683.

33. William S. McFeely, *Grant: A Biography* (New York: W. W. Norton & Company, 1981), 367–368; DuBois, *Black Reconstruction,* 684 (see chap. 3, n. 29).

34. Foner, *Reconstruction,* 457 (see intro., n. 10); Stephen P. Halbrook, *Freedmen, the Fourteenth Amendment, and the Right to Bear Arms, 1866–1876* (Westport, CT: Praeger, 1998), 124.

35. Valelly, *Two Reconstructions,* 109–110; Du Bois, *Black Reconstruction,* 683–684.

36. Quoted in Sipress, *Triumph of Reaction,* 83; *Report on the Condition of the South,* 13.

37. James K. Hogue, "The Battle of Colfax: Paramilitarism and Counterrevolution in Louisiana," Paper presented to the Southern Historical Association Conference, Atlanta, GA, November 6, 1997, 14 n.21; *Report on the Condition of the South,* 13; Bud McElroy notes, Melrose Scrapbook 67, CGH; Committee of Seventy, *History of the Riot at Grant Parish,* 3. For a discussion of white responses to black militia, see Forrest G. Wood, *Black Scare: The Racist Response to Emancipation and Reconstruction* (Berkeley: University of California Press, 1970), 140.

38. *U.S. Army Pension File: Alabama Mitchell*, NARA.

39. "The Colfax Fight," *[Alexandria] Louisiana Democrat*, April 23, 1873.

40. "Condition of the South: On Horseback Through Louisiana," *New York Times*, October 23, 1874.

41. Alcée Bouchereau, *Statement of the Sugar and Rice Crops Made in Louisiana, 1872–73* (New Orleans: Pelican Books and Job Printing Office, 1873), vi.

42. Sipress, *Triumph of Reaction*, 87–89; Joseph G. Dawson III, *Army Generals and Reconstruction: Louisiana, 1862–1877* (Baton Rouge: Louisiana State University Press, 1982), 114.

43. "The Radical Barbeque," *Alexandria Democrat*, October 10, 1872, 1.

44. Henry Clay Warmoth, *War, Politics, and Reconstruction: Stormy Days in Louisiana* (New York: Negro Universities Press, 1930), 161; Tunnell, *Crucible of Reconstruction*, 170; George C. Rable, *But There Was No Peace: The Role of Violence in the Politics of Reconstruction* (Athens: University of Georgia Press, 1984), 123.

45. "A Word of Warning," *Alexandria Rapides Gazette*, October 19, 1872, 1; Highsmith, "Reconstruction in the Heart of Louisiana," 484.

CHAPTER 6

1. George Rable, "Republican Albatross: The Louisiana Question, National Politics, and the Failure of Reconstruction," *The Louisiana Purchase Bicentennial Series in Louisiana History: Volume VI, Reconstructing Louisiana*, Lawrence N. Powell with J. Mark Souther, eds. (Lafayette: University of Louisiana at Lafayette Press, 2001), 698–699.

2. Warmoth, *War, Politics, and Reconstruction*, 242–243 (see chap. 4, n. 43).

3. Perry H. Howard, *Political Tendencies in Louisiana* (Baton Rouge: Louisiana State University Press, 1957), 138; Dawson, *Army Generals and Reconstruction*, 140–142 (see chap. 5, n. 41); William Gillette, "The Longest Battle: Intervention in Louisiana," in *Reconstructing Louisiana*, 677–678.

4. Karl Koenig, *The History of the March* (Abita Springs, LA: Basin Street Press, 1996), 50.

5. Ye Mistick Krewe of Comus, "The Missing Links to Darwin's Origin of Species" (New Orleans: L. Graham & Co., Printers, 1873), WRC.

6. Pierre Duval, *The Carillon Satires*, edited and translated by John Maxwell Jones (Camden, N.J.: [privately printed by John Maxwell Jones, 1978), 6.

7. Mistick Krewe, "The Missing Links."

8. Perry Young, *The Mistick Krewe: Chronicles of Comus and His Kin* (New Orleans: Carnival Press, 1931), 81, 99, 107–109; "The Sleuth, Keen Scented on the Trial of Game" [Woodcut sketches by J. Wells Champney], Leonard Huber Collection, 1974.25.19.26, Williams Research Center, Historic New Orleans Collection, New Orleans, LA; Henri Schindler, *Mardi Gras New Orleans* (New York: Flammarion, 1997), 47–54; Errol Laborde, *Marched the Day God: A History of the Rex Organization*

(New Orleans: School of Design Press, 1999), 6–10; James Gill, *Lords of Misrule: Mardi Gras and the Politics of Race in New Orleans* (Jackson: University of Mississippi Press, 1997), 100–103.

CHAPTER 7

1. *New Orleans Republican,* March 1, 1873.

2. *New Orleans Republican,* May 23, 1873.

3. Ibid.; *New Orleans Republican,* March 1, 1873; *Ninth Census of the United States,* 1870, M593-506, 468 and M593-13, 100; "An Old Timer Passes Away" [newspaper clipping, n.p., n.d.], Melrose Scrapbook 67, CGH (see intro., n. 2).

4. [Letter of George W. Stafford], *Louisiana Democrat,* May 13, 1873.

5. Stafford, "Statement of Colfax Fight"; [Witness testimony], *Condition of the South,* 532.

6. O. W. Watson, "An Incident of My Boyhood Days," Robert DeBlieux Collection, Folder 265, CGH, 2.

7. Quoted in Joel Gray Taylor, *Louisiana Reconstructed, 1863–1877* (Baton Rouge: Louisiana State University Press, 1974), 270.

8. "General Jim's Reminiscences" [newspaper clipping, n.p., July 22, 1905], Melrose Scrapbook 67, CGH; Milton Dunn, "The Record Should Be Kept Straight" [newspaper clipping, *Colfax Chronicle,* n.d.], Melrose Scrapbook 67, CGH; *New Orleans Republican,* March 7, 1874; "Tenting on the Old Camp Ground," Words and music by Walter Kittridge (Boston: Oliver Ditson & Company, No. 277) [scanned sheet music online] http://ny77thballadeers. tripod.com/tenting2.html.

9. Carol Wells, ed., *War, Reconstruction, and Redemption on Red River: The Memoirs of Dosia Williams Moore* (Ruston, LA: McGinty Publications, 1990), 70–71.

10. William Ward to Jacob Johnson, April 5, 1873, Letter offered as Defense Exhibit filed in Case of *U.S. v. Columbus Nash, et al,* Record Group 21: Records of District Courts of the United States, 1685–1991, NARA, Southwest Region, Ft. Worth, TX.

11. Ibid.; *New Orleans Republican,* March 6, 1874.

12. *Horrible Massacre in Grant Parish, Louisiana: Meeting of Colored Men in New Orleans* (New Orleans: Republican Office, 1873), 6; Jonathan I. McCain, "Reconstruction Days in Colfax, Grant Parish, and Montgomery," Judge Jones Collection, Folder 33, CGH (see chap. 5, n. 3).

13. Manie White Johnson, "The Colfax Riot of April, 1873," *Louisiana Historical Quarterly* 13 (July 1930), 403; "J. R. Beckwith testimony, *Condition of the South,* 419.

14. Jonathan I. McCain notes, Melrose Scrapbook 67, CGH.

15. Watson, "Incident of My Boyhood Days," CGH, 1.

16. *New Orleans Republican,* April 10, 1873; *New Orleans Republican,* March 7, 1874; Affidavit of W. R. Rutland filed in case of *United States v. Columbus Nash,*

et al, February 14, 1874, Record Group 21: Records of District Courts of the United States, 1685–1991, NARASW.

17. *New Orleans Republican,* May 21, 1874.

18. "The Riot in Grant Parish," *New Orleans Republican,* April 10, 1873.

19. *New Orleans Republican,* February 27, 1874; *New Orleans Republican,* March 6, 1874; *New Orleans Republican,* May 1, 1874; Johnson, "Colfax Riot," 400, 408–409.

20. *New Orleans Republican,* June 2, 1874 and June 5, 1874.

21. Quoted in *The Campaign Textbook: Why the People Want a Change* (New York: Democratic National Committee, 1876), 133.

22. Watson, "Incident of My Boyhood Days," 3–4; Milton Dunn notes, Melrose Collection, Folder 237, CGH.

23. [Editorial], *Louisiana Democrat,* February 19, 1873; Westy Horn to M. A. Dunn, September 10, 1916, Melrose Collection, Folder 237, CGH; *Alexandria Democrat,* February 19, 1873; "General Jim's Reminiscences"; "Record of Pre-WWII Shipbuilding," Colton Company, Maritime Business Strategies, LLC [data online], http://www.coltoncompany.com/shipbldg/ussbldrs/prewwii/shipyards/otherother.htm; J. E. Dunn to Cammie G. Henry, March 4, 1926, Melrose Collection, Folder 359, CGH.

24. W. L. Tanner to Milton Dunn, Melrose Collection, Folder 237, CGH.

25. George Stafford, "Statement of Colfax Fight," *Alexandria Democrat,* May 14, 1873.

26. *Ninth Census of the United States,* 1870 [database online at Ancestry.com], M593_513, 83, NARA; *Civil War Service Records* [database online at Ancestry.com], Box 589, Record 115; *New Orleans Republican,* March 11, 1874.

27. [Quoted in closing argument of Attorney J. R. Beckwith, *U.S. v. Columbus Nash, et al*] *New Orleans Republican,* March 13, 1874.

28. Quoted in Henry E. Chambers, *A History of Louisiana: Wilderness—Colony—Province—Territory—State—People* (Chicago: The American Historical Society, 1925), 676.

29. "Speech of T. Morris Chester," *Massacre in Grant Parish,* 8.

30. "T. W. DeKlyne, testimony taken in the United States Circuit Court, before the Hon. Judge Woods and a Jury, March 26, 1874, *United States v. Columbus Nash,*" Records of the Select Committee on that part of the President's Message relating to the Late Insurrectionary States, NR 43A-F31.4, NARA; T. W. DeKlyne, "Interview with Mr. Nash," in *Meeting of Colored Men,* 25–26; R. H. Marr testimony, *Condition of the South,* 476–477; *New Orleans Republican,* March 1, 1874 and May 24, 1874.

31. Johnson, "Colfax Riot," 413.

32. Milton Dunn notes on conversation with Baptiste Elzie, circa 1921, Melrose Collection, Folder 237, CGH; Milton Dunn, "Colfax Fight," ibid.

33. George Stafford, "Statement of the Colfax Fight," *Alexandria Democrat,* May 14, 1873.

34. Watson, "Incident of My Boyhood Days," 5.

35. [Testimony of Mrs. E. P. Register] *New Orleans Republican,* March 3, 1874; McCain, "Reconstruction Days in Colfax," CGH; [Testimony of Ward Ross] *New Orleans Republican,* May 27, 1874.

36. Watson, "Incident of My Boyhood Days," CGH.

37. "Statement of a Negro Wounded at the Massacre," *New Orleans Republican,* May 12, 1873.

38. Benjamin Brimm, testimony taken in the United States Circuit Court, before the Hon. Judge Woods and a Jury, March 4, 1874, *United States v. Columbus Nash,* "Records of the Select Committee on that part of the President's Message relating to the Late Insurrectionary States, NR 43A-F31.4, NARA.

39. Brimm testimony, NARA; [Witness testimony] *New Orleans Republican,* February 28, 1874.

40. [Witness testimony] *New Orleans Republican,* February 28, 1874.

41. *New Orleans Republican,* February 28, 1874; Record Group 15, Records of the Veterans Administration, Pension Files, 1861–1934, Alabama Mitchell, 71st U.S. Colored Infantry, NARA.

42. Johnson, "Colfax Riot," 417; *New Orleans Republican,* March 1, 1874 and May 23, 1874.

43. Brimm testimony, NARA; *New Orleans Republican,* March 4, 1874.

44. *New Orleans Republican,* February 28, 1874, March 4, 1874, and May 24, 1874.

45. Brimm testimony, NARA.

46. [Account of the Steamboat *Southwestern, New Orleans Times,* circa April 15, 1873] reprinted in *Massacre in Grant Parish,* 10.

47. [Letter of George W. Stafford], *Louisiana Democrat,* May 13, 1873; "Mr. Stafford's Statement," *Rapides Gazette,* May 17, 1873.

48. "Mr. Stafford's Statement," *Rapides Gazette,* May 17, 1873; *New Orleans Republican,* May 28, 1874.

49. William Whight, testimony taken in the United States Circuit Court, before the Hon. Judge Woods and a Jury, March 26, 1874, *United States v. Columbus Nash,* "Records of the Select Committee on that part of the President's Message relating to the Late Insurrectionary States, NR 43A-F31.4, NARA; T. W. DeKlyne testimony, NARA.

50. "List of Homicides in Grant Parish," in *Use of Army in Southern States,* 514; Harrison and McNeely, *Grant Parish,* 75.

51. Watson, "Incident of My Boyhood Days," 6; Milton Dunn notes, Melrose Scrapbook 67, CGH; Catherine Wall, "Destruction during Reconstruction: The Colfax Riot, 1873" [student paper based on local interviews, July 1965], Colfax Riot Collection, Colfax Public Library, Colfax, LA.

52. Kate Kingston Boyd Grant, "The Battle of Colfax" [unpublished manuscript, April 1873], Colfax Riot Collection, Colfax Public Library, Colfax, LA; *New Orleans Republican,* May 29, 1874.

53. "Speech of T. Morris Chester," *Meeting of Colored Men*, 11; *New Orleans Republican*, March 4, 1874 and June 4, 1874.

54. *New Orleans Republican*, February 28, 1874, March 4, 1874, March 13, 1874, May 27, 1874, May 29, 1874, June 5, 1874.

55. [Dorcas Pittman testimony] *New Orleans Republican*, May 27, 1874.

CHAPTER 8

1. DeKlyne Testimony, *U.S. v. Columbus Nash, et al;* "Report of T. W. DeKlyne," in *Meeting of Colored Men*, 22–26; Ninth Census of the United States, 1870 [database online at Ancestry.com], M593_525, 780, 384, NARA; *New Orleans Republican*, May 23, 1874 and May 27, 1874.

2. Kellogg to Emory, April 15, 1873, Record Group 393, Letters Received, Department of the Gulf, 1873–1877, NARA.

3. "A Second Fort Pillow," *New York Times*, April 19, 1873.

4. "The Louisiana Troubles," *New York Times*, April 20, 1873.

5. Captain W. J. Gentry, 19th Infantry to William B. Hughes, Quartermaster, April 17, 1873, Record Group 393, Letters Received, Department of the Gulf, NARA; *New York Times*, April 19, 1873 and April 20, 1873; William Pitt Kellogg testimony, *Condition of the South*, 263.

6. *New York Times*, April 27, 1873.

7. DeKlyne to Packard, May 8, 1874, Record Group 393, Letters Received, Department of the Gulf, 1873–1877, NARA.

8. E. L. Bossiat, "Death of J. W. Hadnot" and "The Colfax Riot," *Louisiana Democrat*, April 16, 1873.

9. *Alexandria Democrat*, April 22, 1873 and May 14, 1873; *Rapides Gazette*, May 3, 1873 and May 17, 1873; *New Orleans Republican*, May 8, 1873.

10. "General Notes," *New York Times*, May 12, 1873.

11. Watson, "Incident of My Boyhood Days," 6 (see chap. 7, n. 6); O. W. Watson to Milton Dunn, October 18, 1921.

12. Wells, *War, Reconstruction and Redemption*, 73, 78 (see chap. 7, n. 9); Johnson, "Colfax Riot," 419 (see chap. 7, n. 13); Ninth Census of the United States, 1870 [database online at Ancestry.com], M593_513, 101, 203, NARA; Bee Dunn to C. C. Dunn, n.d., Melrose Collection, Folder 356 B, CGH (see intro., n. 2).

13. Wells, *War, Reconstruction, and Redemption*, 78.

14. "The Louisiana Murders," *Harper's Weekly* XVII (May 10, 1873), 396–397.

15. "Letters from North Louisiana," *New Orleans Republican*, May 8, 1873.

16. Manie White Johnson, "The Colfax Riot of April 1873" [manuscript of article published in *Louisiana Historical Quarterly*, op. cit.], Colfax Riot Collection, CPL, 60; "Significant Dates in Grant's Life: May 22, 1873," [posted online at Grant's Tomb], www.grantstomb.org/sgdates.html; "Habeas Corpus," Oxford English Dictionary [database online], http://dictionary.oed.com/

cgi/entry/50101016?query_type=word& queryword=habeas+corpus&first=
1&max_to_show=10&sort_type=alpha&result_place=1&search_id=73hM-
cjCjeK-4493&hilite=50101016.

17. "Louisiana: From Our Own Correspondent," *New York Times*, May
30, 1873.

18. Louis F. Post, "A 'Carpetbagger' in South Carolina," *Journal of Negro
History* 10 (January 1925), 45.

19. Quoted in Sipress, "Triumph of Reaction," 111 (see chap. 5, n. 21).

20. Quoted in Ibid., 110–111; Dawson, *Army Generals and Reconstruction*, 150
(see chap. 5, n. 41).

21. Robert J. Kaczorowski, *The Politics of Judicial Interpretation: The Federal
Courts, the Department of Justice, and Civil Rights, 1866–1876* (New York: Oceana
Publications, 1995), 176; Sipress, "Triumph of Reaction," 108.

22. Wells, *War, Reconstruction, and Redemption*, 76–77.

23. Record of Events: October 24, 1873 and October 26, 1873, Department
of the Gulf, Record Group 393, Entry 1976, NARA.

24. "Our Navy in Buckram," *New Orleans Republican*, May 2, 1873.

25. Mark Swanson, *The Atlas of the Civil War: Month by Month* (Athens:
University of Georgia Press, 2004), 148.

26. "*U.S.S. Ozark-I,*" *Dictionary of American Naval Fighting Ships* [data-
base online], Naval Historical Center, Department of the Navy, Washington,
D.C., http://www.history.navy.mil/branches/org9-3.htm; "River Monitors,"
Dictionary of American Naval Fighting Ships [database online], Haze Gray and
Underway, Naval History and Photography Website, http://www.hazegray.
org/danfs/monitors/river.txt.

27. Sipress, "Triumph of Reaction," 113; Johnson, "Colfax Riot," 408.

28. *Ninth Census of the United States, 1870* [database online at Ancestry.com],
M593_513, 72, 144; Susan Durr Herbert, Notes on Calhoun family history, November
22, 2004, Tybring Hemphill Collection, Sidney, British Columbia, Canada.

29. "Our Navy in Buckram," *New Orleans Republican*, May 2, 1873.

30. Harrison and McNeely, *Grant Parish*, 67.

31. "Off and On," *Rapides Gazette*, November 15, 1873.

32. [Editorial], *Louisiana Democrat*, October 29, 1873; *Ninth Census of the
United States, 1870* [database online at Ancestry.com], M593_528, 5, 11.

33. "Reported Outrages by State Police in Louisiana," *New York Times*,
November 2, 1873; [Editorial] *Louisiana Democrat*, October 29, 1973.

34. Wells, *War, Reconstruction, and Redemption*, 76; "Grant Parish Horror,"
Rapides Gazette, November 15, 1873.

35. Grant, "Battle of Colfax," 10; *Ninth Census of the United States, 1870*
[database online at Ancestry.com], M593_513, 83, 166, NARA.

36. Grant, "Battle of Colfax," 10.

37. M. Layssard, "Statement of the Colfax Outrage," *Louisiana Democrat*,
November 26, 1873.

38. "The Metropolitans," *Louisiana Democrat*, November 5, 1873.

39. "Return of the Ozark," *Rapides Gazette*, November 1, 1873.

40. [Editorial], *Louisiana Democrat*, November 12, 1873; Milton Dunn notes and photograph of tree stump, Melrose Scrapbook 67, CGH; James Madison Wells testimony, *Condition of the South*, 516; "The Grant Parish Outrage," *New York Times*, November 15, 1873.

41. "Testimony of James Madison Wells," *Condition of the South*, 517; Wells, *War, Reconstruction, and Redemption*, 75–78.

42. "Office of the United States Marshal" [report of Henry Lott] in *Use of the Army*, 342–343; James Madison Wells testimony, *Condition of the South*, 516. Another reference had a black prisoner released from the jail and "permitted to go to Little Rock, Ark, on a social visit to Loyd Shorter." [Editorial], *Alexandria Democrat*, January 28, 1874.

43. Quoted in Johnson, "Colfax Riot," 408.

44. [Editorial], *Alexandria Democrat*, April 16, 1873.

CHAPTER 9

1. "Grant Parish, La., Murderers Committed," *New York Times*, December 5, 1873; Commitment filed in Case of *United States v. Columbus Nash et al*, U.S. Circuit Court of the New Orleans Division of the Eastern District of Louisiana, Record Group 21, Records of the U.S. District Courts of the United States, 1685–1991, NARA.

2. Dunn, "Nash—A Tribute," 4.

3. J. R. Beckwith testimony in *Condition of the South*, 409; *Seventh Census of the United States*, 1850 [database online at Ancestry.com], M432_536, 92, 186.

4. J. R. Beckwith to George H. Williams, June 17, 1873, Source Chronological Files: Letters Received by the Attorney General, 1870–1884, M940, Reel 1, NARA; Robert J. Kaczorowski, *The Politics of Judicial Interpretation: The Federal Courts, the Department of Justice, and Civil Rights, 1866–1876* (New York: Oceana Publications, 1985), 176; Sipress, *Triumph of Reaction*, 109 (see chap. 5, n. 21).

5. George C. Rable, "Republican Albatross: The Louisiana Question, National Politics, and the Failure of Reconstruction," in *The Louisiana Purchase Bicentennial Series in Louisiana History: Volume VI: Reconstructing Louisiana* (Lafayette: University of Louisiana at Lafayette Press, 2001), 698; [Proceedings] July 4, 1870, *Journal of the Senate of the United States of America, 1789–1873*, American Memory Project, Library of Congress, http://memory.loc.gov/cgi-bin/query/r?ammem/hlaw:@field(DOCID+@lit (sj064146)).

6. Michael R. Belknap, "Federalism and the Protection of Civil Rights," *Columbia Law Review* 86 (December 1986), 1741–1754; William H. Rehnquist, "Remarks of the Chief Justice, Dedication of the Ohio Judiciary Center, May 15, 2004," Speeches of Supreme Court Justices, Supreme Court of the United States, http://www.supremecourtus.gov/publicinfo/speeches/sp_05–15–04.html; George H. Williams to J. R. Beckwith, February 3, 1874, Letters Sent by the Department of Justice:

Instructions to U.S. Attorneys and Marshals, 1867–1904, M701, Reel 4, NARA; J. R. Beckwith to George H. Williams, May 23, 1874, Source Chronological Files: Letters Received by the Attorney General, 1870–1884, M940, Reel 1, NARA.

7. "The Colfax Prisoners," *Louisiana Democrat* (March 4, 1874).

8. *Ninth Census of the United States,* 1870 [database online at Ancestry.com], M593_513, 116, 233; M593_506, 468, 309; M593_506, 383, 139; M593_513, 86, 173; M593_513, 90, 181; M593_513, 100, 201; M593_512, 24, 49.

9. "The Colfax Prisoners," *The Caucasian,* December 26, 1874 reprinted in *Condition of the South,* 852; W. P. Kellogg testimony in ibid., 246; "The Colfax Prisoners," *Louisiana Democrat,* January 28, 1874.

10. "The Grant Parish Prisoners Fund," *New Orleans Republican,* June 28, 1874; J. R. Beckwith testimony in *Condition of the South,* 414.

11. J. E. Dunn to Cammie G. Henry, March 4, 1926, Melrose Collection, Folder 359, CGH (see intro., n. 2); J. R. Beckwith testimony in *Condition of the South,* 419; "The Grant Parish Prisoners" [report on proceedings], *New Orleans Republican,* February 27, 1874; "The United States Circuit Court," *New Orleans Republican,* May 19, 1874; Claude G. Bowers, *The Tragic Era: Reconstruction after Lincoln* (Cambridge: Houghton Mifflin, 1929), 436.

12. Charles Vincent, *Black Legislators in Louisiana during Reconstruction* (Baton Rouge: Louisiana State University Press, 1976), 175; "The State Penitentiary: Reports of the Committees," *New Orleans Republican,* February 24, 1874.

13. "The Grant Parish Prisoners," *New Orleans Picayune,* June 30, 1874 [article reprint], in *Condition of the South,* 188.

14. "A Republican" to S. B. Packard, April 6, 1874, in *Use of the Army,* 338.

15. J. R. Beckwith to George H. Williams, May 23, 1874, Source Chronological Files: Letters Received by the Attorney General, 1870–1884, M940, Reel 1, NARA.

16. Only three of the original dozens of transcripts of witness testimony have survived. The most comprehensive surviving record appears in the pages of the *New Orleans Republican,* whose editor, T. G. Tracy, attended the trial daily and shared his own notes with the district attorney. See "Testimony taken in the United States Circuit Court," Select Committee, on that part of the President's Message relating to the late Insurrectionary States, HR 43A-431.4, NARA.

17. "Jottings in the Grant Parish Trial," *New Orleans Republican,* March 1, 1874; "Emphatic Swearing," *New Orleans Republican,* May 31, 1874.

18. W.E.B. DuBois, "The Souls of Black Folk," in *The Oxford W.E.B. DuBois Reader,* Eric J. Sundquist, ed. (New York: Oxford University Press, 1996), 116.

19. "Jottings in the Grant Parish Trial," *New Orleans Republican,* March 1, 1874; "Closing Arguments in the Case," *New Orleans Republican,* March 13, 1874.

20. U.S. Circuit Court, *United States v. Columbus C. Nash, et al.,* U.S. Circuit Court, 1874, No. 12, NARA Archival Resource Center [collection online], http://arcweb.archives.gov/arc/servlet/arc.ControllerServlet?&pg_n&rn_1&nw_n&nh_12.htm.

21. "The Grant Parish Prisoners" [witness testimony], *New Orleans Republican*, March 7, 1874; March 8, 1874; March 10, 1874.

22. "The Grant Parish Prisoners" [witness testimony], *New Orleans Republican*, March 8, 1874; Lalita Tademy, *Cane River* (New York: Warner Books, 2001), 383–388.

23. McCain, "Incident of My Boyhood Days," 5.

24. *U.S. v. Cruikshank et al.*, 25 Federal Cases 707 (No. 14,897) C. C. La (1874).

25. J. R. Beckwith to George H. Williams, June 26, 1874, Source Chronological Files: Letters Received by the Attorney General, 1870–1884, M940, Reel 1, NARA; Kaczorowski, *Politics of Judicial Interpretation*, 178; Charles Fairman, *The Oliver Wendell Holmes Devise History of the Supreme Court of the United States, Volume VI: Reconstruction and Reunion, 1864–88, Part I* (New York: The Macmillan Company, 1971), 1378.

26. "The Grant Parish Prisoners" [witness testimony], *New Orleans Republican*, June 2, 1874; *Ninth Census of the United States*, 1870 [database online at Ancestry.com], M593_527, 175, 352.

27. Kaczorowski, *Politics of Judicial Interpretation*, 179.

28. "Lynching in Louisiana—Grant Parish," *New York Times*, June 10, 1874.

29. Ibid., 179; John R. Howard, *The Shifting Wind: The Supreme Court and Civil Rights from Reconstruction to Brown* (Albany: State University of New York Press, 1999), 97; J. R. Beckwith to George H. Williams, June 25, 1874, Source Chronological Files: Letters Received by the Attorney General, 1870–1884, M940, Reel 1, NARA.

30. Fairman, *Holmes History of the Supreme Court*, 1378–1379; Howard, *Shifting Wind*, 99; Kaczorowski, *Politics of Judicial Interpretation*, 179.

31. Newman and Gass, "New Birth of Freedom, 21 (see chap. 5, n. 4).

32. *United States v. Cruikshank et al.*, C.C. La. 1874, Case No. 14, 897, 1 Woods, 308 [available online at Westlaw, 1 Woods 308].

33. 1 Woods 308; Kaczorowski, *Politics of Judicial Interpretation*, 180–183.

34. 1 Woods 308.

35. Gillette, "Longest Battle," 680; Mitchell, *All on Mardi Gras Day*, 66; Augusto P. Miceli, *The Pickwick Club of New Orleans* (New Orleans: Pickwick Press, 1964), 70–71; Elaine Frantz Parsons, "Midnight Rangers: Costume and Performance in the Reconstruction-Era Ku Klux Klan," *Journal of American History* 92 (December 2005), 834.

36. Highsmith, "Reconstruction in the Heart of Louisiana," 485–486; H. Oscar Lestage, Jr., "The White League in Louisiana and Its Participation in Reconstruction Riots" (master's thesis, Louisiana State University and Agricultural and Mechanical College, 1930), 637.

37. William Pitt Kellogg testimony in *Condition of the South*, 246.

38. George H. Williams to J. R. Beckwith, July 17, 1874, Letters Sent by the Department of Justice: Instructions to U.S. Attorneys and Marshals, 1867–1904, M701, Reel 4, NARA.

39. [Editorial], *The Caucasian,* July 4, 1874, in *Condition of the South,* 772.

40. Sipress, *Triumph of Reaction,* 116–117; Arthur W. Allyn testimony in *Condition of the South,* 155–156.

41. James K. Hogue, "The 1873 Battle of Colfax: Paramilitarism and Counterrevolution in Louisiana," Paper presented at the Southern Historical Association annual conference, Atlanta, GA, November 6, 1997 [available online], http://warhistorian.org/hogue-colfax.pdf. See also Raiford Blunt testimony in *Condition of the South,* 214–223.

42. Tunnell, *Crucible of Reconstruction,* 198–201 (see chap. 3, n. 20); "The Coushatta Massacre...Letters from the Victims," *New Orleans Republican,* n.d., in *Condition of the South,* 773.

43. Miceli, *Pickwick Club,* 71; Gillette, "Longest Battle," 680; Tunnell, *Crucible of Reconstruction,* 202.

44. J. B. Stockton to Stephen B. Packard, October 22, 1874, in *Use of the Army,* 307; *New Orleans, Louisiana Death Records Index, 1804–1949* [database online at Ancestry.com], State of Louisiana, Division of Archives, Records Management, and History.

45. Donald McIntosh to Assistant Adjutant General, Department of the Gulf, November 26, 1874, in *Condition of the South,* 75.

46. [Lewis Merrill testimony], *Condition of the South,* 156.

47. Ibid.; Lewis Merrill to Assistant Adjutant-General, Department of the Gulf, November 26, 1874, in ibid., 75.

48. [Witness testimony], *Condition of the South,* 263.

49. John DeLacy testimony in *Condition of the South,* 373, 376.

50. S. Van Dusen to S. B. Packard, November 8, 1874, in *Use of the Army in Southern States,* 402.

51. Bowers, *Tragic Era,* 443.

52. McFeely, *Grant,* 417.

53. A. Mitchell to F. C. Zacharie, January 5, 1875, in *Condition of the South,* 223.

CHAPTER 10

1. Quoted in Edwin A. Davis, *The Story of Louisiana* (New Orleans: J. F. Hyer, 1960), 243.

2. Kaczorowski, *Politics of Judicial Interpretation,* 191; J. R. Beckwith to George H. Williams, December 11, 1874, Source Chronological Files: Letters Received by the Attorney General, 1870–1884, M940, Reel 1, NARA.

3. Halbrook, *Freedmen and the Fourteenth,* 169; Robert M. Goldman, *Reconstruction and Black Suffrage: Losing the Vote in Reese and Cruikshank* (Lawrence: University of Kansas Press, 2001), 76.

4. Ibid., 86–87.

5. Valelly, *Two Reconstructions,* 117–118; "An Act to Enforce the Right of Citizens of the United States to vote in the several States of this Union, and for

other Purposes, May 31, 1870," in *The Statutes at Large and Proclamations of the United States of America, from December 1869 to March 1871, Volume XVI,* George P. Sanger, ed. (Boston: Little, Brown, and Company, 1871), 140.

6. Goldman, *Reconstruction and Black Suffrage,* 87.

7. *U.S. v. Cruikshank,* 92 U.S. 542 (1875).

8. Ibid.

9. Valelly, *Two Reconstructions,* 117–118.

10. Ibid., 76.

11. Dawson, *Army Generals and Reconstruction,* 259 (see chap. 5, n. 41).

12. "Bourbon Ballads: Extra No. 52, Songs for the Stump," *New York Tribune,* September 1879, Library of Congress American Memory Online Archive, http://memory.loc.gov/rbc/amss/as1/as101480/001q.gif.

13. Nell Irvin Painter, *Exodusters: Black Migration to Kansas After Reconstruction* (New York: Knopf, 1977), 181.

14. Ibid., 182.

15. Paul Lewinson, *Race, Class & Party: A History of Negro Suffrage and White Politics in the South* (New York: Russell & Russell, 1963), 68.

16. Painter, *Exodusters,* 96.

17. Ibid., 99.

18. Louis R. Nardini, Sr., "A Grant Parish History," *Colfax Chronicle,* August 24, 1962; Carl A. Brasseaux, Glenn R. Conrad, and R. Warren Robison, *The Courthouses of Louisiana* (Lafayette: Center for Louisiana Studies, University of Southwestern Louisiana, 1977), 82; Howard, *Political Tendencies in Louisiana,* 153–172 (see chap. 6, n. 3).

19. *L. Bouchereau's Statement of the Sugar and Rice Crops Made in Louisiana, 1882–1883* (New Orleans: Pelican Books and Job Printing Office, 1883), v–iv; *Biographical and Historical Memoirs of Northwest Louisiana* (Nashville: The Southern Publishing Company, 1890), 503.

20. Susan Durr Hebert to Tybring Hemphill, November 22, 2004 [private correspondence in author's possession].

21. Ibid.; *Tenth Census of the United States,* 1880.

22. Ibid.; *Thirteenth Census of the United States,* 1910; Julius Grodinsky, *Jay Gould: His Business Career, 1867–1892* (Philadelphia: University of Pennsylvania Press, 1957), 318; Richard O'Connor, *Gould's Millions* (Garden City, N.Y.: Doubleday, 1962), 275; Maury Klein, *The Life and Legend of Jay Gould* (Baltimore: Johns Hopkins University Press, 1986), 473–474, 477.

23. Painter, *Exodusters,* 82, 181–186; Emmett Scott, *Negro Migration During the War* (New York: Oxford University Press, 1920), 4, 78.

24. "Article 5 [no title]," *The Independent—Devoted to the Consideration of Politics, Social and Economic,* March 4, 1875, 19.

25. Pierre Duval, *The Carillon Satires,* edited and translated by John Maxwell Jones (Camden, N.J.: [privately printed by John Maxwell Jones, 1978]).

26. *Louisiana Statewide Death Index,* 1900–1949 [database online at Ancestry. com].

27. Frederick Douglass, *The Life and Times of Frederick Douglass,* in *The Oxford Frederick Douglass Reader,* William L. Andrews, ed. (New York: Oxford University Press, 1996), 296.

28. [Obituary of William Smith Calhoun], *Colfax Chronicle,* January 17, 1891.

29. "Origins of the Colfax Massacre: Correcting a Misstatement of Facts," *Colfax Chronicle,* June 3, 1882.

30. Westy Horn to M. A. Dunn, September 10, 1902; "General Jim's Reminiscences," *Shreveport Journal,* July 22, 1905, Melrose Scrapbook #67, CGH (see intro., n. 2).

31. Quoted in Daniel Brantley, "Blacks and Louisiana Constitutional Development, 1890–Present: A Study in Southern Political Thought and Race Relations," *Phylon* 48 (1987), 51–61.

32. Brantley, "Louisiana Constitutional Development," 57–59; Howard, *Political Tendencies in Louisiana,* 188.

33. Quoted in Howard, *Political Tendencies in Louisiana,* 189.

34. Ibid., 190–191; Brantley, "Louisiana Constitutional Development," 57; Leon Litwack, *Trouble in Mind: Black Southerners in the Age of Jim Crow* (New York: Knopf, 1998), 225.

35. Lewinson, *Race, Class and Party,* 62.

36. George Washington Cable, *The Silent South* (New York: Charles SCribners' Sons, 1885), 168–71.

37. Milton Dunn notes, September 12, 1914, Melrose Scrapbook 67, CGH.

38. "Colfax Monument Unveiled," *Colfax Chronicle,* April 16, 1921; "Historic Colfax Tree Registered in Hall of Fame at Washington," n.d., n.p. [newspaper clipping], Melrose Scrapbook 67, CGH; "Program: Unveiling of Monument [to] Heroes of the Colfax Riot," Melrose Bound Volume 3, CGH.

39. W. S. Ingram, "'Colfax Riots,' Famous in Reconstruction of Entire Dixie Domain," *Colfax Chronicle,* June 13, 1926; Robert Moore [Extension Forester] to N. D. Canterbury [Louisiana State Department of Conservation], November 22, 1929, Dorman Collection, Folder 386, CGH.

40. "Colfax Riot Made History," *Pershing Way Magazine,* n.d. [magazine clipping], Melrose Scrapbook 67, CGH.

41. Quoted in Robert Dallek, *Flawed Giant: Lyndon Johnson and His Times* (New York: Oxford University Press, 1998), 183.

42. Newman and Gass, "New Birth of Freedom" (see chap. 5, n. 4); Frederick D. Wright, "The Voting Rights Act and Louisiana: Twenty Years of Enforcement," *Publius* 16 (Autumn, 1986), 104.

43. John Hope Franklin, "Rediscovering Black America: A Historical Roundup," *New York Times,* September 8, 1968.

Bibliography

Ayers, Thomas. *Dark and Bloody Ground: The Battle of Mansfield and the Forgotten Civil War in Louisiana* (Dallas: Taylor Trade Publishing, 2001).

Baker, A. R. "Reminiscences of Natural Gas in the Oil Country," *Magazine of Western History* 7 (February 1888): 454.

Bell, Derrick A., Jr. "Brown v. Board of Education and the Interest-Convergence Dilemma," *Harvard Law Review* 93, no. 3 (1980): 518–534.

Betts, Edward Chamber. *Historic Huntsville: From Early History of Huntsville, Alabama, 1809 to 1870* (Louisiana: Louisiana State University Press, 1966).

Beveridge, Charles E., and Charles Capen McLaughlin, eds. *The Papers of Frederick Law Olmsted, Volume II: Slavery and the South, 1852–1857* (Baltimore: Johns Hopkins University Press, 1981).

Biographical and Historical Memoirs of Northwest Louisiana (Nashville: The Southern Publishing Company, 1890).

Birney, William. *James G. Birney and His Times: The Genesis of the Republican Party* (New York: Bergman Publishers, 1969).

Blassingham, John W. *Black New Orleans, 1860–1880* (Chicago: University of Chicago Press, 1973).

Blaustein, Albert P. and Robert L. Zangrando, eds. *Civil Rights and the Black American: A Documentary History* (New York: Washington Square Press, 1968).

Bouchereau, Alcée. *Statement of the Sugar and Rice Crops Made in Louisiana in 1881–82, with an Appendix* (New Orleans: L. Graham & Son, Printers, 1882).

Booth, Andrew B. *Records of Louisiana Confederate Soldiers and Louisiana Confederate Commands* (Spartanburg, SC: Reprint Co., 1984).

Brasseaux, Carl A., Glenn R. Conrad, and R. Warren Robinson. *The Courthouses of Louisiana* (Lafayette: Center for Louisiana Studies, University of Southwestern Louisiana, 1977).

Brundage, W. Fitzhugh. *The Southern Past: A Clash of Race and Memory* (Cambridge: Harvard University Press, 2005).

Buyer, Linda. *The Calhoun House: Historic Huntsville* IX (Spring/Summer 1983): 29–36.

Carleton, Mark T. "The Politics of the Convict Lease System in Louisiana: 1868–1901," *Louisiana History* VIII (Winter 1967): 5–25.

Caskey, Willie Malvin. *Secession and Restoration of Louisiana* (Baton Rouge: Louisiana State University Press, 1938).

Chambers, Henry E. *A History of Louisiana: Wilderness—Colony—Province—Territory—State—People* (Chicago: The American Historical Society, 1925).

Champomier, P. A. *Statement of the Sugar Crop Made in Louisiana in 1845–6* (New Orleans: Magne & Weisse, 1846).

Clay-Clopton, Virginia. *Belle of the Fifties: Memoirs of Mrs. Clay, of Alabama, Covering Social and Political Life in Washington and the South, 1853–1866, Gathered and Edited by Ada Sterling* (New York: Doubleday, Page & Company, 1904).

Clayton, Dewey M. "A Funny Thing Happened on the Way to the Voting Precinct: A Brief History of Disenfranchisement in America," *The Black Scholar* 34, Issue 3 (San Francisco: Fall 2004): 42.

"Committee of 70." *History of the Riot at Colfax* (New Orleans: Clark and Hofeline, Books & Joss Printing Office, 1873).

Corley, D. B. *A Visit to Uncle Tom's Cabin* (Chicago: Laird & Lee Publishers, 1892).

Culbert, David H. "The Infinite Variety of Mass Experience: The Great Depression, W. P. A. Interviews, and Student Family History Projects,": *Loiusiana History* XIX (Winter 1978): 43–63.

Current, Richard N., ed. *Encyclopedia of the Confederacy, Volume III* (New York: Simon & Schuster, 1993).

Dallek, Robert. *Flawed Giant: Lyndon Johnson and His Times* (New York: Oxford University Press, 1998).

Davis, Edwin A. *The Story of Louisiana.* New York: J. F. Hyer, 1960.

Dawson, Joseph G., III. *Army Generals and Reconstruction: Louisiana, 1862–1877* (Baton Rouge: Louisiana State University Press, 1982).

Democratic Party National Committee. *The Campaign Text Book: A Summary of Leading Events in Our History under Republican Administration* (New York: Democratic Party National Committee, 1876).

Dennett, Daniel. *Louisiana As It Is* (New Orleans: Eureka Press, 1876).

DuBois, W.E.B. *Black Reconstruction in America* (New York: Oxford University Press, 2007).

Dunning, William A. *Reconstruction, Political and Economic* (New York: Harper and Brothers, 1907).

Durel, Pierre. *The Carillon Satires.* Edited and translated by John Maxwell Jones (Camden, N.J.: [printed privately by John Maxwell Jones], 1978).

Dyer, Frederick H. *A Compendium of the War of the Rebellion, Volume III: Regimental Histories* (New York: Thomas Yoseloff, 1959).

Eaton, Clement. *History of the Old South* (New York: Macmillan, 1949).

Fairman, Charles. *The Oliver Wendell Homes Devise History of the Supreme Court of the United States, Volume VI: Reconstruction and Reunion, 1864–88, Part One* (New York: The Macmillan Company, 1971).

Fletcher, Mary Dell. *Grant Parish Cemeteries* (Bossier City, LA: Everett Publishers, 1990).

Follett, Richard J. *The Sugar Masters: Slavery, Economic Development, and Modernization in Louisiana Sugar Plantations, 1820–1860, Volume I* (Doctoral Dissertation, Louisiana State University and Agricultural and Mechanical College, 1997).

Foner, Eric. *Freedom's Lawmakers: A Directory of Black Officeholders during Reconstruction* (Baton Rouge: Louisiana State University Press, 1996).

Franklin, John Hope. *Reconstruction After the Civil War* (Chicago: University of Chicago Press, 1994).

Freudenberger, Herman, and Jonathan B. Pritchett. "The Domestic United States Slave Trade: New Evidence," *Journal of Interdisciplinary History* 21 (Winter 1991): 457–468.

Fridlington, Robert. *The Supreme Court in American Life, Volume 4: The Reconstruction Court, 1864–1888* (Millwood, NY: Associated Faculty Press, 1987).

Goldman, Robert M. *Reconstruction and Black Suffrage: Losing the Vote in Reese and Cruikshank* (Lawrence: University Press of Kansas, 2001).

Gosnell, Harpur Allen. *Guns on the Western Waters: The Story of River Gunboats in Civil War* (Louisiana: Baton Rouge, Louisiana State University Press, 1949).

The Grant and Colfax Songster: Comprising a Choice Selection of New and Popular Songs and Ballads for Campaign (New York: Beadle and Company, Publishers, 1868).

"The Great South," *Scribner's Monthly* VII (December 1873): 129–161.

Grodinsky, Julius. *Jay Gould: His Business Career, 1867–1892* (Philadelphia: University of Pennsylvania Press, 1957).

Hahn, Steven. *A Nation Under Our Feet: Black Political Struggles in the Rural South from Slavery to the Great Migration* (Cambridge: Harvard University Press, 2003).

Halbrook, Stephen P. *Freedmen, the Fourteenth Amendment, and the Right to Bear Arms, 1866–1876* (Westport, CT: Praeger, 1998).

Hall, Kermit L., ed. *The Oxford Companion to the Supreme Court of the United States* (New York: Oxford University Press, 1992).

Harris, William H. *Louisiana Products, Resources and Attractions* (New Orleans: E. A. Brandao & Co, 1885).

Harrison, Mabel Fletcher, and Lavina McGuire McNeely. *Grant Parish: A History* (Baton Rouge: Claitor's Publishing Division, 1969).

Hatch, Edward. *Recapitulation* (New Orleans: Headquarters Bureau Refugees, Freedmen, and Abandoned Lands, 1868).

Hawkins, Gregg A. *Louisiana Terrorism: The 1873 Colfax Incident* (master's dissertation, Southern University, 1999).

Heitman, John Alfred. *The Modernization of the Louisiana Sugar Industry, 1830–1910* (Baton Rouge: Louisiana State University Press, 1987).

Hewett, Janet B. *The Roster of Union Soldiers, 1861–1865: United States Colored Troops, Volume I* (Wilmington: Broadfoot Publishing Company, 1997).

Hewett, ed., Janet B. *The Roster of Confederate Soldiers, 1861–1865, Volume III: Buff, Aaron to Coirrier, E. F.* (Wilmington: Broadfoot Publishing Company, 1995).

Highsmith, Willam E. "Some Aspects of Reconstruction in the Heart of Louisiana," *Journal of Southern History* 13 (1947).

House of Representatives, 43rd Congress, 2nd Session. *Report of the Select Committee on That Portion of the President's Message Relating to the Condition of the South,* Report No. 101, January 15, 1875 (Washington, D.C.: Government Printing Office, 1875).

House of Representatives, 43rd Congress, 2nd Session. *Report on the Condition of the South,* Congressional Serial Set No. 251 (Washington, D.C.: Government Printing Office, 1875).

House of Representatives, 44th Congress, 2nd Session. *Use of the Army in Certain of the Southern States, Executive Document No. 30* (January 24, 1877), Congressional Serial Set v. 1755 (Washington, D.C.: Government Printing Office, 1877).

House Reports, No. 101, Serial 1657, *Condition of the South: Report of the Committee Chaired by George F. Hoar* (Washington, D.C.: Government Printing Office, 1875).

Howard, John R. *The Shifting Wind: The Supreme Court and Civil Rights from Reconstruction to Brown* (Albany: State University of New York Press, 1999).

Howard, Perry H. *Political Tendencies in Louisiana* (Baton Rouge: Louisiana State University Press, 1957).

Hunter, Louis C. "The Invention of the Western Steamboat," *Journal of Economic History* 3 (November 1943): 201–220.

Ingram, Henry Atlee. *The Life and Character of Stephen Girard, Mariner and Merchant* (Philadelphia: [Self-Published], 1892).

Johnson, Manie White. "The Colfax Riot of April 1873" (master's dissertation, University of California, 1929).

Johnson, Marael. *Louisiana, Why Stop? A Guide to Louisiana's Roadside Historical Markers* (Houston: Gulf Publishing Company, 1996).

Journal of the Convention Framing a Constitution for the State of Louisiana 1867–1868 (Westport, Connecticut: Greenwood Publishing Company, 1867–1868).

Kaczorowski, Robert J. *The Politics of Judicial Interpretation, The Federal Courts, Department of Justice and Civil Rights, 1866–1876* (Dobbs Ferry, NY: Ocean Publications, 1985).

Klein, Maury. *The Life and Legend of Jay Gould* (Baltimore: Johns Hopkins University Press, 1986).

Koenig, Karl. *The History of the March* (Abita Springs, LA: Basin Street Press, 1996.

Kolchin, Peter. *American Slavery, 1619–1877* (New York: Hill and Wang, 1993).

Lestage, H. Oscar, Jr. "The White League in Louisiana and Its Participation in Reconstruction Riots" (master's dissertation, Louisiana State University and Agricultural and Mechanical College, 1930).

Lewinson, Paul. *Race, Class & Party: A History of Negro Suffrage and White Politics in the South* (New York: Russell & Russell, 1963).

Lipsitz, George. "The Possessive Investment in Whiteness: Racialized Social Democracy and the 'White' Problem in American Studies," *American Quarterly* 47, Issue 3 (September 1995).

Litwack, Leon. *Trouble in Mind: Black Southerners in the Age of Jim Crow* (New York: Knopf, 1998).

Lockett, Samuel H. *Louisiana As It Is: A Geographical and Topographical Description of the State,* edited and with an introduction by Lauren C. Post (Baton Rouge: Louisiana State University, 1969).

Loewen, James W. *Lies Across America: What Our Historic Sites Get Wrong* (New York: New Press, 1999).

Lonn, Ella. *Reconstruction in Louisiana After 1868* (New York: G. P. Putnam's Sons, 1918).

Lowery, Walter. "The Political Career of James Madison Wells," *Journal of Southern History* 15 (November 1949): 550–561.

Mak, James, and Gary M. Walton. "Steamboats and the Great Productivity Surge in River Transportation," *Journal of Economic History* 32 (September 1972): 620–624.

Mangan, Katherine S. "Portrait: The History, Routine, and Terror of a Prison System," *Chronicle of Higher Education* 38 (June 3, 1992): 38–39.

Marks, Paul Mitchell. *In a Barren Land: American Indian Dispossession and Survival* (New York: William Morrow and Company, Inc., 1998).

The Massacre in Grant Parish, Louisiana. Meeting of Colored Men in New Orleans: Address and Speeches (New Orleans: Republican Office, 1873).

McDonald, Robert R., John R. Kemp, and Edward F. Haas, eds. *Louisiana's Black Heritage* (New Orleans: Louisiana State Museum, 1979).

McPherson, James B., ed. *The Atlas of the Civil War* (New York: Macmillan, 1994).

——. *Battle Cry of Freedom: The Civil War Era* (New York: Ballantine Books, 1988).

Menn, Joseph Karl. *The Large Slaveholders of Louisiana, 1860* (New Orleans: Pelican Publishing Company, 1964).

Miller, Francis Trevelyan, ed. *The Decisive Battles, The Photographic History of the Civil War* (New York: Castle Books, 1957).

Mills, Elizabeth Shown, and Gary B. Mills. *Tales of Old Natchitoches* (Chicago: Adams Press, 1978).

Mitchell, Reid. *All on Mardi Gras Day: Episodes in the History of New Orleans Carnival* (Cambridge: Harvard University Press, 1995).

Nankivell, John H. *History of the Twenty-Fifth Regiment United States Infantry, 1869–1926* (Denver: The Smith-Brooks Printing Company, 1927).

Northrop, Solomon. *Twelve Years a Slave,* edited by Sue Eakin and Joseph Logsdon (Baton Rouge: Louisiana State University Press, 1968).

O'Connor, Henry. *Republican Political Handbook for Public Speakers and Local Committees* (New York: Evening Post Steam Press, 1880).

O'Connor, Richard. *Gould's Millions* (Garden City: Doubleday, 1962).

Parsons, Elaine Frantz. "Midnight Rangers: Costume and Performance in the Reconstruction-Era Ku Klux Klan," *Journal of American History* 92 (December 2005): 811–835.

Powell, Lawrence N., with J. Mark Souther. *Reconstructing Louisiana, The Louisiana Purchase Bicentennial Series in Louisiana History, Volume VI* (Lafayette, LA: Center for Louisiana Studies, University of Louisiana at Lafayette, 2000).

Pratt, Fletcher. *Civil War on the Western Waters* (New York: Henry Hit and Company, 1956).

Rable, George. "Republican Albatross: The Louisiana Question, National Politics, and the Failure of Reconstruction," *The Louisiana Purchase Bicentennial Series in Louisiana History: Volume VI, Reconstructing Louisiana* (Lafayette: University of Louisiana at Lafayette Press, 2001).

Rable, George C. *But There Was No Peace: The Role of Violence in the Politics of Reconstruction* (Athens: University of Georgia Press, 1984).

Ransom Roger L., and Richard Sutch. *One Kind of Freedom: The Economic Consequences of Emancipation* (Cambridge: Cambridge University Press, 2001).

Rehder, John B. *Delta Sugar: Louisiana's Vanishing Plantation Landscape* (Baltimore: John Hopkins University Press, 1999).

Ripley, C. Peter. *Black, Blue and Gray: Slaves and Freedom in Civil War Louisiana* (doctoral dissertation, Florida State University College of Arts and Sciences, 1973).

Rodrigue, John C. *Reconstruction in the Cane Fields: From Slavery to Free Labor in Louisiana's Sugar Parishes, 1862–1880* (Baton Rouge: Louisiana State University, 2001).

Rohr, Nancy M. *An Alabama School Girl in Paris, 1842–1844: The Letters of Mary Fenwick Lewis and Her Family* (Huntsville, AL: Silver Threads Publishing, 2001).

Roland, Charles P. *Louisiana Sugar Plantations During the American Civil War* (Leiden, Netherlands: E. J. Brill, 1957).

Rubin, Richard. "The Colfax Riot: Stumbling on a Forgotten Reconstruction Tragedy in a Forgotten Corner of Louisiana," *Atlantic Online* (July/August 2003).

Schindler, Henri. *Mardi Gras Treasures: Invitations of the Golden Age* (Gretna, LA: Pelican Publishing Company, 2000).

Scott, Emmett. *Negro Migration During the War* (New York: Oxford University Press, 1920).

Sefton, James E. *The United States Army and Reconstruction, 1865–1867* (Baton Rouge: Louisiana State University Press, 1967).

Shallat, Todd. "Engineering Policy: The U.S. Army Corps of Engineers and the Historical Foundation of Power," *The Public Historian* 11 (Summer 1989): 6–27.

Shugg, Roger W. *Origins of the Class Struggle in Louisiana: A Social History of White Farmers and Laborers during Slavery and After, 1840–1875* (Baton Rouge: Louisiana State University Press, 1968).

Sifakis, Stewart, ed. *Compendium of the Confederate Armies: Louisiana* (New York: Facts on File, 1995).

Singletary, Otis A. *Negro Militia and Reconstruction* (Austin: University of Texas Press, 1957).

Sipress, Joel M. *The Triumph of Reaction: Political Struggle in a New South Community, 1865–1898* (Ph.D. dissertation, University of North Carolina at Chapel Hill, 1993).

Smith, Caroline Patricia. "Jacksonian Conservative: The Later Years of William Smith, 1826–1840" (Doctoral dissertation, Auburn University, Auburn, AL, 1977).

Smith, Murphy D. "The Stephen Girard Papers," *Manuscripts* (Winter 1977): 14–23.

Stafford, G. M. G. *The Wells Family of Louisiana, and Allied Families* (Alexandria, LA: Standard Printing Company, Inc., 1941).

Stowe, Charles Edward, and Lyman Beecher Stowe. *Harriet Beecher Stowe: The Story of Her Life* (Boston: Mifflin Company, 1911).

Stowe, Harriet Beecher. *Key to Uncle Tom's Cabin* (Cincinnati: American Reform Tract and Book Society, 1856).

Swanson, Mark. *Atlas of the Civil War, Month by Month: Major Battles and Troop Movements* (Athens: University of Georgia Press, 2004).

Tademy, Lalita. *Cane River* (New York: Warner Books, 2002).

——. *Red River* (New York: Warner Books, 2007).

Taylor, Joel Gray. *Louisiana Reconstructed, 1863–1877* (Baton Rouge: Louisiana State University Press, 1974).

Taylor, Judge Thomas Jones. *A History of Madison County and Incidentally of North Alabama, 1732–1840* (University, AL: Confederate Publishing Company, 1976).

Thurman, Allen G. *Bayonet-Government in Louisiana: Speech on the Hon. A. G. Thurman of Ohio in the Senate of the United States, January 27, 1875* (Washington, D.C.: Government Printing Office, 1875).

Trelease, Allen W. "Who Were the Scalawags?" *Journal of Southern History* 4 (November 1963): 445–468.

Tunnel, Ted. *The Crucible of Reconstruction: War, Radicalism, and Race in Louisiana, 1862–1877* (Baton Rouge: Louisiana State University Press, 1984).

Valelly, Richard M. *The Two Reconstructions: The Struggle for Black Enfranchisement* (Chicago: University of Chicago Press, 2004).

Vandal, Gilles. "Black Violence in Post-Civil War Louisiana," *Journal of Interdisciplinary History* 25, no. 1 (Summer 1994).

——. "Property Offenses, Social Tension and Racial Antagonism in Post-Civil War." *Journal of Social History* 31, Issue 1 (Fall 1997): 127.

——. *Rethinking Southern Violence: Homicide in Post-Civil War Louisiana, 1866–1884* (Columbus: Ohio State University Press, 2000).

Vincent, Charles. *Black Legislator in Louisiana During Reconstruction* (Baton Rouge: Louisiana State University, 1976).

Vincent, Charles, ed. *The Louisiana Purchase Bicentennial Series in Louisiana History, Volume XI, The African American Experience in Louisiana, Part B: From the Civil War to Jim Crow* (Lafayette, LA: Center for Louisiana Studies, University of Louisiana at Lafayette, 2000).

Waldo, J. Curtis. *History of the Carnival in New Orleans from 1857 to 1882* (New Orleans: L. Graham & Son, Printers, 1882).

Warmouth, Henry Clay. *War, Politics and Reconstruction: Stormy Days in Louisiana* (New York: Negro Universities Press, 1930).

Wells, Carol, ed., *War, Reconstruction and Redemption on Red River: The Memoirs of Dosia Williams Moore* (Ruston, LA: McGinty Publications, 1990).

Wells, Mary Ann. *A History Lover's Guide to Louisiana* (Baton Rouge: Quail Ridge Books, 1990).

Wells-Barnett, Ida B. *On Lynching: Southern Horrors, a Red Record, Mob Rule in New Orleans* (New York: Arno Press and the New York Times, 1969).

White, Barbara A. *The Beecher Sisters* (New Haven: Yale University Press, 2003).

White, Howard A. *The Freedman's Bureau in Louisiana* (Baton Rouge: Louisiana State University Press, 1970).

Whittington, G. P. "Rapides Parish, Louisiana—A History," *Louisiana Historical Quarterly* Volume 18 (January 1935).

Wikberg, Ron, E. J. Carter, and Floyd Webb. "Tragedy at Colfax," *The Angolite* 14 (November/December 1989).

Wildes, Harry. *Lonely Midas: The Story of Stephen Girard* (New York: Farrar and Reinhart, 1943).

Wilson, Charles Regan, and William Ferris, eds. *Encyclopedia of Southern Culture* (Chapel Hill: University of North Carolina Press, 1989).

Wilson, James. *The Earth Shall Weep: A History of Native America* (New York: Grove Press, 1998).

Winters, John D. *The Civil War in Louisiana* (Baton Rouge: Louisiana State University Press, 1963).

Wood, Forrest G. *Black Scare: The Racist Response to Emancipation and Reconstruction* (Berkeley: University of California Press, 1970).

Wright, Frederick D. "The Voting Rights Act and Louisiana: Twenty Years of Enforcement," *Publius* 16 (Autumn 1986): 97–108.

Zacharie, F. C. et al. *Argument on the Law and the Evidence before the Congressional Committee on Louisiana Affairs* (New Orleans: A. W. Hyatt, Printer, 1874).

Index

Adams, Henry, 159, 161
African Americans
    Civil War participation by, 41
    in post–Civil War period
        land ownership, 88
        liberation, 47
        population decreases, 47
    voters, 158–159, 165, 170
Agriculture
    in 1872, 79
    Civil War effects on, 46–48
    cotton, 8–9, 15–16, 19, 79
Alabama
    Huntsville, 12, 19–20
    Indian removal from, 14
    secession of, 39
    slave market in, 10, 11, 13
    slavery in, 7–8
    Smith's ownership of land in, 8–9
Alexandria, 35–36
Alexandria Democrat, 61
Allen, Benjamin L., 98–99
Allen, Lev, 72, 92, 98, 101
Amendments
    10th, 39
    13th, 64

14th, 64, 146
15th, 66, 144, 146
"An Incident of My Boyhood Days," 109
Antoine, C. C., 85
Army Appropriations Act of 1867, 65
Artillery, 96–97
Atchafalaya River, 5

B. L. Hodge, 95, 113
Banks, Nathaniel P., 37–38, 42, 50
Battle of Canal Street, 149–150
Battle of the Wilderness, 37–38
Bayou Boeuf, 116
Beckwith, J. R., 92, 112–113, 118–119,
    132–133, 140, 145–146
Beecher, Charles, 28
Biossat, Edward, 125, 129, 135
Black Codes, 48, 53, 134
Black gunslingers, 72
Black suffrage, 54, 66
"Blue whistlers," 91, 95
Boardman, Billy, 97
Borland, Peter, 72–73, 92, 98
Boulard, Antoinette, 24
Bowie, Jim, 29
Bradley, Stephen J., 140, 142–143, 145

Brantley, Green, 93
Breda, Ernest J., 115, 119
Brimm, Benjamin, 104, 106, 140
Buffalo Soldiers, 98
Butler, Major General
    Benjamin Franklin, 85
Butler, O. J., 92

Caddo Indians, 4
Caddo Lake, 4
Calhoun, Eugene, 161
Calhoun, Gustavus, 12–13
Calhoun, John C., 6
Calhoun, John Taylor, 33
Calhoun, Marie Marguerite Ada, 33,
    53, 160–161
Calhoun, Mary, 30–31
Calhoun, Meredith
    artwork owned by, 31
    in Europe, 30–31, 33–34, 39, 53
    in France, 33–34
    Girard's influence on, 9–10
    global travels of, 22–23
    in Huntsville, 19–20
    Mary Smith Taylor's marriage to, 9
    moral education of, 10–11
    as opium trader, 11
    Paris residence of, 30
    residence of, 19
    as Simon Legree, 26–28
    slave ownership by, 12–13
    slave transport operations, 10–11
    supercargo position of, 10
    views on Negro race, 22–23
    violent human interactions
        witnessed by, 11–12
    wealth of, 20
Calhoun, Meredith Jr., 33
Calhoun, William Smith
    attempted attacks on, 129–130
    Colfax Courthouse battle response
        by, 122
    death of, 163–164
    description of, 13

education support by, 49–53
Guerin's work with, 33–34
health problems of, 35, 55
Hooe's capture of, 94–95
injury to, 32–33
James Madison Wells and, 38–39
marriages of, 52–53, 161
obituary for, 163–164
Olivia Williams and, 52–53, 123, 161
Olmstead's writings about, 34–35
Ozark support, 122–123, 134
physical disabilities of, 32–33, 35, 55
plantation rebuilding by, after
    Civil War, 49
plantation supervision by, 35
political ambitions of, 53–56, 64
renting of land to Freedmen by, 49
as Senator, 64
threats against, 57
Calhoun, William Smith Jr., 123, 161
Calhoun plantations
    armed confrontation on, 93–94
    crops grown on, 19, 25
    description of, 13, 18
    ditch digging on, 24
    execution of slaves on, 25
    Firenze, 49, 51
    life on, 23–25
    Mirabeau, 19, 44
    whipping of slaves on, 25–26
    Willie Calhoun's management
        of, 35
Campbell, John A., 155
Canal Street, 87
Cane River, 35
Casey, James F., 135
Catahoula Parish, 59
Caucasian, The, 147–148
Cazabat, Alphonse, 87, 160
Chamber, Pinkney, 102
Champion No. 3, 42–44
Champion No. 5, 42
Cheneyville, 116–117
Cheneyville Rifles, 36

Children
  education of, 50
  post-Civil War changes to, 47
  schools for, 50
Choctaw removal, 14
Cholera, 15
Civil Rights Acts
  of 1866, 48
  of 1964, 170
Civil War
  African Americans service in, 41
  agricultural destruction caused by,
    46–48
  description of, 36–38
  economic losses caused by, 46–48
Cloutierville, 35
Coffle yokes, 17
Colfax
  African American population in, 78–79
  development of, 3–5
  Red River slave transport arrival in,
    17–18
  sale of land in, 5
  schools in, 51
  white families in, after Civil War, 92
Colfax Chronicle, 164, 169
Colfax Courthouse battle
  arrests after, 119
  artillery, 96–97
  black defenders of, 101–103
  black families return to Colfax after,
    115–116
  Calhoun's response to, 122
  commemoration of, 164
  days after massacre, 108
  deaths at, 104–105, 107, 109
  DeKlyne's response to, 118
  description of, 87, 101–102
  economic costs of, 116
  escalating tensions at, 95–96,
    99–100
  execution of prisoners, 105–106
  federal and state law enforcement
    response to, 120–121

first deaths at, 100–101
grand jury proceedings after, 115
Hadnot's shooting at, 103–104, 107
hanging of prisoners, 109
indictments after, 118–119, 156
militia defense of, 92
monument for, 167–168
mutilation of dead bodies, 110
Nash–Allen meeting, 98–99
newspaper reporting of, 117
19th U.S. Infantry dispatch to, 113
prisoners of, 103–105
Radical Republicans in, 87
remembrance of, 164, 167
Republican control of, 88
roof fire at, 102
scene at, 113–114
seizure of, 90
survivors of, 162
U.S. Army response to events
    at, 113
victims of, 108–109, 111–112,
    126–127, 167–168
white offensive at, 100–101
white victims of, 103–104, 107,
    167–168
Committee on Private Land
    Claims, 6
Confederate States of America, 36
Congressional Acts, 75
Conscription Act, 36
Convict leasing, 166
Cosgrove, James, 150
Cotton, 8–9, 15–16, 19, 79
Credit Mobiliér, 134
Cricket, 42–43
Cruikshank, William, 48, 136, 154. See
    also U.S. v. Cruikshank et al.
Cuney, Samuel E., 55
Cuny's Point, 101

Dancer, Edmund, 41–42, 92
Dare, Edward, 96
Darwin, Charles, 84

DeKlyne, Theodore W., 111–112, 118
DeLacy, John, 150–151
DeLacy, William J., 55
Devil's Backbone, 57
Disenfranchisement, 165
Ditch digging, 24
Douglas, Stephen, 38
Douglass, Frederick, 163
DuBois, W.E.B., 139
Dunn, Christopher Columbus, 90,
    96–97, 160, 164
Dunn, Milton, 90, 105, 164, 167
Durrell, Edward H., 82 118, 137

Economic subjugation, 166
Edgerton, Frank, 149
Education. *See* Public education;
    Schools
Election Day, 60, 80–81
Elections
    1868, 67–68
    1872, 82–83
Ellis, Bully, 92
Ellis, John, 136
Elzie, Baptiste, 100, 105
Elzie, Etienne, 105, 139
Emory, William H., 80, 113
Enforcement Acts
    of 1870, 75, 77
    of 1871, 118
    Bradley verdict effect on, 148
    revision of, after *U.S. v. Cruikshank
        et al.*, 157
Europe, 30–31, 33–34, 39, 53
Execution of slaves, 25
Exodusters, 161

Field, David Dudley, 155
15th Amendment, 66, 144, 146
Firenze Plantation, 49, 51
Flowers, Eli, 92, 95
Fort Jessup, 27–28
14th Amendment, 64, 146
France, 33–34

Frank Leslie's Illustrated Weekly, 117
Franklin, John Hope, 170–171
Frazier, Hal
    description of, 62–63
    murder of, 63–65
Frazier, "Old Buck," 37
Frazier's Mill, 62
Freedmen
    description of, 47–49
    renting of land to, 49
    schools for, 50
Freedmen's Bureau, 48–52, 58
Fugitive Slave Act of 1850, 73
Fulton, Robert, 3

Gaines, Loyal (Cuffy), 41–42, 78, 92, 163
Girard, Stephen, 9–10
Gould, Jay, 161
Grand Duke Alexis of Russia, 83
Grand jury proceedings, 115
"Grandfather clause," 165
Grant, Ulysses, 28, 38, 59, 75–76
Grant Parish
    conservatives from, 87
    description of, 49, 63–65
    klansmen arrested in, 76–77
    map of, 2
    militia congregation in, 90
    White League in, 146–147, 149–150
"Great Day," 40
Great Raft of the Red River, 3–5
Greeley, Horace, 80
Guerin, Dr. Jules, 33–34

Habeas corpus writ, 151
Hadnot, A. J., 37
Hadnot, J. P., 136
Hadnot, James W.
    death of, 103, 114
    description of, 37, 87, 92
Hadnot, Luke, 105
Haitian Revolution, 154
Harper's Weekly, 117
Harris, Charles, 91

Harris, Sidney, 103, 167
Hazen, Alfred, 60
Henderson, Hampton, 127
Henry, Cammie G., 169
Hickman, John, 5
Hickman, Peter, 5
Hickman, Thomas, 105, 136, 141
Holloway Prairie, 59
Hooe, J. G. P., 60, 68, 94, 101, 115
Hunter, Robert P., 147
Huntsville, 12, 19–20
Huntsville Democrat, 40

Ice House Hotel, 58
Indian migrations, 15
Indictments, 132–133, 143–145
Irwin, Bill, 89, 102, 136

Jackson, Andrew, 6
Jackson, Stonewall, 37–38
John T. Moore, 96–97
Johnson, Andrew, 53
Johnson, Lyndon, 170
Jones, Meekin, 106

Kansas, 162
Kellogg, William Pitt, 80, 82–83, 86, 147
Kelso, George Y., 55
Key to Uncle Tom's Cabin, 28–29
Kimball, Adam, 100
Knights of the White Camellia, 89
Ku Klux Klan, 58–60, 68–71, 75, 167
Ku Klux Klan Act, 75–76

LaBelle steamboat, 94
Lacour, Cordelia, 126–127
Lacour, John, 126–128
Ladies of New Orleans, 137
Lafitte, Jean, 29
Land ownership, 88
Lane, Ada, 160–161
"Last Cargo of Slaves, The," 28–30
Lay, Henry C., 20
Layssard, Captain Valentin, 127

Lee, Robert E., 4, 28
Legree, Simon, 26, 28
Lemoine, Denis, 37, 89
Lemoine, Prudhomme, 136, 141
Lewis, Alfred, 136, 142
Lewis, Mary Fenwick, 34
Lincoln, Abraham, 39
Longstreet, General James, 37–38
Louisiana
    description of, 3, 36
    election of 1868 dispute, 67–68
    legislature in, 66–67
    post–Civil War, 88
    public education for black children
        in, 50
    Reconstruction efforts, 134
    secession of, 39
    state government power in, 65
    U.S. Army troops departure from, 158
    voters in, 54
    wartime losses, 46
    white supremacy in, 65, 160, 170
Louisiana Democrat, 126, 130
Louisiana Purchase, 6
Louisiana Returning Board, 67
Louisiana White League, 146–147,
    149–150
Lynch law, 167

Mardi Gras, 83–85, 151
Marr, R. H., 136, 154
Marsh, George R., 115, 138
Massacre. *See* Colfax Courthouse battle
McAlpin, Robert, 27
McCain, John, 93, 141
McEnery, John, 80, 82
McIntosh, Donald, 150
McKinney, Jesse
    black civilians response to, 89–90
    burial of, 115–116
    murder of, 88–89, 91–92
McKinney, Laurinda, 89, 139
Mechanics Hall Statehouse, 86
Merrill, Lewis, 150

Miles, John, 97–98
Mills, Baptiste, 108
Mirabeau Plantation, 44, 89, 99
"Missing Link," 85
Mississippi River, 5
Mistrial, 141–142
Mitchell, Alabama, 41, 78, 92, 104, 140, 163
Montfort, Thomas, 38
Moore, Dosia Williams, 120
Moore, Thomas O., 44
Murder, 58
Mystick Krewe of Comus
    description of, 83–84
    parade of 1872 by, 84–87

Nash, Christopher Columbus, 37, 52, 71, 87, 97–99, 117, 131–132, 149
Natchez Trace, 14
Natural disasters, 46–47
Nelson, Levi, 135
New Orleans, 83–86, 137, 147
New Orleans Metropolitan Police, 66, 125–126, 128
New Orleans Republican, 95
New York Daily Times, 22, 26
Newsham, Joseph P., 67
19th U.S. Infantry, 113
Norris, A. B., 142
Norris, Tom, 142

Odd Fellows Hall, 87
Ogden, Frederick N., 149
"Old Time Ku Klux Klan," 89
Olmsted, Frederick Law
    description of, 21–22
    New York Daily Times, 22
    Red River travels by, 22
    Willie Calhoun as described by, 34–35
Opium trade, 11
Osborn, John, 74

Packard, Marshal, 114, 121
Packard, Samuel B., 112, 118
Parades, 83–87

Paris, 30
Parish, Stephen, 100–102
Parishes. *See specific parish*
Paul, David, 37, 104
Penn, Clement, 37, 105, 139, 141
Phillips, William B., 56–57, 59, 71, 121–123
Pickwick Club, 83
Pinchback, P.B.S., 82
Pittman, Dorcas, 110
Pittman, Lank, 110
Plantations
    armed confrontation on, 93–94
    cotton cultivation on, 19
    crops grown on, 19, 25
    description of, 13, 18
    ditch digging on, 24
    execution of slaves on, 25
    Firenze, 49, 51
    life on, 23–25
    Mirabeau, 19, 44
    revenues from, 19
    whipping of slaves on, 25–26
    Willie Calhoun's management of, 35
Plessy v. Ferguson, 166
Porter, Admiral David D., 42–44, 121–122
Posse Comitatus, 73–74, 91, 97
Prudhomme, Jean Baptiste, 5
Public education
    curriculum, 51
    federal support for, 50
    freedmen's contributions to, 50
    state funds for, 166
Pump-boats, 43
Purvis, Cora, 161

Radical Reconstruction, 54
Randell, John H., 44–45
Rapides Gazette, 115
Rapides Guards, 28, 35–36
Rapides Invincibles, 36
Rapides Parish
    description of, 46–47

Grant Parish developed from, 63–64
restrictions on land ownership, 48
voter violence, 61
Reconstruction Act of 1867, 54, 165, 169
Red River
commerce on, 4
flood of, 46
Great Raft of, 3–5
slave transport on
coffle yokes used for, 17
Colfax steamboat landing, 17–18
costs of, 17
timing of, 17
switchbacks of, 5
transportation needs, 121
Red River Campaign of 1864, 40–42
Red River Parish, 63
Red River Republican, The, 28
Register, R. C., 86, 92, 119
Republican Party, 54, 56, 80
Rex, 83, 86, 147
Richardson, W. L., 92
Rigolette de Bon Dieu, 5, 18, 35, 63
Rillieux, Norbert, 18
Robarts, William Hugh, 27–28
Robinson, Jesse, 63
Rock Island, 57–58, 70, 97
Rosenthal, A. M., 150
Rosenthal, Jonas, 130
Rutland, Jim, 92
Ryan, Michael, 67–68, 125

Sabine Rifles, 37
Scarborough, George W., 92, 105, 115
Schools
in Colfax, 51
curriculum in, 51
federal support for, 50
at Frazier's Mill, 62
opposition to, 51–52
political orientation of, 51–52
teachers in, 50–51
threats against, 62
Schumann, Sidney, 116

Segregation, 165–166
70th United States Colored Infantry, 41
71st United States Colored
Infantry, 41
Sexual paranoia, 117
Seymour, Horatio, 61
Shackleford, Sam, 96
Shaw, Daniel, 86, 98, 123
Shelby, Alfred, 71–72
Sheridan, General Philip, 38, 53, 151
Shorter, Loyd, 128–129
Shreve, Captain Henry, 3–4
Slaughterhouse Cases, 135, 142
Slave(s)
Calhoun's ownership of, 12–13
execution of, 25
mortality of, 29
separation of families, 16
Smith's ownership of, 13–14
surplus of, 13, 16
transport of
from Africa, 29
description of, 14
on Red River, 17–18
whipping of, 25–26
Slave brokerage, 13
Slavery
abolition in France, 154
in Alabama, 7–8
description of, 4
Smith's support of, 7–8
Southern support for, 37
Smith, Eliza, 89
Smith, William
death of, 18
investments by, 7
land ownership by, 8–9
political convictions of, 7
resistance to public financing for
improvements, 7
slave ownership by, 13–14
slavery support by, 7–8
as South Carolina senator, 5–6
westward migration by, 9

Smithfield Quarters, 97
Snagboats, 3–4
Southwestern, 106
St. Martin Parish, 114, 118
Stafford, George, 107–108, 147
Stafford, Leroy, 36–37, 90
Stafford Guards, 36–37
Stafford Plantation, 48
Stockton, J. B., 150
Stowe, Harriet Beecher, 26–28
Sugar, 18–19
Sugarhouse Bayou, 18
Supercargo, 10
Sweet potatoes, 48

"Tariff of Abominations," 6
Task ditch, 24
Taylor, Mary Smith, 9
Taylor, Richard, 44
Teachers, 50–51
10th Amendment, 39
"Tenting on the Old Camp
     Ground," 91
Texada, Joseph, 48, 89
Texada, Lewis, 48
13th Amendment, 64
Thomas, Sarah, 16
Tillman, Alex, 112, 132–133
Tocqueville, Alexis de, 15
Transport of slaves
     from Africa, 29
     description of, 14
     on Red River, 17–18
Tulane, Louis, 153
Tulane, Paul, 153–154
Tulsa Riot, 171
Twitchell, Marshall, 55, 149

Uncle Tom's Cabin, 26–28
Union soldiers, 41
United States v. Columbus Nash et al., 131
U.S. Army Corps of Engineers
     Great Raft of Red River cleared
          by, 3–5

snagboats, 4
U.S. v. Cruikshank et al.
     black enfranchisement affected by,
          158–159, 165
     defendants
          absence of, 116–118
          alibis for, 141
          capture of, 131–132
          defense of, 136–137, 140–141,
               155–156
          indictments against, 132–133,
               143–145, 156
          lawyers for, 136
          mistrial of, 141–142
          "not guilty" verdict, 142–143
          prosecution of, 133–135, 137, 140
          support for, 136
          testimony against, 138–139
          transport of witnesses against,
               137–138
          trial of, 132, 137
     description of, 142–144
     legal outcome of, 157–158
     remembrance of, 169
     verdict, 146–150, 154, 156
     voting rights affected by, 156
     Waite's opinion, 156–157
     White League formation after
          verdict in, 146–147, 149–150
U.S. v. Reese, 156
U.S.S. Easton, 43
U.S.S. Ozark
     Calhoun's presence and support of,
          122–123, 134
     1864 song about, 124
     1873 song about, 120
     government support in, 134
     Grant Parish posse on, 122–124
     physical description of, 121–122
     risks for, 123
     troops on, 123–124

Voters
     African American, 158–159, 165, 170

registration of, 54, 75
Voting Rights Act of 1965, 170

Waite, Morrison, 156–157
Ward, William
 arrests by, 73–75
 assassination attempt on, 151
 Calhoun's support for, 79
 description of, 72–73
 illness of, 95
 last years of, 162
 military reputation of, 79
 militia of, 77–78, 91–92
 on *Ozark*, 138
 physical description of, 77
 political victory by, 81
 state penitentiary project, 138
Warmoth, Henry Clay
 assassination attempt on, 82
 description of, 61
 impeachment of, 82
 Liberal Republicans, 80
 metropolitan police organized by, 66
 political appointments by, 65–66

Watson, Oscar, 93, 109, 116
Weathers, Bella, 57
Wells, James Madison, 28, 38, 53
Wells, Montfort, 28
West and Kimbrell clan, 64–65, 70
Wheat's Louisiana Tigers, 72
"When the Lincoln Gunboats
 Come," 124
Whight, William, 111–112
Whipping of slaves
 description of, 25–26
 legal punishments for, 65
White, Baptiste, 106, 108
White, Delos W., 51, 56–58, 63–64,
 70–71
White, Shack, 102
White, Zach, 101
White League, 146–147, 149–150
Williams, George H., 119, 134–135, 148
Williams, Olivia, 52–53, 123, 161
Winn Parish, 63–64, 70
Women, 47

Yawn, Jeff, 105